THE SPONSORED FILM

THE
SPONSORED
FILM

by Walter J. Klein

COMMUNICATION ARTS BOOKS

HASTINGS HOUSE, PUBLISHERS

New York 10016

LIBRARY OF CONGRESS CATALOGING IN PUBLICATION DATA

The sponsored film.
 Klein, Walter J

 (Communication arts books)
 Includes index.
 1. Moving-pictures in advertising. 2. Moving-pictures in industry. 3. Moving-pictures, Documentary, I. Title.
HF5844.K54   1976   659.1'52   76-18311
ISBN 0-8038-6734-4

Published simultaneously in Canada by
Saunders of Toronto, Ltd., Don Mills, Ontario

Designed by Al Lichtenberg
Printed in the United States of America

CONTENTS

PREFACE

The world is full of a number of things that no one has ever examined, identified, described, defined, measured or isolated.

We know it's so because virtually all of our present-day communications and promotional sciences didn't exist a generation or two ago. We realize that another generation or two from now will see new sciences, new arts, new phenomena to involve society as importantly as television does today. We can see it in transition at this very moment. The corporate executive watching his own commercial doesn't realize the building he seems to be circling never existed; it was created entirely as an exercise in computer animation. The crowds at the trade show don't see any difference in the TV image, even though it came from a videodisc. Many of us are aware of holography and laser sciences but do not yet live in that age when they will be as essential to communications as the telephone is today.

In spending more than a generation making sponsored films, I frequently got the feeling I was in a world in dynamic transition, so mercurial, moving so rapidly that our own professionals were often being left behind. At lunch in our company lounge I can frequently hear in the idle talk of our staff the professional prejudices of different time periods.

I realize that every five years is a generation in sponsored films. There will be a generation gap between this year's cinema school graduate and the graduate five years from today. They will talk shop in different terms—attack a new sponsored film production in different ways—find different values in the films they watch.

Amid all this, I yearned to nail it down, to capture it somehow in a snapshot, to stop it all just long enough to examine it, identify it, describe it, define it, measure it, isolate it.

I was reluctant to write a book about sponsored films because surely there were excellent volumes on the subject. I looked in our company and public libraries. Among the many books on film production, public relations and theatrical films I found nothing on sponsored films. Nothing.

We've hired a large number of professionals in the 28 years we've been in business. I've wanted to give each new employee something more than the company orientation booklet and a walking tour of the studios. I wanted to hand them a book about our industry. There was never anything to hand them.

Rather uncomfortable, this feeling of spending a career in an industry that could offer the world tens of thousands of excellent films *but not one book*. So I wrote it. It is done not out of pride, nor as an ego trip, but out of necessity to describe a very real communications manifestation called the sponsored film. Be assured this book is not "complete." If it were possible to encapsulate all knowledge about sponsored films neatly within one book, each copy would surely explode from the energy of the subject's dynamism.

ACKNOWLEDGEMENTS

The reader must first be thanked. He created the demand for this book that made it a reality.

The good people who provided the information that gave it factual integrity—they must next be thanked. It was not easy for them. For in creating this book I was not so concerned with the ounces of film cement each sponsored film producer consumed as what professional battles he was losing and winning. So I asked difficult, complex questions that drew difficult, complex replies.

They came from dear friends all over the world, principally fellow producers in our trade association, IQ. They came from giants like Tom Hope, Graeme Fraser, Jack Hennessy and Ott Coelln whose names are renowned in the sponsored film industry and whose 20/20 perspective gave me priceless material.

Then I find it right to thank my loving family, who were reluctant to see this book published. They visualized all the hard-won information, techniques and trade secrets (if there are any) of our corporate operations spread out open in a book for anyone to buy for a few dollars. They are to be thanked for setting aside their better judgment, knowing I wanted to share this information.

INTRODUCTION:

What Is a Sponsored Film?

Sponsored films. It is a term so little known that its enunciation elicits blank stares or a quick nod of the head of a person who fancies he knows all about it, like knowing all about railroading from watching a freight train "schlep" past a crossing.

Actually the term slips out of your fingers while you are gripping it, trying to define it. Certainly we can leave it at a combination of the definitions of its two words: *a motion picture paid for by an industry or person.*

That may satisfy millions, but not the readers of this book. Nor can it satisfy me and my fellow producers of sponsored films, who deserve at least a more profound inspection of our careers.

A motion picture paid for by an industry or person? What's that? Aren't *all* films paid for by an industry or person? What's implied? Is this a vanity thing, like books authored by successful businessmen who couldn't write gripping graffiti on a washroom wall? Does it say we will tell a story—any story—for a buck? Is brainwashing involved? What was that business some years ago about subliminal communication, using one frame at a time in a TV film? And how about the 14 toothbrushing films Goldwater said the taxpayers bought? Is that what we're talking about when we say "sponsored films"?

You bet your sweet life it is.

It's all that and more. The good and the not-so-good. The failures and successes. The hackneyed and the inspired. The selfish and the unselfish.

Sponsored films, to coin a phrase, cover a multitude of sins. They escape definition for reasons other than their diversity. Sponsored films are, like humanity, still evolving. You no sooner have your pat little concept worked out in your damp sandpile than a wave arrives to make you start over. No sooner do you identify "sponsored films" as everything listed in a Modern Talking Picture Service mailer than you watch a sponsored film capture an Oscar in Hollywood and hear of another being seized in Uganda as dangerous propaganda. And you quickly realize This Thing Is Bigger than Either of Us.

Technology and allied arts are in there swinging, too. Are there sponsored *tapes*? Sponsored *discs*? Are they the same or different? If they are the same, why don't we include sponsored *books*? Sponsored *music*? Sponsored *art*? Sponsored *people*?

Paul Wittgenstein lost his right arm in World War I and commissioned Maurice Ravel to write his exquisite *Concerto in D Major for Piano Left Hand and Orchestra* so Wittgenstein could show the world that he was still a virtuoso. Wittgenstein and Ravel argued over its content and Wittgenstein won out. That is sponsored music.

Most of Congress is sponsored. In Washington we have sponsored people, politicians underwritten by political parties, industry, individuals and tax funds. Or are politicians simply bankrolled? Are these political sponsors all wrapped up in guiding the destiny of the politicians they back? *Are you kidding*? Of course they are. That isn't simple bankrolling; it's *sponsorship*.

So motivation is clearly involved in our word Sponsorship. Whoever or whatever *sponsors* a film, tape, disc, book, work of art or music—or human being—*has the intent to influence the ultimate work*. That intent can be pure as a Shirley Temple doll or as sinister as certain lobbies. (I really shouldn't use the word "sinister." I'm left-handed and would not oppose being drafted to head an organization to restore one original meaning of "sinister" as simply "left-handed.")

That is not to say that film producers have little or nothing to say about what goes into their creations. Most producers are involved in producing films that are *not* sponsored. An example would be an educational film destined for classroom use. The producer pays the production bills himself and recoups his investment and a profit by selling prints to schools. The producer has the right to say or do anything lawful within his motion picture, without outside influence. He may well call upon educators or professionals as counsel, but he is boss. He is owner of the mentality of his film as well as its tangibles.

But when that same producer solicits or accepts proffered funds for a film from an individual (rare), industry, government, trade association, organization, institution, union, political party, fresh-air camp or sled-dog racer, his control is transcended by his sponsor. The producer either writes the script or causes it to be written by an independent writer. But its content is clearly directed by the sponsor.

Does all this sound like Pharaoh calling the shots on hieroglyphic history? Too much so. The Pharaohs, we have come to learn, told it like it *isn't*. They controlled the press and twisted their stony records so they might arrive in Egyptian heaven and let humanity think they were gods.

Thus the *quality* of motivation demands detailed consideration in any work on sponsored films, even though it is only at best implied in a definition. Definition? Perhaps we are ready to try one on now.

A sponsored film is a moving picture, in any form, paid for by anyone controlling its content and shown for public entertainment or information. Is that enough? Of course not. There is so much more. . . .

Chapter One

Perspective

Drawing a bead on sponsored films from among all other types of films is a difficult but rewarding experience. It is also necessary if one is to gain any perspective on this "unique critter." Appreciating the value and importance of sponsored films depends in part on understanding their relationship to other kinds of films.

Motion pictures can be categorized in several ways: *Theatrical—Non-Theatrical*. The simplest is to separate the field into theatrical and non-theatrical films—those shown in movie theaters and those that aren't. Theatrical or feature films are largely made for entertainment, using dramatic techniques. Non-theatrical films largely are factual and employ informational techniques.

Another breakdown distinguishes films by their source: *Commercial—In-Plant—Independent*. Commercial filmmakers create movies with their own or borrowed funds for sale or rent. In-plant production units make movies within a company, college, government agency or other definable structure. Independent producers make films on commission from any fund source, for any purpose.

Still another way of dividing up motion pictures is by their subject matter: *Religion—Government—Industry—Education—Medicine & Health—Sports—Agriculture—Travel*.

Many in the industry find it useful to separate films by their use: *Training—Sales—TV News Releases—Lecture—Forensic—Annual Report—Public Relations—Archives*.

Motion pictures are often divided up among their various delivery formats: *8mm—16mm—35mm—Transfer from Videotape*.

And to distinguish one from another they are categorized by production techniques: *Live Action—Animation—Copying of Still Material—Computer—Cinema Verité—Documentary—Experimental.*

Less often one finds films differentiated by their technical form: *Trigger—Motivational— Informational— Entertainment.*

Now, where does the sponsored film fit in all these film pie slices?

Let's take it one at a time. In the first case, sponsored films belong only among non-theatrical films. Next, a sponsored film can be the product of either an in-plant or independent facility, but is not the product of a commercial filmmaker.

Insofar as subjects are concerned, sponsored films cover virtually all of them; there is no limit.

But when we examine the *uses* of films, sponsored films fit very few categories: public relations, image, publicity, sales promotion, public service, information and education are the words most often heard.

Sponsored films can be issued in any delivery format, from 8mm to videodisc. And they can and do employ every production technique in commercial use. Finally, sponsored films can take any technical form.

Having digested this, we can better appreciate the following table of 1973 sponsored film expenditures as published by *Hope Reports, AV-USA, 1973-1974:*

Produced by	Number of Sponsored Films	Spent on Production	Spent on Prints	Spent on Distribution	Total Spent
Business & Industry	2,265	$49,100,000	$41,600,000	$ 9,200,000	$ 99,900,000
Schools	80	900,000	1,000,000	100,000	2,000,000
Colleges	105	1,400,000	800,000	200,000	2,400,000
Government	1,120	20,700,000	15,700,000	3,000,000	39,400,000
Medicine & Health	290	5,600,000	4,200,000	500,000	1,700,000
Community Agency	170	2,000,000	1,100,000	700,000	3,800,000
Religion	30	500,000	700,000	200,000	1,400,000
Totals	4,060	$81,300,000	$65,400,000	$14,200,000	$160,900,000

More than 4,000 sponsored films are identified as produced in America in one year. *Hope Reports* documents some 17,320 total film productions in all non-theatrical categories that same year: 9,000 television documentaries; 11,340 in-plant films; 1,920 short films released in Super 8mm form, mostly silent.

Sponsored films comprise 24 per cent of all non-theatrical films researched by the Hope organization. They cost 25 per cent of all funds spent on non-theatrical films. Broken down by source, the 17,230 non-theatrical films comprised the 4,110 above sponsored films, 11,340 in-plant, and 1,780 commercial films.

In another analysis, *Hope Reports* puts 1973 sponsored film production expenditures in the context of all AV spending, including hardware, software, TV and administration:

Software	$ 453,200,000	In-plant film and	
Hardware sales	613,600,000	tape productions	509,200,000
Export sales	127,700,000	Administration	1,070,000,000
Dealer services	65,700,000	Capital expense	151,600,000
Film and tape rental	125,800,000	Public radio & TV	187,900,000
Sponsored film and			
tape productions	184,100,000	Total	$3,488,800,000

Sponsored films are involved in a large share of this $3.4 billion investment. They are not simply represented by the 5 per cent of the total shown as production costs. They are also connected with hardware, software, rentals, in-plant production and administration.

By looking at many of the broader aspects of non-theatrical motion pictures, we can now shake our test tube and watch the sparkling crystals of sponsored films precipitate to the bottom and look more closely at their unique chemistry.

PUBLIC RELATIONS AND THE "PR FILM"

The sponsored film is inevitably considered a *public relations film* both by the producer and sponsor.

"Sponsored film" is a term for broader perspectives and for outsiders. Within the industry, producers must continually define each new assignment. They would never say, "General Electric signed with us yesterday for a new sponsored film." Rather you would hear about a training film, TV news release, sales film or *public relations* film.

It's the same at the sponsor end. If a public relations director of a corporation were making an annual report statement to stockholders, he would certainly refer to his products as *sponsored films* at some juncture. And if he's closeted with an Association Films representative about distribution reports, he's using that term again. But in day-to-day use, he'd say *PR film* to delineate his new film on energy management.

This use of the term *PR film* by a PR professional is a vital matter. *The fortunes of PR films have varied directly with those of PR professionals.* When public relations people in leading corporations were little more than mimeograph operators and dispensers of publicity handouts, sponsored films had much less stature than they enjoy today. As publicity evolved into public relations or public information, and duties of PR professionals broadened and deepened, the PR film came into its own.

There is little doubt that if PR professionals fell from grace or were hybridized, sponsored films would suffer substantially.

Industry sponsors films for their public relations values. As industry's appreciation for public relations effectiveness grows, so does their purchase of sponsored films. As public relations executives expand their influence within, so sponsored film stock goes up. Today, PR executives work in corporate communications, public affairs, corporate relations, external relations specialties, employee and other intra-company communications, community relations, federal and local government relations, environment, safety, financial information, corporate advertising and corporate identity. Once the PR director was lucky to get a raise when the others around him did. Now he can be right in line for the presidency. Today industry is working feverishly to sense the future reactions of public and government, to forestall damaging shock. Their public relations people are usually wrapped up in this predicting and pulse-taking. One of the important steps taken to turn public minds around to the corporate way of thinking—and to soften the shock—is sponsored films.

Sponsors readily realize that their PR films are capable not only of reflecting conditions but of turning the public around to the sponsor's way of thinking. A South African travel film may seem benign at first glance, but watch closely and you will see how happy the black people appear. After that, you may well wonder what this Apartheid fuss is all about, and the film has done its job handsomely.

I was once motoring along the California coast on a junket with Mrs. Lady Bird Johnson. That famed conservationist was very vocal until a huge timber truck carrying great redwood logs passed us. She fell silent for some time. That was a terrible turnoff. Yet a couple of months later I watched a PR film on forestry management, sponsored by one of the timber giants. I was left with the feeling that America's forests could not be in better hands than Weyerhaeuser's and Georgia-Pacific's. (Yes, even in the business, I watch, enjoy and am swayed by many sponsored films.)

There are very few members of the Public Relations Society of America today who do not budget at least one sponsored film a year. It may be a "loner"—a film project that runs on its own momentum. More likely it is part of a year's broad program or campaign, wherein many media play a part. In any case, the public relations director will arrange to measure results of the PR film investment as precisely as possible, because he is more sensitive than anyone in industry officialdom to criticism that public relations values cannot be measured, and are therefore not deserving of priority attention and budgeting.

Public relations professionals in industry are not the only executives who buy sponsored films. Presidents, vice presidents, chairmen of the board, sales, marketing, advertising, corporate and government relations people are also actively caught up in decision making. They may even elect to split the film's budget, sort of like co-insurers sharing the risk on a big underwriting contract.

From title page to the listing of Ron Ziegler in the index, *The Creation of Consent* (Hastings House) takes up 315 pages. In Dr. Charles S. Steinberg's very readable book on public relations, the subject of films covers precisely 3-1/2 pages out of those 315. Television publicity takes up another 4-1/2. The book was published in 1975.

Take any book about public relations off the library shelf in the year 1997 and 100 pages will be devoted to the visual media. These are days when corporations hire full-time soothsayers to anticipate corporate shock. Why, then, are astute public relations professionals still so concerned over print?

Evidently that's where most of the trouble starts. The boss is walking a lot faster this morning. He has a clipping in his hand. He isn't talking to anybody. Heading right for PR. Oh, boy, all hell's going to break loose. Until videotape recordings of last night's 11 o'clock news are popularly made at home, bosses aren't so likely to be marching *tape* in hand as *clipping* in hand. It will take another generation to convert our print-oriented society to a true screen-oriented society. Graying executives are still much more at home correcting a press release than the picture side of a TV release.

But the transition has nevertheless begun and has moved progressively forward. Corporations are growing restless over the plethora of print they turn out and the dearth of proof of readership. Some top executives fear they are annually papering the universe. The awards come in right on schedule for exemplary typography and use of paper stock. But even the guys in marketing down the hall forget about the image piece PR put out last year and publish another this year, much to J.B.'s disgust. In short, the public is *getting* more print than ever before in history, and *reading* it less than ever before in history.

What to do? Management might well take the opportunity to include print in the corporate-wide economy wave. Training manuals will henceforth be printed in-house as one-page releases for periodic replacement. Scrap paper will take the place of inter-office memos imprinted with the names of personnel. Only the short-form annual report will be published this year. The "vanity paperback" public relations asked to put in the budget will be put off indefinitely. Etcetera.

That's a rather counterproductive remedy, and it couldn't last. I've always suspected that executive types take a certain satisfaction from contracting for something constructive and get another thrill out of cancelling a year later. They think they are getting points for being innovative when they buy and being shrewd executives when they cancel in the name of Economizing.

Cutting back the print deluge is only part of the process of appropriating important funds for the screen. In the near future, the alteration of promotional budgets in favor of the screen will be nothing short of explosive. Many consumer-product corporations have long since allocated the bulk of their time and space advertising to television. In the advertising department, the switch is already old hat. But move over to PR, sales and marketing and you may witness an embarrassing paradox. In those areas that same corporation is print-heavy.

"But how are we in sales promotion supposed to switch from print to screen?" a hard-working up-and-comer might ask. "I've got to get out promotion kits. Direct mail programs. Contests. Incentive programs. Ad reprints. Convention paraphernalia. Just what magic am I to use to convert all that to the screen?"

The question may sound rhetorical to some. But to the trendy people, there are real answers. Merchandising kits can indeed be put on motion picture film. And direct mail programs. And contests. And incentive programs. And reproductions of TV ads. And convention promotional materials. All lend themselves to the dynamics of motion pictures.

The only reasons sales promotion people don't convert their print to screen is that they are: 1) scared; 2) unfamiliar with production; 3) not too bright.

Let us pray that number 2 covers the vast majority of sales promotion people. If so, the problem is soon remedied. The person who could learn about color registration, bearers, repro proofs and texture screens can just as readily learn about workprints, A&B rolls, opticals and interlocks. After that, producing a sales-incentive spring catalog in motion picture form can be even more challenging and rewarding than doing it in bound booklet form.

With all the in-house propaganda switching heavily toward the screen in the next decade, one may expect the external propaganda to do the same. Industry will steadily divert external print funds to external screen funds: sponsored films. The childish miniature newspapers that telephone companies insert with their invoices will be dropped as readership disasters and the funds put into solidly distributed sponsored films with gutsy messages. The rathole "institutional" ads that companies put into peripheral periodicals will be scrapped in favor of well-programmed sponsored films.

Ad managers want out of the many traps that confront them, most of which are print traps: double-billing, co-op ads, handouts, store-opening promotions put together by local space salesmen, coupons, handbills, and special editions.

Public relations directors also want out of their special traps: personnel orientation brochures, annual reports, press handouts, giant portraits of the president for each branch office, and programs for the Christmas dinner.

All of these low forms of creativity can be upgraded to highly honorable and productive forms by translating them to the screen.

SPONSORED FILMS AS A PROMOTIONAL MEDIUM

The sponsored film industry wants very much to evolve into a clearly defined and controlled promotional medium, with all the trappings, jargon, mystique and investment of television commercials.

Such an evolution appears to be well on the way, but to identify sponsored films today as a universally accepted medium would be at best premature. What might the criteria be for judging whether an activity would qualify as a "medium"?

Let us inspect a high-profile medium to get a feeling for these criteria. Newspaper advertising space is surely the granddaddy of all advertising media, and the American Newspaper Publishers Association assures us its members run their hands through more advertising dollars than any other medium, although television's incursion on the newspapers' domain continues to take over. Classified, retail display and general display advertising are *measurable*—they are ordered and prepared in terms of lines and column inches. They are *positionable*—their placement within today's newspaper is a matter of business concern. Ads can be specifically ordered into a position such as on the theater page, for which a special rate may apply. Or they can be requested, without a special rate, to appear adjacent to live news matter or above the fold.

Newspaper ads may come as single insertion or as part of a series. When part of a series, they may appear with *frequency*, another quality of a promotional medium. The publication will induce the advertiser to run ads regularly on a frequency discount. This encourages repetition of the same ads, thus saving composition costs, and keeps the advertiser's investment spread out in time as well as space, so that the newspaper can minimize a costly runup—adding two more pages to tomorrow's paper to accommodate one large ad.

The newspaper, of course, takes money for all this service, and that is called *consideration*.

Newspaper ads are ordered, prepared and published according to certain *trade standards* by which the entire industry abides, more or less. Advertisers generally know what to say and what not to say in their ads; if not, they are quickly told. They may not lie, exaggerate to the point of misleading, deceive, or damage. The newspaper may restrict the advertiser in his use of solid black areas, running ads upsidedown, or any other artifice that would junk-up the appearance of the newspaper. Thus, there is *regulation* of the individual for the good of the majority.

Newspaper ads contain messages that are designed to motivate readers to act, ordinarily in behalf of the commercial enterprise which is the advertiser. So they have a *clear commercial purpose*. The message can be hard-sell or soft-sell, institutional- or product-sell, pioneering or competitive, factual or flamboyant. Whatever the message, the ad has a specific duty and the reader knows it. Here we can say that the medium is *recognizable as promotion* by the reader, the newspaper and the U.S. Postal Service which does not cotton to any half-ad, half-news matter if a newspaper wishes to keep its franchise to mail at reduced periodical rates.

Advertising agencies' media buyers are importantly concerned with *cost-per-thousand* (or cost-per-million) in computing the best advertising buys for their clients. Therefore, in their eyes and most others, one *sine qua non* of a legitimate medium is the ability to apply the cost-per-thousand evaluation. Time buyers consider this an exact science not to be trifled with by promoters who allege that "34,200 individuals pass our garbage cans with your message inscribed thereon, five days a week."

An accepted medium is *regional, national or international in scope*. One promotional enterprise, no matter how old or large, cannot fit the definition if it cannot relate to similar enterprises elsewhere. A trade journal must be part of the trade press. A sign is only a lonely sign or snipe until it fits the qualifications of a 13-sheet bulletin in the medium of outdoor advertising.

A promotional medium must surely be *constant and controllable*. If circulation of the newspaper were to rise and fall with each edition, advertising rates would become meaningless and advertisers could not intelligently buy space. If column numbers changed from eight to six once, that's troublesome enough. But if they varied from day to day, the advertiser never knowing with certainty how many columns of what width would appear in his newspaper, the publication would soon lose its right to call itself a proper medium.

I would suggest that a medium, to be such, must attain a certain *age and importance*. Gray hair may not be necessary, but diapers cannot swaddle a promotional enterprise eager to be accepted. Which leads to our final criterion, *acceptance*. The presence, legitimacy, activity value, effectiveness and validity of a medium are widely *accepted*. The medium is not subject to broad doubt of its virtues.

We arrive now at the comparison of sponsored films to universally accepted promotion media as a means of determining its present-day legitimacy. Let us take them in the same sequence as our above inspection of newspaper advertising.

Are sponsored films *measurable*? They surely have form, with specific running times in minutes and seconds, a general width of 16mm, photographic reproduction of picture and sound on a single length of film on a standard reel.

Are sponsored films *positionable*? Suddenly the alarm goes off. The warning light flashes. Something is awry. The comparison is not parallel.

For newspaper advertising is a medium in which the advertisements are prepared by the newspaper for its own readers. The sponsored film appears in contrast to have no base of dissemination of its own. A sponsored film has no circulation *per se*. It must first present itself to a television station for examination and transmission, or to a school for classroom projection, or to a theater for showing just before the feature attraction. It's like a truck traveling the public roads, in contrast with a train moving along its own tracks on its own right-of-way.

We could agree that sponsored films are positionable, in that they can be dependably assigned to a productive life of television, theater and community audience showings. We cannot state that a sponsored film can be positioned on a TV station schedule as scientifically as the station's own ad schedule. It is hardly a trade secret that many sponsored films are used to fill holes in a station's schedule. Relegating is not positioning. Many sponsored films do appear at times predetermined by the station film director, and these times are quite often prime times. That is assuredly positioning at its finest. But we find sponsored films in a less than admirable position on this criterion.

Do sponsored films have *frequency*? The majority of sponsored films are one-shot productions, and like one-shot ads, they don't have the frequency quality. But thanks to enterprising television stations and distributors, sponsored films with common interests are often block-booked to comprise a series. Schools will also arrange for booking several sponsored films to match course subjects, creating their own series.

Is *consideration* involved with sponsored films? One of the strengths of sponsored films is its availability on free loan. While some are rented, the rental pattern is self-defeating and sponsors will not hear of it for fear of limiting the audience for which the film was made. So television stations, theaters, schools, churches, resorts, reception rooms and all the rest get their films free and the only consideration involved is return postage. But consideration is involved in the billing of each confirmed showing by distributors to sponsors. Those dollars are just as real as advertising, public relations and marketing dollars.

Trade standards—do sponsored films have them? Certainly. The Society of Motion Picture and Television Engineers (SMPTE) provides articulate and strict technical standards on sponsored films, such as the color temperature of prints for television and off-television use. Prints are delivered with academy leaders, optical tracks, and wound ready for projection. The content of sponsored films is regulated not only by ethics and standards of the film production industry, but by the television, education, religious and other fields, each of which has its own moral and ethical code. If the sponsored film has to abide by many industry standards in addition to its own, it surely qualifies as a medium on this score.

Paradoxically, sponsored films may have an obstacle to qualifying by reason of *regulation*. As pointed out elsewhere, sponsored films are peculiarly devoid of government regulation. (Harry Golden would here insist on repeating several incantations to ward off the Evil Eye, which would surely attack after the mention of such a blessing as "No Government Regulation.") Still, television stations impose their regulations when they accept or reject sponsored films using their own strict criteria. A station will not run trash; that's a truism. A station will not run over-commercialized sponsored films; that's another. Television commercials often step over the bounds of taste. Occasionally stations will reject paid advertising offered them because they cannot find it in themselves to run commercials about overly-intimate products. Stations never face this with sponsored films. Incredibly, sponsored films are devoid of violence, sex or other unwanted qualities found widely in the media. The purity of sponsored films deserves a chapter of its own. Suffice to say that sponsored films deserve an "A" on the criterion of regulation.

Get another "A" ready on *clear commercial purpose*. While sponsored films may often be gentle, even polite in their commercial intensity, there is no attempt to hide their purpose or the identity of their sponsors. Commercialism may be explicit or implicit, but it is inevitably present. The sponsored film has a duty to its sponsor and fulfills it.

Now we face another paradox in judging whether sponsored films are *recognizable as promotion*. It is easy to picture a late arrival sitting down to look at the screen and misinterpreting a sponsored film for a documentary film or network news special. Sometimes television stations cut a showing short in order to squeeze in an extra commercial or public service announcement, and the end titles are partially or totally lost. That act could leave audiences wondering about the source of the show they just viewed. But these actions—coming in late or cutting off the identification—are not those of the sponsored film producer or sponsor, and we might not wish to fault them. Certainly sponsored films cannot be classed with publicity, which by definition and intent succeeds only when it is *not* recognizable as the promotion that it is. Planting a story in a periodical or causing a commercially-oriented news film to be shown on free-TV would put publicity at the foot of the class on the criterion of their being recognizable as promotion.

Comes now the case of *cost-per-thousand*. In a 1970 article in the *Saturday Review*, Will A. Parker, well-known film counselor, stated, "I don't talk to a client in terms of how much it's going to cost to distribute the film, I talk in terms he can understand—in cost per thousand. And in those terms the sponsored film is a better medium buy than any other. Take a picture such as *The Big Question*, which has been in circulation eight years for New York Life Insurance Co. It comes down to a cost of $3.93 per thousand, and that's for a 28-minute message. Compare that with a $7.55 cost per thousand for one full page in *Life*."

Distributors talk cost-per-thousand with sponsored films, too, especially since media buying has swung from general mass audiences to selective audiences such as those sponsored films deliver. If a sponsor performs his own distribution or retains a producer who does that work gratis, his cost-per-thousand drops dramatically with each additional showing, because his investment was essentially a one-time affair, and there are few continuing costs.

Are sponsored films *regional, national or international in scope*? Yes, they are.

Their distribution inevitably takes sponsored films out of the local or provincial category. Their content also goes beyond local parameters. The entire concept of sponsored films is one of transcending geographic limitations in the spreading of the film story.

There is wide disagreement in judging whether sponsored films are *constant and controllable* in media terms. Advocates of sponsored films would certainly want everyone to think they are. But media-oriented people, especially older ones, tend to view sponsored films as a mercurial medium, difficult to pin down when the one considers distribution specifics. The professional distribution houses have traveled light years in improving this image. Their monthly certification of showings breaks down circulation by bookings and showings. Attendance at showings is categorized by men, women, boys and girls. Exact monthly and cumulative totals are confirmed in clear printouts. Doubters can examine the breakdowns and see that Show No. 2537 was for three showings of *Rewarding Careers in Agriculture* seen by 35 boys and 20 girls at Gibson City High School, Gibson City, Illinois, on January 8.

Age and importance could be argued, too. There are those who look at sponsored films condescendingly as peripheral, outside the mainstream of promotional importance. Sponsored film people would rebut with the opinion that loud people are not necessarily important people, nor quiet people ineffectual. Sponsored films are accepted as being an old enough field, since it predates television substantially.

The final criterion, *acceptance*, must be left in limbo. The sponsored film industry would not be turning out upwards of 15,000 films a year if they were not *accepted*. American industry would not be divesting itself of half a *billion* dollars a year in sponsored films if they were not *accepted*. But producers and distributors are first to admit that the surface has only been scratched, and the lack of acceptance is the largest obstacle to growth.

Are sponsored films, therefore, a promotional medium by most, if not all, criteria? The reader may decide for himself. Few pros would deign to decide on a yes-or-no basis. Rather, sponsors, media buyers and other customers would rank their promotional investments in accordance with "priorities." This could bless or damn sponsored films, depending on their importance with each buyer.

For example, a sponsor could look at a sponsored film project as a smart way to economize—cancelling part of a costly media buy and substituting a sponsored film program, where the TV time was free. Or conversely, another sponsor could cancel a sponsored film project as an equally smart way to economize—considering it a lower priority buy than his media program.

And that is exactly what happened during the energy crunch in the mid-1970s. As many American corporations *bought* sponsored films for economy's sake as cancelled them.

THE "COMMERCIAL" ASPECTS

There is droll relation between film and explosives. The early flammable motion picture stock, nitrate film, and the nitrated organic compounds used for military high explosives are chemical country cousins.

That relationship between film and explosives persists today, even with the use of safety film stock. Motion pictures frequently disrupt nations, marriages and the public mentality with explosive force.

These explosive qualities of film are less apparent but nevertheless extant in sponsored films. There are three general categories of non-theatrical films shown to the public: television commercials; sponsored films; educational films.

These film forms vary in commercial content as well as information content. TV commercials, the most assaulted of all three, are short and contain 100 per cent commercial material. TV viewers react adversely more often than favorably, not to their commercial or informational content but because the commercials interrupt the shows viewers are watching, which is considered a breach of TV manners.They also react adversely to repetitious, hard-sell intrusions of the privacy of their brains. A large percentage of viewers react happily and excitedly to clever commercials, memorizing them, repeating their catchlines and imitating their memorable characters.

Educational films are purer than the driven snow (remembering that snow is now polluted), entirely free of commercial material. Their content is directed entirely to informing the audience, and they are underwritten by sources unwilling, unable or unconcerned with influencing their editorial content.

Sponsored films could be considered the hybrid offspring of an educational film father and a TV commercial mother. Whether the child displays the best of both family lines is something else again. Commercially speaking, the sponsored film is never at peace. The TV commercial and the educational film know where they stand at all times—on one side of the commercial wall or the other. But guess where the sponsored film sits: on the wall, like Humpty Dumpty, the fiddler on the roof and other precarious characters.

This posture is not agreeable to everyone. Sometimes I wonder if it is agreeable to anyone. Our family once drove to the Duke-Carolina game, and we were subjected to somewhat hostile glances as our car joined the football throngs on the highway. At the time we had children enrolled in both Duke and Carolina, and both decals appeared on our window. At the game, as always, we sat near the end zone, no pennants to specify our allegiance. This is known as the Great Discomfort, and it is like unto sponsored films, yea verily.

Witness the following excerpts from a letter to Richard Klein, of our shop, from one William H. Genne of the mighty National Council of the Churches of Christ. He is reacting (oh, is he ever) to Richard's script for the sponsored film, *How Do You Explain Death to Children?*

As preliminary information, let me say that our firm felt a sort of pride when the Coggins·Granite people in Elberton, Georgia, agreed to sponsor this film. The theme had been the subject of an excellent book by Rabbi Earl Grollman but no film had ever been made on it that we could find. It is a valid and timely subject, inasmuch as Americans are ever so busy teaching their children all (sic) about sex and nothing about death. Dr. Grollman was wonderful about helping us plan and write the script, and so were several medical, educational and religious organizations, including the National Council of the Churches of Christ.

Near the end of the script, our sponsor asked the inevitable—to include some self-serving words about granite monuments like the Kennedy graves, Iwo Jima, and Tomb of the Unknowns. We felt fine about it. The alliance of commercial with education interests at that script point was sensitive and constructive, just what we aimed for. The film characters were in a cemetery, and little children's voices reacting to death were being heard on the track.

Well, William Genne, William Fore and Emily Gibbes read Richard's script and here is what we got in the mail:

I did not realize from your earlier letter that the "documentary" on which you were working was a commercial for gravestones. Perhaps this explains why there is no mention of cremation as a less expensive, less ground-consuming way of honoring the deceased. How would you answer the child who asks, "Was he (the deceased) boxed or was he burned?" Certainly in this day of ecological awareness, we should mention that as an alternative.

Certainly we must take exception to lines 18-21 in the sound text which states ". . .it is the granite memorial that best commemorates that remembrance." This seems to us to be a crass, tasteless commercial intrusion into otherwise helpful material. . . .

Since you indicate that this is a presentation of a granite company, we must request that you do not identify the National Council of the Churches of Christ in the USA in any form or manner as having any relationship whatsoever with your production.

We think you have much excellent material in your presentation but wish it were presented in a more acceptable context.

There was obviously no way to turn around such reaction to a rational point of view, but I did believe the organization should rethink the concept of sponsored films. So they got this reply:

Your October 21 letter was certainly a disappointment. You bless us for some excellent material in our script for *How Do You Explain Death to Children*? and then cut us to pieces for working for the Coggins people who mine granite in Georgia for monuments.

It all reminds me of *Guys and Dolls* and other stories where the prim and proper folk were shocked to find their good works were supported by gambling and liquor money. Why, virtually every TV show today is broken up by someone's commercials. *It is a way of life.*

I really think you have overkilled with your accusations of "crass, tasteless commercial intrusion. . ." The few lines at the end thrown to the good people who put up $40,000 are, I believe, little enough return for the gesture of making this film possible, the only one on the subject.

In strange contrast to your precipitous reaction, Dr. Grollman and other religious, medical and educational organizations and sources have reacted to this script most pleasantly and positively. Some did suggest modifying the wording of the monument reference, which we did right away, but did not use any language close to yours of your next-to-last paragraph.

Regarding cremation, nothing in the film plunks for burial over cremation. Indeed, granite monuments are used in cremations, too. Another entire film could be devoted to your point of ecologic and economic values of cremation, but you seem way off course in suggesting that our film on explaining death to children is the proper forum.

We will comply with your wishes and leave the National Council of the Churches of Christ out of the film altogether, though we regret that you did not simply and calmly ask us to resubmit the script after making suggested changes.

You seem to harbor an innate bitterness about "gravestones" and espouse cremation as the one proper conclusion for the body. In spite of many books and exposures of funeral and burial abuses, most Americans, including the undersigned, still find comfort burying our dead and marking the grave. You in your position should respect that truth and not insist that all this is a matter of right and wrong.

I have but one purpose in writing this letter: to ask your organization to maintain an open mind about sponsored films. I believe it is valid and worthwhile for American industry to spend its money to back needed films that otherwise would never be produced for lack of funds. You obviously prefer to damn industry if they include a few self-serving words in their own films, and I think that is unfortunate.

Our people have worked many years to cultivate industry to turn from printing catalogs and making sales films and spend their funds on public-need films. They have not only agreed, but have gradually reduced their commercial values in such films to unbusinesslike levels. We wish your organization would take an attitude of welcoming such a trend rather than turning your back on it.

Perhaps I should have gone on to tell the story that our friend Dr. Georg Munck wrote in the University of Dusseldorf Annual. Dr. Munck heads Leonaris-Film in Boblingen, Germany, maker of superb sponsored films, especially in the medical and scientific fields. "During the Great War, 300,000 soldiers of all countries concerned died of malaria in the Balkans. (I myself have seen their graves in Salonika and Athens.) In the same region during the Second World War, there were less than a hundred deaths from malaria. True, quinine had been replaced by Atebrin, but says Ernst Rodenwaldt in his work *A Doctor's Life in the Tropics*, there was also a film: '. . .this film gave tens of thousands of soldiers in Greece, Russia, Italy and the islands an insight into the mechanics of malaria and the importance of prophylactic action and protection from mosquitoes. . .'"

That film was *The Enemy—Malaria*, produced in 1942 by the Berlin Academy of Military Medicine. A few years later the film would just have likely been a Leonaris-Film production, sponsored by Merck, Hoechst or Ciba-Geigy. In such a case, I wonder if the armies watching it would find the sponsor's commercial segments to be a "crass, tasteless commercial intrusion into otherwise helpful material. . ."

Let us not avoid the often obvious fact that sponsored films are indefensibly commercial at times, and no one knows better than the producer.

Tom Hodge manages Cathay Film Services in Singapore, a very substantial production house where sponsored films are made for clients all over Southeast Asia. He fights the same battle for commercial subtety that we producers fight all over the world, from Sydney to Oslo.

"We were making a film for an oil company about service to a developing area," Tom told me. "It was an idea film with ample room for creativity. But as we got into it, the company's public relations department was merged with their marketing department. Suddenly the marketing manager was judging our film on the frequency of the firm's name appearing on trucks, hoardings and gas stations. The result was that we couldn't find an audience for the film because everyone, correctly, reacted by saying it was just an advertising pretense."

Tom Hodge once tried to sell an airline on making a sponsored film about what an exciting place Southeast Asia is, only to be asked, "How many times are you going to show my planes?" He finds travel films to be the worst (or best) example of wasted money in the sponsored film field.

"The hotel, car rental and airlines people look at a travel film and think, 'Boy, what a terrific tourist film! Full of hotels. Restaurants. Plugs. Plugs. Plugs!' They see it solely in advertising terms, little realizing that the film will earn next to no showings anywhere simply because it *is* full of advertising."

WHAT'S WRONG WITH SPONSORED FILMS?

Elsewhere we point out the many things that are *right* about sponsored films, such as their disciplined morals. Now let us ask, what is *wrong* with sponsored films?

If we consider the wealth of creativity, months of production work and long suffering with committees that sponsored film producers deliver for around $40,000, the answer would have to be: practically nothing. Using the $40,000 per half-hour sponsored film as a basis, producers deliver sponsored films for $160,000 per two hours of film. A TV network two-hour special prices out at around $500,000. A Hollywood two-hour film costs its backers perhaps $6 million. So, considering the amount of work and creativity sponsored filmmakers are willing to devote to their product, we should not spend too many hours around the water cooler poking verbal holes in sponsored films.

But the temptation is just short of overwhelming—underwhelming, as it were. Producers are highly self-critical, as well they should be, and are not too reluctant to talk about other producers' work as well.

Start, please, with triteness. Those who have seen many, perhaps too many, sponsored films see some disturbing patterns. They see clearly a tendency for producers to imitate not only other sponsored films but *their own*. Some filmmakers think that once they've done something successfully, they should build on it by doing it again and again. Others think that an art form should develop in sponsored films, just as in ragas and karate. There may be merit in these repetition rationales, but they are no excuse for creating trite films. Four-year-old children are adept at doping out the outcome of Saturday morning animated films. Ten-year-olds can master the ending of any police TV show within ten minutes of its start. It's a game people play. Of course, if the players stay to the end to see if they were right, something is accomplished in the way of viewership. But if the viewer wins the game, the sponsor loses.

Trite films all too often come from old producers who should have been shot or retired years ago. Tom Hope says, "Older producers are not current in their style." That is a kind way of saying they are turning out hack. The opening tease is hackneyed. The opening and closing titles are hackneyed. The talking heads are hackneyed. The music is hackneyed. The narration is hackneyed. The most one can say for some of these films from old-time houses is that they are true replicas of sponsored films made in the 1950s and 1960s.

Sponsored films go wrong in length. The requirement to fit films to TV quarter-hour and half-hour lengths sometimes spreads out a shorter story instead of compressing a longer one. Editors are told to cut the film to 14:30 and very little else, so that's what they do: cut to 14:30 and very little else.

Sponsored films go wrong in narration. Voices are stentorian, staid or static. A seasoned viewer can *hear* the narrator getting his cues, being told to stretch, compress and emphasize. He can *hear* the narrator *read*. Is that an offense? Top grade offense. The good narrators do not read or recite. They communicate.

But not too much. Tired sponsored films get that way because some idiot insists on wall-to-wall running at the mouth.

Sponsored films go wrong with talking heads, especially rotten ones. Theatrical casting directors know so well that 99 out of 100 good mainline Americans aren't worth their weight in used trusses when it comes to projecting their own personalities to an audience. But somehow sponsored filmmakers rank among the naive. They accept the sponsor's request to show Gertrude Godzilla as the expert in her field on camera for seven minutes. Gertrude, unfortunately, has a tic, a predilection for saying *vis à vis,* and a tendency to say in a thousand words what non-experts say in ten. Even good talking heads turn films into junk when they dominate the film and their charisma runs out.

Sponsored films go wrong with their form. Writers and producers should ask themselves whether their films *must* open with an early sample of what is yet to come, *must* show things chronologically complete with flashbacks, *must* hear tracks of narration over a bed of stock *all-purpose neutral* music, *must* involve presentation of a problem followed by evolution of the solution, and *must* end with a sunset, montage, zoom-to-longshot or somebody, anybody, *smiling* ("Ah, Pancho! Ah, Cisco!").

Sponsored films go wrong by underestimating their audience. Someone is still quoting and following the old saw that the average movie mentality is 11 years.

A sponsor just recently asked me to change *dialog* to *two-way discussion* on the grounds the audience might not understand the word. Another recently told me he had a hard time with his A-V people keeping our word *confounder* in his script because they thought most viewers would not know it. A teacher or writer knows to uplift and stimulate his followers with fresh words and fresh word usage. They don't lose their students or readers, they activate them. But sponsored film writers and filmmakers sweat to simplify. They hold this fear that 17½ per cent of the viewers will get lost if any specifics are quoted in the metric system. Small wonder some sponsored films outperform sleeping pills three-to-one.

Two professional sources that perpetrate bad sponsored films are narrators and stock music houses. Old-time TV personalities think half their success is wrapped up in their ability to modulate their voices through two octaves—the old "50-kilowatt voice." Those days are gone forever. Viewers are little concerned with the chest measurements of a bass-baritone radio announcer trying to sound like Marc Antony. They go for straight-shooting dispensers of information offered in clear tones and terms.

Stock music catalogs, even today, contain carefully prepared lists of stings, fanfares, bridges, main titles and tags. Stock tapes bear music so dated it could be matched up with art deco exhibitions. Twice we contacted CBS Records' EZ Cue Library about newer material and were told nothing new was available. They fully expect producers to use their stuff reverently for eternity plus six months. The arrival on the scene of the synthesizer came just in time.

Sponsored films go wrong when they are illustrated lectures and not motion pictures at all. Historic materials especially succumb to this treatment. The picture side of the script reads like this: "Archive shot of Scott in youth," "Battlefield scene from contemporary book" and "Zoom to closeup of rifle in etching of Scott in battle."

These weaknesses are not those of sponsored films alone. But sponsored films are those with the big audiences and that is reason enough to improve them.

Misuse of the medium is a failure pointed out by Tom Hodge in Singapore. Some sponsors and producers consider sponsored films a proper medium for conveying information. "Anyone can draw information from encyclopedias, directories and pamphlets," Hodge reminds you and me. "A sponsored film should make you *feel* something. It should *involve* you. It should *motivate* you into action or thinking leading to action, because you have *felt* something. The first thing I ask any sponsor is, Let's pretend your film is finished. The audience has seen it. They're on their way home. What do you want them to feel inside about what they've seen? *Not* what you want them to *know*; only what you want them to *feel*?" That is sponsor preparation of the highest order and something all producers could well follow.

Recently Tom Hodge saw a short film in a Singapore cinema. He knew it was a sponsored film because the producer-director is a friend of his in New York who makes only sponsored films. But there was no indication whatsoever in the story line of the film or in the title credits as to the sponsor identity. "It was a fascinating film selling nothing but ideas," Hodge reported. "I wrote my friend to find out what intelligent sponsor had paid for such a wonderful film with no credit and no plugs. It was *DuPont*." Hodge philosophizes that most sponsors are like most religious lay persons: they are not content to see the good work done. They want credit for it, too.

Lastly, but not finally, too many sponsored films are forgettable. I would like to tell you about each of them but I've forgotten them. Sponsored films in this respect are like folks. One lady can run at the mouth for an hour straight and the only things you remember are the thoughts that ran through your mind while she droned. (My brother-in-law says knitting is something women do to occupy their minds while they are talking.) Another lady can add verbal condiments to her conversation and you can't get her discussion out of your mind.

Sponsored films can bust your brain or send you sleepy-bye. I once saw a sponsored film about dumps. It wanted to make the point that piling rubbish in a city dump was not a proper answer, and that organic materials do not readily decompose as some would have us believe. Now how would you go about making that point unforgettable? Would you up and say, through the narrator, "Piling rubbish in a city dump is not a proper answer. Organic materials do not readily decompose as some would have us believe"? This to the accompaniment of charts showing rates of decay of vegetables, paper, fabric and wood?

The film I witnessed did it right. The crew went into the dump and got a fast *cinéma verité* interview with the operator of a tractor whose job was to spread the incoming rubbish. Here is the essence of what he said:

"You tell me all this stuff is biodegradable? That's garbage, man. Here. Watch. I'll go down a foot. There. Look. There's a page from the Chicago Tribune of August 17, 1961. You can read every damn word on the page."

Can you forget that image? I couldn't. It haunts me. I will go to my grave with it. God bless the sponsor and producer who left me with that magnificent imagery. It told me so much so quickly so permanently. It told me that sponsored films can be gorgeous.

One of the most profound critiques of sponsored films as a species comes from Irene Wood, editor of non-print reviews for *The Booklist*, the respected publication of the American Library Association.

Many producers consider getting a film reviewed in *The Booklist* to be tantamount to a national festival award. Hundreds are passed by for every one Ms. Wood writes up. And those that are reviewed are thrown as many rocks as roses. Ms. Wood observes:

My objections are not to the sponsorship of films in itself, *if* the sponsorship is just that—a low-keyed sponsor mention and not a blatant commercial hard-sell. Most sponsored films do underplay the commercial interest and so must be considered in light of their worth as films, that is, the technique and content of the finished product.

Unfortunately, that is where most sponsored films miss their marks. The film techniques used in the production are hackneyed or ordinary. Frequently, the acting is stiff and lacks credibility. In essence, if a sponsored film could stand on its own as a *film,* there certainly would be no objection to its sponsorship; in fact, viewers would be most impressed that a corporate sponsor would underwrite such a fine production.

Ms. Wood catches the sponsored film producer with his cinematic pants down. She accuses him of using the umbrella of sponsored films to keep the rain of criticism from his mediocrity. In a polite way she reminds our industry that if a sponsored film is a loser, it is so not because it is sponsored but because the people who made the film turned out a failure *per se*. It is a lesson sponsored filmmakers dare not forget.

Chapter Two

The Sponsored Film Industry

EVOLUTION

The unacquainted might guess that an industry investing upwards of $40,000 in each film would have its footprints all over it. I'm happy to say that is not the case.

Back in the early days, heavy-handedness was the *sine qua non* of sponsored films. More often than not they were two-reel commercials entertaining viewers with *The Story of Shoes, The Story of Oil, The Story of Laxatives,* and *The Story of Boilers.**

Hapless, helpless producers cranked out *industrials*, knowing full well that there just wasn't anything else, after theatrical entertainment, to put on film. I remember Mr. Sterling, a New Englander who opened Sterling Industrial Films in Charlotte, North Carolina, right after World War II. He thought he'd have the market all to himself; that he did. He plugged away at it, honestly and in dignity to the end, never to profit from the infant television which could have been his professional rebirth.

I was making up *The Charlotte Observer*, and selling display space as well. Mr. Sterling bought a small year-to-year contract from me just so he could approach my boss, P. H. Batte, about making *The Story of The Charlotte Observer*. He figured that Batte would welcome him as a valued customer and then he'd parlay that into a sale. He didn't know Pryor Hamlin Batte, who kept him on the string, promising to take the matter up with Curtis Johnson (God) for a couple of years. All that time poor Mr.

---

* Sad to report that one current sponsored film directory lists no fewer than 27 films beginning, "The Story of. . . ."

Sterling kept buying that weekly card in the *Observer* and praying. I don't think he ever realized that Batte sold Sterling instead of Sterling selling Batte.

And now I remember Duke Sanchez. He was a millworker who had to quit textiles because he was allergic to the stuff. He taught himself photography and opened Duke Photo in downtown Charlotte. Made a decent living the rest of his life with sittings, proofs, hand-tinted portraits—the whole bit. When TV revved up in 1949, he was there with an early Bach Auricon, ready to help our infant company. The first TV commercial in our part of the world was a 60-second hard-sell pitch for Hostess Venetian Blinds featuring two-year-old Richard Klein raising hell with a Hostess blind. He climbed up it, tied it in knots, set fire to it, stomped it and beat hell out of it. I still have a few outtakes but the original is long since gone. We transmitted the thing the night before WBTV went on the air in September 1949, on a closed-circuit show in the old Armory Auditorium, and on the air for months afterward. Station time cost $23 per spot and it didn't pull a single order. But the client and we had a stake in history.

Duke shot that and many other early commercials for us with his trusty Auricon in his Trade Street studios. He also did a few industrials, including some for his old textile friends. They followed the genre of all such pre-TV films. Everything was scripted chronologically, so viewers wouldn't get confused. No shot lasted fewer than seven seconds, because anything shorter was considered choppy and unsuitable for the viewer to absorb. Just about every item in the manufacturer's catalog got some exposure, as well as the officers, directors, staff and the sponsor president's family. Those early sponsored films were first cousins to the Sunday rotogravure supplements that itinerant salesmen promoted for local newspapers. If the advertiser wanted his wife's church Sodality group in his roto space, he got it, so long as he took out an ad.

Their only similarity to *The Plow That Broke the Plains* and *The River* was that they were all on 16mm black-and-white film. Beautiful educational films like those—and a few forgettable ones as well—were shown during school assembly programs all over America. After school you might catch Reginald Denny and Charlie Butterworth in a 16mm reduction of a Hollywood epic for ten cents, shown in a half-empty school auditorium.

But you rarely saw an industrial in a school. Or a church. Or at a civic club. Not *unless* there was a special audience interest in a particular subject available from an industry source. That was the key: a matching of interests. It was a frail thing at first, almost an accident. American industries that had been underwriting industrials for sales purposes discovered a peripheral market in showing their film to schools, churches and civic clubs. The boss was invited to address the Evanston Rotary

Club. He popped a couple of smart pills in his mouth and took a projector, screen and his new film, *The Story of Soap*, with him—might as well get some extra mileage out of that fat $3,500 investment, he figured.

When "The End" flashed upon the screen, the boss was startled to hear his fellow Rotarians applauding. Suddenly he saw himself a success in Show Biz. And even better, his friends were asking questions. "I never knew soap was so interesting, Joe," one said. "Joe, you're in a fascinating business there," another remarked, shaking his hand.

Was that the way sponsored films were born? Certainly. The scene was repeated, with variations on the theme, thousands of times all over America. The successful program chairman in a fraternal organization was the fellow who knew where to put his hands on a film and a projector at least once a month. (It's still that way, right?) Then Lion president Jim Whitaker would stand up and say, "Let's give old Barney here a hand. He's been the best program chairman we've had since I've entered the chairs. Brings us great films, just like the one we just saw, *The Story of Bananas*." (Applause)

In the neighborhood theaters, audiences would get the full treatment: two full-length features, two shorts, previews and commercials produced by Motion Picture Advertising Service in New Orleans or Alexander Films in Colorado Springs.

So there yet was no hybrid. No combination of soft-sell with hard-sell. No mix of PR values with marketing values. What you saw in theaters, schools, clubs, churches, camps and resort hotels was either straight entertainment or straight sell.

Then a few industrial film pioneers *learned the exquisite power of understatement*. It didn't really take American industry so long to adapt this weapon that they had used for generations. If you were selling a Pierce Arrow motor car, you understated its virtues rather than reciting them in scandalously large type.

An executive of Lipton once spent more than an hour with me reciting the pleasures he had filming the Lipton Regatta each year. "Do you pour any tea on screen?" I asked. "Never," he replied. "What do you spend each year?" "Oh, including foreign language versions and world distribution, about a quarter of a million dollars." "What commercial benefit do you get from it?" His answer: "We get enormous value from it simply by identifying the films as *The Lipton Regatta*."

That was Style. And if anything needed style, it was early sponsored films. You couldn't blame the producer for heavy-handedness. If the client wanted to jam more commercial exposure in a film, closely followed by his ad manager and ad agency, the producer buckled and complied. But when clients began appreciating the full spectrum of public relations, the sponsored film came closer to becoming an honest woman.

Sponsored films could never have germinated if a number of non-theatrical production houses were not already in business to form the seed bed. According to *Hope Reports*, the oldest known non-theatrical producer still in operation is the Reid Ray Film Company of St. Paul, Minnesota. It started in February, 1910, as Raths-Seavolt Motion Pictures. Today, Reid Ray teaches cinematography at Rochester Institute of Technology. Just a few months later Jamison Handy began his timeless, famous house in Detroit, the Jam Handy Organization. We in the business imagine we've seen the name Jam Handy on everything from candy bars to windmills, it's such a byword. Founder Handy "still actively heads his production company, although it has been divested of many divisions to form other companies," Tom Hope writes. "Now it is only a small shell of the former non-theatrical giant."

Bray Studios opened in New York in 1911. Wilding began in Detroit in 1914. Jamieson Film Company started in Dallas in 1916. Filmack, known best for its theatrical trailers, began in 1919 in Chicago. Other well-known producers who were flourishing before World War II include Jerry Fairbanks, Calvin, Neil Douglas, Hardcastle, Audio Productions, Sarra-Chicago, Lasky, F. K. Rockett, Walter S. Craig, and Crawley.

Hope finds that as a rule non-theatrical film producers—the ones turning out sponsored films—are more stable than feature film producers. He cites more than 40 industry filmmakers that opened before World War II are still very much in business.

Industry use of films dates back almost to the invention of motion pictures. Jim Card, Curator of Eastman House in Rochester, has pictures from the 1890's that we would classify today as sponsored films. Standard Oil of Indiana was into film early in the 1900's. Jamison Handy remembers his first client in 1911 was National Cash Register. General Electric backed one in 1907 and International Harvester bought film in 1911. Caterpillar Tractor credited their film with helping to market 10,000 earthmoving machines to the Allies before and during World War I.

With all due respect to the pioneers of the industry, the public deserves most of the credit for the robust growth of sponsored films out of infancy. You can see it in the statistics on sales of 16mm film projectors. In 1934 50—count 'em—50 projectors were sold, all to industry. Next year 800 were bought, 600 of them by business and industry. In 1936 sales reached 1,500 units, but only 600 of those were purchased by industry. Schools, churches and libraries were getting into the 16mm format in a positive, significant way. By 1939, as World War II began in Europe, 16mm projector sales had reached 5,000 a year, and 4,000 of those were going to the public.

During the war years fabrication of projectors was stopped except for armed forces' use. 1944's figure of 10,000 projectors zoomed to 18,000 in 1945 and 32,200 in 1946. Growth after that was only gradual to a high of 76,200 in 1972. Today, some 266,000 are in active use in business. Perhaps another million are *around*, some in operation, some being cannibalized for parts. I am continually shaking my head at the ancient 16mm projectors I see around. DeVrys, RCAs, Ampros and Movie-Mites are even today in active commerce among used equipment suppliers, and not to supply vintage projector collections either. The First Methodist Church may well own two spanking new self-loading Bell & Howells, but they are still holding onto their early Kodak projector. It looks like too important a piece of machinery to throw out, and nobody wants to buy it. Every so often it is pressed into use in Sunday School and it works just fine.

Growth of sponsored films during the 17 years *Hope Reports* has traced it has been modest in comparison to the growth of in-house training and sales films. These are Tom Hope's figures for sponsored films made by industrial producers:

1956	1,400
1957	1,600
1958	1,500
1959	1,700
1960	1,500
1961	1,480
1962	1,700
1963	1,900
1964	2,170
1965	1,960
1966	2,500
1967	2,200
1968	2,560
1969	2,760
1970	1,980
1971	2,070
1972	2,100

In the same period in-plant productions by industry grew from 2,595 to 8,000 films. But do not be misled. While the numbers of non-theatrical films other than sponsored films might grow enormously, it is still the sponsored films that have the giant audiences. There is no formal distribution investment in training films, sales films, orientation films, engineering films and all the other non-theatrical categories. But there is a vast investment in distribution in sponsored films. And the investment in each sponsored film *production* far exceeds the investment in all other non-theatrical types. The sponsored film may average $40,000. A training film is lucky to market at $14,000. So numbers are not the most vital criterion in determining the growth of the importance of sponsored films.

The comparison can be taken another step. The entity of the sponsored film as it emerged after World War II as a new medium took on an awesome stature. Suddenly the product of a Reid Ray or a Jamison

Handy was no longer only a commodity bought to serve a specific need, like teaching warehousemen at distributors in the field how to unpack crates without damaging the merchandise. The new sponsored film was creative, sensitive, written like a short story, paced like a theatrical drama, inquisitive like a *Post* reporter, and full of the heady qualities of the feature film. It was hard for the training film on unpacking crates to fail. It was all too easy for the sponsored film to fail. The stakes were big. Industry could not permit their friendly sales-film producer to touch the the propaganda machine called the sponsored film in which they were now investing. Newer producers who understood media psychology were retained to make sponsored films.

As television grew from an oddity watched by sidewalk superintendents staring at sets in store windows to a tiger of a new medium, stock industrial films could no longer be used as public relations vehicles. Industry and producers had to come up with films that thought and provoked thinking. The sponsored film of 1950 told Optimist Club members how fortunate they were because America was the richest oil nation in the world, and their way of life was superior because of it. The sponsored film of 1976 was telling another generation of Optimist Club members how to squeeze more miles out of every gallon of scarce gasoline, and this time they believed and were paying close attention to everything they saw.

Television grew in all directions. Millionaires were created with the granting of franchises to go on the air by the Federal Communications Commission. VHF stations proliferated until UHF channels had to be opened up. Coaxial cables joined isolated stations to become real-time networks. Programming hours spread from a few nighttime hours to 18 and more hours per day.

That did it. Old feature movies had been plugging programming holes for many a TV station. By the mid-60's, stations were hurting for fresh material. Reruns of made-for-TV sitcoms were limited and drawing not-so-great ratings. Too much children's programming was scaring away adult-product sponsors. Old movies were run four to eight times each on one station because stations made contracts for unlimited runs at one flat fee, and the audiences were in pain.

Stations looked around for new programming sources. Their eyes fell quickly on sponsored films. *Advantage:* they were free. *Disadvantage:* they came mostly as single titles and not as series productions. *Advantage:* they were wonderfully flexible, filling embarrassing gaps before and after sports events and at seasonal time changes. *Disadvantage:* so many of them were insipidly dull or loaded with commercial plugs. *Advantage:* there were some real gems among them, worthy of promotion. *Disadvantage:* program directors had to scrounge all over to bring the prints in to preview. *Advantage:* they made great spot vehicles for increased local profits.

The sponsored film came of age. It was to be an important source of information and entertainment as long as audiences with projectors and TV sets wanted to see fresh shows.

RESEARCH

Yesterday

There is little that offers more gratification than having time on your side and looking back a few years on the work of researchers to see how smart they were at doping the present and future of their trade. We all have that opportunity now as we examine the finest survey ever conducted in the sponsored film business—up to the year 1954.

It's called *The Dollars and Sense of Business Films* and it was published that year by the prestigious Association of National Advertisers in New York. The ANA film steering committee that prepared the study was illustrious:

John Flory—Eastman Kodak Company, Chairman
Dr. V. C. Arnspiger—Encyclopedia Britannica Films, Inc.
William M. Bastable—Swift & Company
Leo Beebe—Ford Motor Company
Gordon Biggar—Shell Oil Company
Eyre Branch—Standard Oil Company of New Jersey
John J. Dostal—RCA Victor Division, Radio Corporation
of America
Harold F. Driscoll—Bell & Howell Company
John K. Ford—General Motors Corporation
William Hazel—Standard Brands Incorporated
Thomas W. Hope—General Mills, Inc.
J. Whitney King—American Can Company
Willis H. Pratt, Jr.—American Telephone and Telegraph Company
William E. Sawyer—Johnson & Johnson
Virgil L. Simpson—E. I. du Pont de Nemours and Company, Inc.

Well, you are already wondering, did these good folks hit the mark or blow it, way back there in 1954?

In 128 pages of charts, graphs, lists, illustrated paradigms, homilies and platitudes, the committee appears to have come up with facts and conclusions that extended further into the future than they would have dared to imagine.

Oh, yes, some of their statements look a little quaint today:

Color films are favored nearly four-to-one. With color television now materializing, this ratio can be expected to swing even further in this direction.

Television, instead of competing with the traditional type of institutional film, seems to be furnishing to sponsors a valuable extra means of distribution.

The screen can enlarge or reduce the actual size of objects.

. . . .It is surprising to note that 89 percent of all the films here surveyed were originally intended for school and college distribution as one of their prime audiences. This may indicate an increasing tendency on the part of American industry to present its message to future consumers and voters while they are forming lifelong habits and opinions.

But the majority of their findings were valid in their day and valuable to the industry today. Not the least of such findings was an opening statement by John Flory that concluded, ". . .The business film has definitely come of age as an important medium of public communications."

The committee carefully examined 157 sponsored films in active distribution in 1954. Theirs was original research, and they quickly felt the need of additional continuing research, something that is still being vocalized today. They singled out the need for research in selective audiences for sponsored films. "Many of today's films seem to be aimed at too many audiences. Research is needed to prove the relative value of designing a film to appeal to a single type of audience—or at most, to a few homogeneous ones—as against a film designed for a number of different audiences." Now that was and is true wisdom.

The committee called for documentation of case histories of successful sponsored films. (They would have been better researchers if they had called for such work on unsuccessful films as well.)

They proposed establishment of a National Audio-Visual or Audience Registry to compile and maintain data on number, location and type of audiences for sponsored films. (The volume you are now reading is probably the first published effort to detail all such audiences; see Pages 103-130.)

Facilities and trade practices of distributors should be published and uniform distribution records encouraged, the ANA committee suggested, and their hopes became reality.

"Special surveys are needed not only to explore existing methods of reaching audiences but also to trail-blaze new ones," they went on. "For example, television is a field of prime interest; the export market (now that magnetic projectors are available); and the farm and educational fields need constructive re-examination." Little did they know that one day a TV network just for Alaska pipeline workers would be showing sponsored films, or that awed children and parents would be rollercoastered *into* projections of sponsored films at Disney World.

In their infinite wisdom, the group recommended a checklist on responsibilities of the sponsor and distributor, to compare to the ANA's excellent publication, *A Check-List for Producer and Sponsor Responsibilities in the Production of Motion Pictures*, which has been in useful service for many years.

Another recommendation: "The wide applicability of films to the various needs of business organizations and the relatively modest investment required to produce an effective film suggest the need for alerting all levels of business management to the value of the film as a tool and the best means of employing it." To which an interested person could add only, *Amen*.

The committee saved the most profound recommendation for last. "Vast progress has been made since the end of World War II by social and psychological scientists in studying audience reactions and the factors contributing to effective film production. These findings should be codified and translated into terms understandable and useful to both sponsor and producer."

Today

Two of the wisest moves the Eastman Kodak Company made to support and encourage the sponsored film industry were to hire two specialists as consultants. Bringing John Flory, an industrial film producer and, later, Tom Hope, an in-plant film and A-V man, into the fold as advisers on non-theatrical films provided assistance to countless producers, business sponsors, organizations and government agencies involved in motion pictures. Kodak generously allowed Flory and Hope to spend the necessary time to help their customers succeed.

Shortly after Hope joined Kodak in 1954, he and Flory were asked about the economics and potential of the young non-theatrical film and audio-visual field. Since no such data existed, the two were urged to see what they could come up with as an analysis of this growth industry. In 1958 Flory, with Hope's assistance, issued a report on the economic impact of the non-theatrical film, followed the next year by a jointly authored major study of the nature and scope of a by then $200 million industry. Another $50 million was being spent on all other media. Once the Society of Motion Picture and Television Engineers published it, executives in the industry found the information so valuable that they urged that annual updates be made.

The reports grew in stature, depth and size. After the initial broad study, the annual reports grew from one page in 1960 to 16 pages nine years later. Seventeen thousand reprints were sold in 1969. Doing the reports outside his regular duties at Kodak, Tom Hope's "labor of love" became too much labor. He regretfully announced in the 1969 edition that the reports would be discontinued.

Calls of dismay poured in. He was told the reports had filled an otherwise empty hole for the sponsored film and A-V industry. So Hope explored various possibilities to have the reports continued. Several associations which showed interest found that what Hope had done voluntarily would cost at least $20,000 a year. One highly interested private research firm, if it took the projection, would sell reports for

$2,000 each! That would have generally reduced buyers to the few largest firms; it ran against the Hope grain.

After considering three offers from different companies who wanted Hope to join them and devote much of his time to the now widely-used A-V market reports, he and his wife decided to set up their own company, *Hope Reports*. Hope left Kodak in April, 1970. The first edition of *Hope Reports AV-USA 1969* was issued the following September.

From the single volume, the *Hope Reports* output has grown to a dozen different annual publications and a varying quantity of private studies and surveys done under contract for corporations and organizations.

The Hope organization conducts 80 to 100 surveys a year. The basic data come from the manufacturers. Surveys of film labs, videotape duplicators, industrial producers, dealers, end users and other segments bring different perspectives. Every year several surveys entirely cover certain aspects and segments of the industry. After that, models are established and follow-up surveys are made which each year encompass a sample of carefully selected respondents. Government data and industry surveys are utilized.

Tom Hope heads a staff of eight, five who do research, at the Rochester, New York, office. An additional nine knowledgeable individuals based in Rochester and seven other cities across the country augment the full-time Rochester staff for big surveys, especially major ones done for clients as private studies.

Like archeologists, the Hope people gather little, unrecognizable pieces and fit them together into meaningful, industry-wide performance records and trends. They gather such information as a firm's annual film output in detail, employment changes, capital expenditures, net profit, and plans and forecasts for the future. From manufacturers they gather sales data for cameras, other production equipment, projectors and so on.

Using the *Hope Reports*, subscribers can match their own track record against that of the industry which includes among others their direct competitors. But much more can be gleaned from the reports. "It's surprising that some businessmen operate with blinders on," Tom confides. "They think only of their particular product line and their immediate competitors, not realizing that an entirely different medium or line could seriously affect their future business."

Tom could be referring in part to me and my peers who make it in 16mm film production and tend to ignore the presence of videotape and the possibility of a videodisc someday. He, of course, is right. Recognizing him as the guru of the industry, one can appreciate his transcending view of the many narrow parts and people that make up our total industry. That is what makes *Hope Reports* valuable.

Take one report for example. *Hope Reports Industry: AV and*

Training lists the 500 major producers by name, chronologically arranged. It does not list producers who folded up over the years, just those who survived. Another table has a tally of more than 3,000 film producers listed by cities. Of the 3,090 which identify themselves as producers (as listed in telephone directories), Tom Hope considers 2,000 actually in the production business on a full-time basis. Who are the other 1,000? Hope replies, "Oh, maybe a retired cameraman or a part-time producer who will do a little free-lance or part-time work." Another 560 list themselves as audio-visual producers.

Hope's nose does not appear to be all-powerful in photographs of him, but it is a mighty nose nevertheless. He can smell a trend in the sponsored film industry before anyone else realizes a change is taking place. For example, he sees many new production companies formed by young filmmakers coming off the campuses as giving the well-established firms some genuine competition. "Tough as that is, this development has a positive result, too. Some older producers should retire. The young filmmakers have a much lower overhead cost. They do not expect as much salary as someone who has been in the business for 30 years and is now drawing pay well up in the five-figure bracket. This pressure keeps the free enterprise system on its toes." Hope also notes that it seems that for every sponsored film producer who folds up, several new ones spring up. He does not project that point further, but he could easily say that there is going to be one whale of a lot of film boutiques, or a lot of casualties, or both.

Another book, *Hope Reports Video II*, reveals facts and trends of videotape production as well as film production. Compared are production costs, duplication (printing), distribution costs, and such.

The report shows that there are 95 full service videotape producers and another 222 TV program production houses using videotape. Furthermore, 56 motion picture producers have videotape capability. Of the total 373 producers, 178 are in the east, 69 in the central states and 126 in the west.

So far, most videotape production is being done in-house rather than by independent producers. Because of the difference in technology and approach to production, Hope envisions most work continuing in the film medium with videotape only taking over that production for which film is not ideally suited in the first place, the recording of a live talk or presentation on a quick basis. Where a story or plot is to be used, the film medium is superior to that of tape, according to Hope. "There is a challenge to sponsored film producers to do a better job, possibly using both media. But the capability of making good motion picture prints from videotape at a reasonable cost still does not exist. The 16mm film is the only motion medium which can be used any place in the world on anyone's projector. Film format super-8 is also a compatible worldwide standard today, but the cartridge (packaging) aspect is far from uniform. The use of super-8 film stands to become a major medium used by business and industry in the next decade. It is the only medium which is highly portable with good quality."

Coming up with these trends after examining tens of thousands of figures, Hope reminds me of my brother-in-law. During World War II he was a school teacher with 20/2000 vision but 20/20 perception. His hobby was collecting postmarks—not postage stamps or covers, but postmarks. He would send out thousands of postal cards to little post offices asking the postmaster to return his postal card cancelled there. As a part of this avocation, he requested and received regular directories of new and closing post offices, and changes in the volume of existing ones. One day he noticed something strange. The post offices in Oak Ridge, Tennessee, and Hanford, Washington—places he never heard of before—had doubled in volume in only a few months. He'd never seen anything like that before in the U.S. Post Office bulletins. When the next publications came in, he couldn't believe his eyes. The volume was now multiplying in both those post offices and nowhere else in America. My brother-in-law was onto military targets of exquisite importance to the enemy: the sources of the first atomic bombs. And he found it in unclassified government bulletins. So he put one and one together—his lips, that is—for the duration of the war.

That's how Tom Hope works—reading things from figures that seem to catch everyone else blind as the proverbial bat. He calls 'em like he sees 'em, no matter who goes into shock. Sample: *the sponsored film business boom is leveling off and growing at a much slower rate now*. Business among the older, well-established producers is falling off, but that is more than being offset by the new, small filmmaking companies that are springing up everywhere. Hope should know. He has, and reports to his subscribers, the annual expenditures for sponsored films and for commercial distribution, the only source for such data.

The Television Market

When distributors talk to television stations about sponsored films, the names are changed. Industrial films or sponsored films suddenly become "free films" (Modern Talking Picture Service) or, more accurately, "free-loan films" (Association Films, Inc.). The distributors are using the terms the stations want to hear. Film directors and program managers at TV stations, whether commercial, public or cable, do not want to be reminded of the funding source when they plan their station programming. They would rather be reminded of the financial savings in booking a number of "free films" as opposed to the syndicated material for which they must pay for each performance. There is also some confusion in the minds of station personnel when the word "sponsor" is used.

Stations are very careful about what they show. Their management is concerned and committed to transmit programs that will attract the largest possible audience at given times, that will draw local public praise, and that will keep the Federal Communications Commission satisfied with the station's responsibility. They are simply not interested in running "filler," a word often used as an epithet to denote the worthlessness of segments run between important shows, or close to the station's sign-on or sign-off times. The sponsored films they use are chosen by the stations, and are not imposed on the stations by means of unsolicited shipments. When an occasional sponsored film is sent to a station without prior arrangements, the station will return it with the admonition to ship only when requested. Thus, stations select only one sponsored film at a time from among thousands available. And then, they will order them for preview prior to possible transmission.

Because of this, sponsors, distributors and producers are keenly interested in what stations want, and what the trends are in such interests. Modern conducted a survey among 1,477 program people at TV stations, most of whom had used "free-loan films" at some time or another. Cable systems were not included.

The 1,477 questionnaires went to personnel at almost 900 stations then on the air. Only 201 replied, 32 of them women, which leaves one to wonder what the remaining 1,276 thought, or did with the questionnaire forms sent by Modern. That is the scourge of the survey field. Are the non-respondents of the same mind as the respondents, or quite the opposite? Personal surveys are obviously more valid because the survey professional derives answers from virtually everyone contacted. Personal surveys are also much more expensive.

First question asked was, "What subjects do you prefer in free films?"* Here is how the answers were tabulated:

Travel	56%	Science	33%
Sports	54%	Consumer information	31%
Public service	38%	Farm	19%
		Religion	8%

The individual remarks of the respondents displayed some discomfort with Modern's choice of the above categories, which fit Modern's products better than a TV station's programming needs. Stations said they could use films about or for:

Holidays	Small investors
Historic subjects	Nature
Educational subjects	Fishing and hunting
Women's news	Public affairs
Children	Outdoor living and recreation

* Obviously several indicated more than one preference, resulting in a total exceeding 100 per cent.

Although only 76 respondents listed public service films among those they prefer, Modern derived specific information about public service programming from most of the 201 who returned their forms. 71 per cent preferred environment films (this was in the early '70s), 49 per cent preferred youth subjects, 38 per cent said art was a preferred subject, 33 per cent the world scene, 26 per cent the cities and 21 per cent the economy. Individual comments reflected regional problems—minority problems in Illinois, agriculture in Kentucky and social welfare in Georgia.

Modern was performing a service for its clients, the sponsors, and for producers at the same time it was learning much from this survey for its own future. Subject areas received coolly by TV stations mean trouble for everyone, and it is to everyone's service to know as early as possible what subjects are not in demand. Whether the TV station managers have the moral *right* to so determine what their viewers should see is the subject of other books and articles. Suffice to say that the stations have little interest in putting blinders on public eyes and want only to be watched as avidly as possible.

Modern asked its station people which women's subjects were preferred and here is how the answers came in:*

Consumer information	47%
Family living	31%
Foods and cooking	26%
Home decoration	25%
Clothing styles, care, sewing	24%
Careers	21%
Grooming	13%

That was all the subject questioning Modern did. Next, they asked the stations which running time was most helpful and the overwhelming answer was half-hour (71%), in comparison to quarter-hour length (38%) and short films (32%). Modern has always found the half-hour length to be preferred by stations, but that does not mean TV stations do not welcome one-hour, quarter-hour and 3- to 5-minute short films. Stations *think* in terms of half-hour segments, the way they think in terms of 13-week schedules. Of course, many stations block-book two quarter-hour shows of similar content to make up a half hour.

Modern looks for opportunities to block-book their myriad individual sponsored films as a common-interest series. If they can build a clientele of stations willing to welcome and transmit 13 sponsored films at a time instead of one, the distributor has taken three giant steps. So Modern asked the stations which method of booking they prefer—individual titles or series. The replies indicated 77 per cent favored one sponsored film at a

* Multiple replies resulted in percentages exceeding 100.

time and only 17 per cent preferred a series. It was then that Modern realized they blundered in writing the question. In previous surveys they had asked, "Do you like the idea of series?" and got a walloping 80 per cent positive response. In practice, many stations work with some sponsored films on a series basis, but even they are uneasy about someone outside the station deciding what goes into a conglomerate program of this type.

The survey struck the soft underbelly of sponsored films when it came out and asked stations how such films could best be improved. Stations replied that less commercialism would help; 59 per cent said so. One might wonder if stations did not offer this criticism automatically, what with their unceasing suffering from public criticism about "too many commercials on your stations." Twenty-five per cent of respondents suggested human interest would help the sponsored films they show. Star names would help, according to 22 per cent. Better production quality was suggested by 18 per cent, as was humor. Fourteen per cent allowed as how more information would improve sponsored films, and 12 per cent voted for stronger story lines.

What about sponsored videotapes, Modern asked? Thirty-nine per cent said they'd use them, 33 per cent said they wouldn't. Sixty-three per cent preferred 16mm film over videotape and 16 per cent chose videotape over 16mm film. Such figures can be interpreted to suit one's predilection. Modern would do well to ask the identical questions of the identical station personnel three years later to sense a trend. One cannot determine weather trends by observing a barometer only once.

Where Sponsored Film Investments Go

One of the most valued resources in the sponsored film industry has been the *Free Film Source Book*, published by the Broadcast Information Bureau in New York for many years to supply television stations and cable systems with intelligence on thousands of sponsored films available to them.

Free Film Source Book meticulously catalogued 9,724 different sponsored films varying in length from 30 seconds to two hours. All were in current use. A few were released in the '50s and '60s but most were produced in the '70s. The field providing the largest number of titles was the Religious and Inspirational category with a massive 3,900 titles. This figure was swollen by the presence of a number of series productions that have been rolling for a generation. Half-hour religious films outnumbered the quarter-hours two-to-one. With 40 per cent of all the listed sponsored films falling in the religious area, and those films being mostly long ones, we might draw the conclusion that the religious enterprise does not know when to stop talking, filming and collecting funds. While only 37 short films (less than 10-minutes) were religious films, 99 short films fell in the sports field, 53 in travel and 35 in safety. Simply stated, a lot of vital information can be packed into five-minute films but religious film sources pay little attention.

After religion the largest single source of sponsored films is— surprise—the United States Army. With 1,187 titles, they make almost every other sponsor look like novices. The approximate total viewing time of these 1,187 listed U.S. Army titles is 522 hours. If a recruit were seated before a screen immediately after induction and made to view these Army movies, it would take him 65 eight-hour days to see them all—over two solid months of movie watching. What a way to prepare for battle.

The financial might of the Army over other branches of the service shows up clearly on the list of sponsored films. The Air Forces total is but 387. The Navy lists only a puny 100 films. Marine Corps is down for 77. The Coast Guard offers 15.

Following religion and the armed forces, travel covers the largest influx of sponsored films to the marketplace with 713. Sports is next with 505. Here is the summary:

Religious	3,900	Space	149
Armed forces	1,766	AEC	122
Travel	713	Safety	105
Sports	505	Women	82
Industry	286	Food supply	76
Health	228	Education	71
Documentary	223	Nature	63
Agriculture	208	Transportation	47
Social welfare	175	All other	1,003
		Total	9,722

The complete analysis of all films by category and running time follows. Bear in mind this list does not include all sponsored films currently available, but all sponsored films that were intentionally listed by sponsors with the Broadcast Information Bureau for free telecasting. Many thousands of other sponsored films are available. Of those, a great number have not been cleared for television use (full music and talent rights not paid for). Many others were made for specialized audiences.

One can learn a good deal by studying these figures. The preferences of certain industries for certain film lengths is apparent. The degree of commitment to sponsored films by industry, government branch, subject and geographic area is evident.

Research people boldly defend their survey methods and results as scientifically correct. No competitive research expert, no writer, no client can tell a Gallup, a Nielsen or a Harris that his analysis is faulty and get away with it. There is only one ultimate judge of the research expert's work: *time*.

FREE FILM SOURCE BOOK 1975 – NUMERICAL BREAKDOWN OF SPONSORED FILMS

	40–120 minutes	23–29 minutes	11–22 minutes	1/2–10 minutes	Total
		Number of Films			
Agriculture:					
General	–	11	7	10	28
Bees	–	1	–	–	1
Conservation	–	–	2	–	2
Equipment and facilities	–	3	2	–	5
Farming	–	10	26	–	36
Forestry	–	21	13	7	41
Horticulture	–	10	9	2	21
Marketing	–	–	4	–	4
Other lands	–	2	13	–	15
Research	–	–	5	–	5
Soil and water	–	4	7	4	15
Animal and Poultry Husbandry	–	16	8	–	24
Animals:					
General	–	9	6	2	17
Pets	–	–	4	0	4
Pet care	–	1	–	–	1
Arts and Crafts:					
General	3	6	3	2	14
Ceramics and sculpture	–	3	5	–	8
Hobbies	–	2	3	1	6
Other lands	–	5	16	2	23
Photography	–	4	5	–	9
Printing and publishing	–	1	–	–	1
Theater	–	1	1	1	3

	Number of Films				
	40–120 minutes	23–29 minutes	11–22 minutes	1/2–10 minutes	Total
Business	–	9	14	–	23
Child Care	1	–	–	–	1
Civil Defense	–	13	2	5	20
Commerce – General	–	5	–	–	5
Communications	–	3	11	4	18
Documentary:					
General	–	35	27	7	69
Biography	1	9	–	–	10
Other lands	4	37	88	17	146
People	2	37	27	6	72
Religious	–	5	–	–	5
Ecology – Energy	5	12	14	4	35
Economics	–	10	8	1	19
Education:					
General	–	14	8	–	22
Community	–	–	2	1	3
Institutions of learning	–	8	3	–	11
Other lands	–	6	6	4	16
Youth	–	4	12	2	18
Farm Life:					
General	–	2	4	–	6
Equipment and facilities	–	2	–	–	2
Food Supply:					
General	–	12	18	7	37
Fruit and vegetables	–	5	8	3	16
Meat and fish	–	5	17	1	23

	Number of Films				
	40–120 minutes	23–29 minutes	11–22 minutes	1/2–10 minutes	Total
Foreign Language Tracks:					
Afrikaans	-	1	-	-	1
Arabic	-	1	-	-	1
Chinese	-	2	-	-	2
Finnish	-	1	-	-	1
German	2	2	4	1	9
Italian	2	2	1	-	5
Japanese	1	4	5	-	10
French	3	3	14	1	21
Norwegian	1	-	-	-	1
Portuguese	2	5	3	-	10
Spanish	5	10	15	3	33
Swedish	1	-	-	-	1
Government	3	15	8	4	30
Health:					
General	3	20	46	13	82
Dentistry	-	3	6	4	13
Medicine	1	19	17	8	45
Other lands	-	-	2	-	2
Pollution	-	2	5	-	7
Rehabilition	1	7	15	1	24
Research	-	7	9	2	18
Treatment and institutions	1	9	5	-	15
Vision	-	2	3	3	8
Youth	-	6	6	3	15
History	3	13	22	3	41

	40–120 minutes	23–29 minutes	11–22 minutes	1/2–10 minutes	Total
		Number	of Films		
How To Do	–	–	1	1	2
Human Relations	–	13	–	–	13
Industry:					
General	–	18	27	4	49
Auto	–	2	4	2	8
Aviation	–	7	21	16	44
Buildings and homes	–	11	11	1	23
Coal and minerals	–	9	4	–	13
Electricity	–	6	–	1	7
Iron and steel	–	17	2	–	19
Natural resources	–	12	–	–	12
Oil and gas	–	10	5	1	16
Other lands	1	15	28	8	52
Rubber	–	2	–	2	4
State and city resources	–	4	–	–	4
Transportation	–	–	3	–	3
Textiles	–	2	4	–	6
Insects and Pests	–	2	4	2	8
Juvenile	1	11	69	68	149
Labor	–	2	2	–	4
Literature	–	3	–	–	3
Music	–	7	17	4	28
Nature and Wildlife	–	25	22	16	63
Parades and Festivals	–	5	3	–	8
Products – Manufactured	–	5	7	2	14
Recreation	–	4	3	2	9

	Number of Films				
	40–120 minutes	23–29 minutes	11–22 minutes	1/2–10 minutes	Total
Religious and Inspirational	11	2,693	1,159	37	3,900
Safety:					
General	–	3	17	6	26
Fire	1	8	6	–	15
Highway	–	9	7	18	34
Home	–	2	3	–	5
Job	–	2	–	–	2
Research	–	4	–	–	4
Water	–	5	4	11	20
Space	4	70	37	38	149
Science:					
General	1	8	14	–	23
Aviation	1	–	–	–	1
Chemistry and physics	–	3	–	–	3
Engineering	–	8	7	–	15
Industry	–	3	–	–	3
Oceanography	–	5	4	–	9
Research	4	40	19	8	71
Series – Diversified	–	1	17	160	178
Social Welfare:					
General	–	16	57	12	85
Community	–	13	12	9	34
Other lands	–	9	7	7	23
Rehabilitation	–	2	11	1	14
Youth	1	8	7	3	19

	Number of Films				
	40–120 minutes	23–29 minutes	11–22 minutes	1/2–10 minutes	Total
Sports:					
General	–	96	35	70	201
Auto racing	–	29	10	–	39
Baseball	–	14	–	–	14
Basketball	–	4	1	–	5
Fishing and hunting	–	31	32	5	68
Football	–	60	4	–	64
Golf	–	12	5	–	17
Horseracing	–	–	4	1	5
Riflery	–	1	–	–	1
Skiing	–	17	24	2	43
Tennis	1	2	–	–	3
Track	–	–	–	1	1
Water	–	11	12	21	44
Transportation:					
General	–	2	–	–	2
Auto and highways	–	5	5	–	10
Aviation	–	7	9	1	17
Railroad	–	2	3	1	6
Research	–	–	–	2	2
Ships and waterways	–	4	6	–	10
Travel and Geography:					
Attractions	–	7	22	1	30
Other lands	3	143	234	33	413
Travelogs	3	49	27	1	80
U.S. cities and states	10	80	82	18	190

	Number of Films				
	40–120 minutes	23–29 minutes	11–22 minutes	1/2–10 minutes	Total
U.S. Air Force	10	113	231	33	387
U.S. Army	13	877	259	38	1,187
U.S. Atomic Energy Commission	4	60	46	12	122
U.S. Coast Guard	–	–	13	2	15
U.S. Marine Corps	1	20	53	3	77
U.S. Navy	–	83	17	–	100
Vocational Guidance	–	17	20	1	38
Women's:					
General	–	3	10	9	22
Beauty	–	–	4	1	5
Child care	–	2	3	–	5
Fashion and fabrics	–	4	6	2	12
Home economics	–	3	13	11	27
Interior decorating	–	2	5	4	11
Totals	115	5,341	3,414	852	9,722

SPONSORED TAPES AND DISCS

Cross-pollination—let's look at it in terms of film and videotape formats as delivery media bringing the sponsor's story to the public. Elsewhere we have discussed cross-pollination in the distribution of sponsored films, but here we will be talking about a mixture of technologies rather than human effort.

When videotape first went commercial, battle lines were drawn and professionals were challenged to decide which army they would join. Many TV commercial and film producers jumped into the expense of tape production and lost their shirts. Others stayed exclusively with film and watched many of their clients switch to tape.

In time, the communications and A-V industries came to realize that theirs would always be a hybrid society in which many technologies would mix, and that it was an exercise in futility to champion film or tape alone. They had only to remember that 45 rpm audio discs were marketed without destroying 78s, that 33 rpms were marketed without destroying 45s, that reel-to-reel tapes were marketed without destroying 33s, that cartridges were marketed without destroying reel-to-reel, and that cassettes were marketed without destroying cartridges. Today, the audiophile is quite likely to own equipment to feed all of these formats into his hi-fi amplifier.

So we must adapt our minds to the natural evolution of the *sponsored tape*.

To look at *The Video Bluebook*, published by Knowledge Industry Publications, Inc.* and Esselte, Inc., you would think they are already on the market in healthy competition to sponsored films. But look again. The 368-page, handsomely typeset volume, edited by Patricia Goff, contains thousands of listings of video programs available on ¾-inch U-Matic cassettes, ½-inch EIAJ reel-to-reel, ½-inch FIAJ cartridges and other formats. But virtually all of them were originally produced on film and merely transferred to tape format in order to accommodate the TV stations, industries and government who want to obtain their programs in tape form instead of on film.

In fact, a vast number of the producers listed as the source of these programs have not spent even a dollar transferring their programs from film. They are simply waiting for the first order to come in for a videocassette to send their negatives to the lab for transfer. One might well wonder if publication of *The Video Bluebook* was necessary, since government and industry owners of videotape players can just as easily

* 2 Corporate Park Drive, White Plains, N.Y. 10604.

order out of any film catalog and ask the source to transfer the titles to tape. Of course it is not every directory, film or tape, that lists 23 soft-core pornographic titles like *Dr. Feelgood* and *Sexual Freedom in Brooklyn* along with *Strategies for Handling Executive Stress* and other management training subjects. But then the two categories may be more closely allied than it appears.

Of course the publishers and editor of *The Video Bluebook* and similar directories of the future look forward to the day when the majority of their listings will cover programs originally produced on tape. There are production techniques involved with videotape that film producers cannot touch, and vice versa. Training tapes made as a series in one location can usually be made less expensively than films. Multiple split screens, mixed action supers, freezes, slow replays and other effects that, in film, require complex instructions and optical printers, are much more simply executed on tape when the producer is properly equipped. Computer animation is a tape and not a film phenomenon. These special tape techniques properly belong in sponsored tapes, and sponsored tapes should not be merely a wholesale conversion of films.

But whatever the production methods, sponsored tapes will be a viable manifestation so long as there is hardware to show them. At last count, there were 57 manufacturers producing equipment to display tape programs. Annual sales of videotape recorders have soared from 2,000 in 1964 to 45,000 in 1972. Business purchases of such recorders doubled between 1971 and 1972. A large percentage of these units will be employed to produce original tape programs. But they are also being used to transfer needed and wanted films to tape format. Many sponsored films are involved in this transfer and adaptation movement, often at great cost to producers who are not being paid for such work.

The inevitable should be obvious to all, but sometimes it isn't. Television was inevitable in the evolution of communications. Throughout the 1930s and early 1940s, radio shows would contain the expression, "I wish television were here. . ." A fashion commentator would tell her radio audience about the design tricks of an Italian couturier and then bemoan the fact that "television isn't here yet" to reveal in moving pictures what she was describing in inadequate words. The *New York Times* ran Sunday columns on television's development as a new communications science for non-scientific readers.

The emergence of color television was no surprise, either. Its progress on both technical and marketing fronts seemed agonizingly prolonged when all the world seemed anxious to get on with it. But evolve it did, and now it is an accepted fact. If a prospective sponsor asks a producer today if his new production will be *in color*, the producer looks at him rather skeptically. One heavy-circulation directory today quaintly describes sponsored films as being "in full color," which is like saying, "a genuine talkie." Color in sponsored films and television can compare to safety in banks—universally practiced but frequently violated.

A few years ago I attended a VIDCA convention in Cannes and saw for the first time the trade exhibitions of the then two leading videodisc recording and reproduction systems: MCA's Discovision and Decca/Philips' combined effort. A healthy representation of the world's television and film people were there to see color television shows professionally reproduced from flexible, mirror-finish plastic discs about the size of an LP. This display came at the time that Sony's videocassette format was in the ascendancy, as well as other videotape formats.

It was clear that lines were being drawn for the ultimate battle for a lasting format to record pictures and sound that would follow, if not supersede, photographic film. The American entry was clearly the favorite. The show caused at least one U.S. sponsored film producer to announce for Discovision no matter how long it took to universalize, and to bypass the transitional tape formats.

Why would sponsored film producers seize on videodiscs as the Great New Hope rather than espouse better-known and more widely-used videotape recording? Survival is the principal reason—simple, naked survival. Virtually every producer of sponsored films throughout the globe has endured the fear or the reality of his films being stolen. Most producers, you must understand, sell prints to make money. Their sponsors usually pay all production expenses, but it's an unchallenged trade practice for producers to profit modestly from the occasional or organized sale of prints of the sponsor's film. Sponsors welcome the practice since it provides an incentive for the producer to disseminate the film more widely and thus add to its audience—a prime objective of any sponsored film project.

The thievery was limited, almost controllable so long as sponsored films remained on photographic film stock. Occasionally a blackguard would find a lab to run off clandestine prints from a borrowed print, and sell them without paying the producer. This is known in the trade as "dirty pool." But it didn't disturb trade associations or the government in the same way that unlawful duplication of music cartridges and cassettes did.

When videotape made its appearance, however, thousands of clever minds began going clickety-click. Schools, those unblemished guardians of the world's cerebella, quickly became the *mafia* of the sponsored film industry—jumping into videotape with both feet. They saw the wonderful flexibility, exciting lifelike qualities and measurable economy of in-house videotape facilities over photographic film production. Educational TV shows could be prerecorded for later telecast. Tapes could be circulated from school to school and system to system—and erased for reuse.

Nothing to complain about so far. But then educational institutions began borrowing films from all kinds of sources, and transmitted them on scholastic TV stations and closed-circuit networks. Worse, the borrowing and taping often evolved into a well-oiled centralized facility serving scores, even hundreds of schools.

So you had a benign situation suddenly turning sinister. Schools borrowed films in apparent innocence, either free in the case of sponsored films, or for a rental fee in the case of non-sponsored films. They taped them and returned them in a day or so. The distributor or sponsor would receive them in due form and suspect nothing. Meanwhile, back at school, these films were getting played to death in tape form with no record or recompense to the producer or rental service. A producer whose prime business is to make scholastic films at his own expense in order to sell prints to schools could face painful death that way.

Producers and distributors got wind of all this, of course, and howled. They began putting warnings on all their prints, such as: "Reproduction of this motion picture by photographic or electronic means without written permission of the copyright owner is strictly prohibited." They extended the protection of the copyright to more or all of their productions, publishing copyright notices within the film titles. They printed warnings in their catalogs and on the papers accompanying loaned prints. They responded to requests for prints by reminding borrowers that the prints would be shipped for one-time showing-and-return and not for tape reproduction.

Producers would agree to reproduction sometimes if the school would agree to buy one honest print. Others would hold out and refuse to sell prints if any duplication were to follow, feeling that token selling of one print was condoning the very illicit practice the industry was combating.

The unlicensed taping of film productions reached far beyond the limits of sponsored films, of course, and the practice seems destined to continue so many years this author prays to live that long. Keeping it alive would be all those sentimental, gray-area situations. "Our orphanage has no funds to buy films, but we would like to tape your wonderful production, *The Story of Owl Pellets*, to show our children through the years. . ."

So there we can see why the sponsored film industry would cling to videodiscs as the format of the future. Not that the industry is disenchanted with 16mm motion picture film. The dependability, stability and popularity of photographic film have created more than a few millionaires, many thousands of decent jobs, and a growing industry. If videotape had been developed *before* motion picture film, it is doubtful the sponsored film industry would exist today.

The delight for producers appears to be that videodiscs cannot now, and will never be easily replicated. The reproduction process remains in the hands of a few professionals whose actions can be watched and controlled under law. Is this concept against the interests of a public bent on copying everything they see on television for their own family consumption? No, not so long as videotape continues as an available process.

Envision the communications center of the home of the near future. It contains a variety of necessary services:

Intercom	Home movie reproduction
Security system	(film to TV screen)
(closed-circuit TV)	Video library (videodisc)
Radio	Music by disc
Television (off the air)	Music by cartridge
TV recording (videotape)	Music by cassette
	Music by reel-to-reel

Such a console, in one piece of furniture, would cost quite a figure. But, then, so does the automobile which is not used as often. More than a consolidated console, separate hardware scattered throughout the home would be the norm, just as it is today. The videodisc playback would take its logical place in the home just as TV recording devices using videotape will come into their own. Each format has its place; they need not compete in deadly battle. *That* is the inevitable that is sometimes not obvious.

Look closer. The home, with its videodisc playback machine, contains a number of discs, wonderfully stacked in a small niche. Unlike photographic film and VTRs, the discs take up so little room they can be slipped under a door, rolled up in a glove compartment, mailed like a letter, and blown off by a wind. A vast wealth of information is stored on the side of one videodisc, the most sophisticated information storage ever to enter a private home.

It should come as no surprise that an important number of these videodiscs will be sponsored. Whether bought and owned outright by the homeowner, or borrowed from his public or private library, videodiscs will be sponsored. Sponsored discs will put the sponsored film industry into the big time, because the numbers will be big. Producers and sponsors who think they will be ordering videodiscs by the 10's and 20's had better return to earth from Saturn. It will be like paperback books; runs of 1,000 will be accepted coldly and orders of 10,000 or more will be the norm. Ten *thousand*? Whoever heard of 10,000 16mm color prints of a sponsored film? No one. That is why this industry will develop into something much bigger than it is today. A fine sponsored film will get the green light from a large corporation and the videodiscs will roll like *Reader's Digest*. Discs will be given away, loaned, sold and rented.

Service stations will give away sponsored videodiscs for Christmas to their patrons. Chainstores will mail videodiscs to credit card customers so they can have a preview of sale merchandise. Production farmers will study the proper use of their new harvesters from the videodisc directions that came with the vehicle title.

Modern and Association Films and all the other distributors will be circulating discs just as they circulate 16mm film prints. And where will film prints be? *Right where they are today*, strong and productive as they have been for a generation or more. For the great majority of sponsors, short-run needs will fill their entire requirements. Prints in quantities of 250 down to a dozen will still be made up in the 16mm format and shown on 16mm projectors. Productions designed for larger audiences will continue to be made in the higher-quality photographic mode.

Videodiscs will surely emerge as an important *additional* format.

Chapter Three

Buying and Selling Sponsored Films

Conceiving successful new sponsored films is a skill restricted to relatively few people. Only a few thousand sponsored films are originated each year, all over the world. The decisions are made by precious few. They are rarely the result of a groundswell of demand from any sector. It's almost like the geologists who study gravimeter and magnetometer readings, maps and geophone records and tell investors where to drill for oil.

THE DECISION MAKERS

The decision makers are the sponsors in 90 per cent of the cases, the remaining 10 per cent being shared by producers and distributors of sponsored films. It is a much easier decision for an executive when a sales or training film is involved. The general sales manager or training director has only to spell out the need for dynamic tools to generate a formal requisition for the new sales or training film.

But with sponsored films destined to motivate special or general audiences, the decision making is more complex. There is a greater risk of failure. A greater chance of missing the mark. Or over-generalization. Or limited coverage. Or bad timing. Or incorrect creative approach. Picking the right subject for the right use at the right time is about as safe as taking an afternoon stroll through an unmarked minefield.

The people who feel and express the need and wisdom for a new sponsored film are trend people, a few men and women who sense the thinking and the inclinations and prejudices of the small, immediate

50

masses who can make or break the corporate future. Such decision makers are supersensitive to the vagaries of labor unions, consumers, federal agencies and competitors. They can often predict what the *Wall Street Journal* will front-page next week in the way of business trends, tax tricks, and unfair practices.

Generally the people who make sponsored film decisions are also deciding which medium is best to attack the problem. The sponsor's millions of old faithful customers are getting too old to sustain the company, and younger generations must be warmed to the sponsor's products. The assault to win young customers may be on many fronts, including sponsored films. Or films alone might be used for this special purpose.

Once the decision is made to make a new sponsored film, the approach must then be refined. Should we tell the public our version of the truth of the matter? Or should we go to our old friend who is respected as the leading expert in the field to tell our story for us, at arm's length? (The arm of the director.) Can we infiltrate the consumer mind better with a documentary approach, or would an entertainment film get into the customer better? Should the protagonist be a famed Hollywood star, or would a little girl get to the audience's heart more disarmingly? Is our contention strong enough for us to show both sides of the story and leave it to the viewer's good judgment to side with us? How will we document our story—by enacting things exactly as they should be, or send out crews to show things as they are in life? And should we do it just once in exquisite depth, or show it many times, with variations, under different circumstances? Will we use professional actors or ask the real cast of characters to play themselves? Should we be as realistic as we can, or should we transcend realism and work with animation and other representations?

The simplest reasons for embarking on a new sponsored film project would be (1) to repeat an old success, or (2) match what a competitor has done. Other prevalent rationales include reaction against government pressures, turning around adverse consumer trends, winning over the unfriendlies, introducing new hardware or software, image-building for the sponsor, morale building for personnel, explaining the sponsor's activities when printed matter has failed, demonstrating products or services that would not otherwise be seen by the viewer, setting incorrect records straight, selling individual personalities important to the sponsor, planting seeds for needed legislation, and softening public reaction to sponsor failures.

Experts in our field can read a definite trend in the decision- making process. They already see the decision makers opting for much more specific rationales than the old image-building. The new wave of sponsored films deals with one challenge at a time, in very specific ways. Executives approve a series of short films and reject one all-encompassing long film. They approve new sponsored films as coordinated parts of a multi-media whole.

SELLING SPONSORED FILMS

The selling of sponsored films does not differ in substance from sales of any other kind of non-theatrical motion picture.

As a matter of fact, a producer may not be thinking at all about what kind of film will be created when he makes his sales calls on his clients or potential customers. The time-honored way of selling requires making calls, lots of calls, on the theory that regular contacts alone will develop satisfactory business.

That line of reasoning is followed faithfully by the great majority of film producers. They are out on the street, driving into the suburbs, riding the elevators and summoning the taxis to make eyeball contact with as many *live ones* as possible. If the producer is a small operator, he may well find himself selling a film, producing it, selling another and producing it. Such hand-to-mouth procedure creates a rather rocky sales graph and too often leads the small producer through a feast-and-famine life replete with periods of borrowing and belt-tightening.

As a result of not knowing just when a new film will come into the house, the small producer will live a modest business life. One able producer I know operates out of his New Jersey basement, making about one $50,000 picture a year. When famine sets in, he has only to report back to the television network he used to work for. They give him production and editing work to tide him over. His work is impeccable, so this is not a case of for-old-time's-sake handouts.

Small Producers

Small producers avoid investment in substantial equipment, staff and studios. They rent equipment, hire crews and reserve studios only for the hours or days they need them. Such people and facilities are available in most cities, so it isn't necessary for small producers to cluster in the largest cities as they once did.

The small producer finds he must master many trades. He is the salesman. The director. The scriptwriter. The editor. The sound man. He may well be the typist. Such switch-hitting has its merits. The producer keeps very sharp in his profession, performing so many duties, and there is surely no communications gap between scriptwriter and director. When a client hires a small producer to do a new picture, he knows he is going to get a whale of a lot of one-person service from the Boss himself, and that's comforting to a corporation executive frustrated by careful separation of duties.

The corporate client also finds an attraction in the zest of the small, independent producer, and feels that the price will be Right. Of course the size of the producer will limit the type of film he can produce. When the small producer is making his calls, he hopes to sell TV commercials, sales films, training films and straightforward industrial films which make up the bulk of his work. These are his genre, and the prospective client knows it. "Are you into sponsored films—quarter and half-hour PR films for television and public groups?" the executive might ask. The answer from the small producer is usually an enthusiastic Yes. But the executive soon learns that the producer's experience in sponsored films is limited to coverage of a Little League tournament, the construction of a large chemical plant, and *The Story of Cholmsford College*.

Small producers enjoy repeat business from faithful clients just as much as large producers. In fact, they may often fall into a comfortable niche with one or two customers who favor them through the years with a steady flow of films of all kinds. The late Matt Farrell wasn't the biggest producer in New York City but his following was the most faithful, and his family never went hungry. Hercules Corporation was his prime source of business; I doubt if there was ever a harsh word exchanged between them during their long professional life together.

Large Producers

Where do we draw the line between small and large sponsored film producers? We might do it by describing an arbitrary line between annual sales figures, above and below a figure like $250,000. But I know a better way. Just ask the producer how much time he spends in the air. If he flies so much he no longer keeps track of the number of miles, airlines, airports and countries, he's a large producer. If he finishes a vodka martini at the airport bar and turns right toward gate 39 thinking he's in Newark when he should have turned left because he's actually in Cincinnati, he's a large producer. Your more substantial filmmakers are often on their way to Montreux before they've recovered from their Tokyo jet lag. And these are not jet-setters who revel in telling you they met the president of Chile last night, while you were watching Elvis at a nearby drive-in. They are very hard-working, long-suffering executives who wished there were a better way.

Larger producers work differently. Their sales work is either in the hands of the head of the firm, who does little or no production work, or with one or more sales specialists. The terrority of the small producer is generally limited to the city region in which he is established. But the larger producer is more dynamic in his sales efforts. He or his salesmen are frequently flying about the country, following up leads, making callbacks, attending trade conferences, birddogging and making cold calls. Jack Hennessy is President of John J. Hennessy Motion Pictures in South Pasadena, California. He is a large producer who does all his own selling and a good part of his client contact work, which keeps him beset with jet lag most of the year. He would like to bring in a salesman to take the load off his shoulders. But he maintains he has never found a producer who had hired a successful salesman, so he isn't optimistic.

To whom did he tell this? To none other than Graeme Fraser, himself the world's supreme example of a successful film salesman who is not a producer. Fraser helps run Crawley Films in Ottawa, Canada, largest private producer in that nation. Of course, Fraser is probably the exception to prove Hennessy's rule. Hired by Budge Crawley a generation ago to handle sales, promotion and public relations for Crawley Films, he has been a legendary success at it. Within a year of his association with Crawley, he was turning in film contracts.

Through the years Graeme Fraser has built an impenetrable wall of sales steel around the Crawley house. Through his being a principal in a separate PR firm, he is probably the only accredited member of the Public Relations Society, Institute of Association Executives and other organizations whose contacts are priceless, who is a full-time film producer.

Government Contracts

Both small and large producers seek out government business. Small producers hear that the federal government favors "small business" and erroneously deduce that they are the small business the government has in mind. Actually, by federal standards, every non-theatrical producer in America, large and small, fits into the "small business" category, unless he's owned by a parent corporation. The paperwork usually frightens off most of the swarm of applicants to the various federal agencies listed in trade directories as letting film contracts. Some producers subscribe to the U.S. Department of Commerce *Business Daily* where they can spot official listings of new film bid requests, and read the news about who was awarded each contract. They will also read, to their considerable dismay, many records of film contracts already awarded without the benefit of bidding. Bill Legg, the late president of Paragon Productions in Washington, D.C., used to say that most of the film contracts let by federal agencies were wired—that is, pre-arranged to go to a favored producer. That was a bit cynical; most are quite fairly, even meticulously, offered and judged. In fact, some agencies demoralize film producers by their very efforts to be impartial. The Consumer Product Safety Commission once proudly announced the winner of a film contract who had nosed out 149 other producers. A producer generally figures it costs him $500 to prepare a government bid. That being the case, the CPSC cost 150 American small business firms $75,000 in the letting of a film contract worth perhaps $40,000!

Quite often small producers hang doggedly in and win government film contracts with fresh concepts and low bids. The result can bring certain prestige to the producer. It can even bring profit, provided the producer didn't forget vital costs in his computations, in which case it's his hard luck. The small producer can ill afford to wait for his payments, but wait he does. More than a few U.S. producers refuse to bid on government film contracts because of often scandalously slow pay, unending script changes, bureaucratic production delays, too many picky-picky requirements and no hope of repeat business.

If the reader pauses here to wonder whether government films can be sponsored films, let him or her be assured that they certainly can. Most government films appear in catalogs to be very necessary instructional and informational works. But special interests are most definitely served in virtually all government films. While the subject may be quite objective, the treatment within each film of the contracting branch or agency is loaded with PR values. Did you ever see a Navy film that failed to sell and flatter the Navy? No, and you never will. This isn't insidious. The agencies believe it is their specific duty in making films to promote chauvinistically their particular office. They would like nothing better to hear one day from their boss that a showing of their film to a Congressional committee kept their annual budget from being cut.

Organizations

Where else beside industry and the government do producers turn for their sales? Organizations are a prime prospect for sponsored films. In this category appear trade associations*—fraternal, women's, youth, sports, professional, educational, political, labor, health, recreational, civic, scientific, travel, financial, social, sociological and many other organizations. (Gail Research Company lists over 17,000 in its *Encyclopedia of Associations*.)

When such organizations are substantial enough to have at least one full-time professional, they are usually in position to consider one or more motion pictures to serve their particular interests. Large and small producers know this all too well, and the elevator floormats in Chicago and Washington are worn thin by producers making calls in those two most important organization headquarters cities.

Organizations like to sponsor films, which are an attractive and dramatic way to show their members that they are doing important things in return for their dues payments. The first love of organizations is, of course, literature—pamphlets to suit every need and market, available to members on a self-liquidating basis and relatively inexpensive to produce and update. But films follow closely as their second choice.

Many organizations are uncomfortable with the mechanics of filmmaking and are frightened at the seemingly high cost of making one.

* See Pages 69-74 and 81-86.

They are often concerned about their film being used politically. If certain high-ranking members appear in it and others don't, accusations of unholy favoritism might abound. Another fear is often very real with a smaller organization. The financial impact of a film production can actually jeopardize the salary of the executive secretary, or at least threaten his or her budgeted raise. So producer salesmen are wise to talk out this sensitivity early in their solicitation. If the threat is real, the producer can suggest such remedies as membership contributions or taxes to raise the film fund, rather than intrude on the annual budget.

Institutions

Institutions are also underwriters of sponsored films. Many hospitals back "image films" and their distribution in order to build the effective medical team and staff they need to succeed. Camps, homes for the aged, universities, retirement complexes—all are sponsored film customers. With colleges and camps, the producer's biggest competition is amateur. Many colleges pride themselves on their ability to produce their own films within their cinema schools or clubs. One college I know proudly shows as its only recruitment film a pitiful thing done by a student as her thesis. Another, Bob Jones University, completed a superb film that any professional producer would be proud to call his own. For years this university built up a mammoth Hollywood-epic style capability in Greenville, South Carolina, to turn out self-serving college and religious films of the DeMille genre. The poor students would slave at unimportant jobs while the faculty did the vital work. Their films were corny and overproduced. But then they got smart and brought themselves into the 20th century. They still make a mob scene out of every film, but divide up sequences and hand them out to small production units. Later the film is assembled and polished so the varying styles don't show. The result is a film with great flavor, excitement, and innovation.

All this bodes ill for the independent film producer, who looks upon colleges and government agencies that make their own films as the bitterest enemy. Not that college films are all that attractive to producers. After all, have you ever seen a college film that failed to document one entire year's activities, from enrollment to graduation? That's a rather gloomy assignment for any producer. He finds himself continually on call to shoot football games, faculty teas and holiday festivals. He may well wish that students would take the footage, no matter how mediocre, and leave him to do the post-production work. Which is exactly what many colleges do—contract with producers only for post-production, and do the script, camera work and wild recording themselves, using the sometimes good and always free offices of the student body.

The University of Virginia planned an image film not long ago and called in several producers to make presentations. The film committee was a student organization with a faculty adviser. Each producer was thoroughly brainwashed with the Charlottesville mystique and was soon convinced that Thomas Jefferson was alive, well and walking on campus that very moment. The bidders bought it graciously until the Committee of Seven story came out. The students proudly said they had the money, plenty of it, to make the film. But they said they were to come by it rather unusually. Seven mysterious alumni would provide $50,000 or so. Their identities were and would remain secret. How do you communicate with them, each producer inquired? Oh, by way of the tree. The *tree*? Oh, yes. Whenever we want to communicate with the Committee of Seven, we simply leave a note attached to a certain tree on campus. We go back there in a day or so and the reply is waiting.

Is that how we will get paid, the producer would than ask anxiously? Yes, indeed, was the reply. The whole thing sounded so much like a flim-flam operation run by high school sophomores, that I imagine the producers took the next pogo stick out of there. Can't you picture the contracting producer going to his attorney months later to complain he didn't get paid, and the attorney says why not, and the producer says, "My $50,000 check wasn't on the tree"?

Business by Invitation

Note that I mentioned that several producers were summoned to bid on the Virginia project. This is the final and by far the most important way a producer gets his sponsored film business—by invitation.

Any student of business cinema who thinks such invitations are accidents has another thing coming. Producers work hard for years to set the stage for invitations to bid on or produce a new picture. Professional age is of prime importance. Buyers of sponsored films are aware of the transient and slippery nature of the film production business, particularly among those who make television commercials. They do not want to get involved with a firm that can't make its payroll and folds in mid-production, leaving the customer with liens instead of films.

So they look around for producers who have been around many years. They will settle for a newer firm made up of heavyweights with many good years as successful professionals. Thus young production houses can get walk-in business just as well as long-established ones.

Another criterion is proximity. The sponsored film customer thinks about a film producer in terms of a professional or semi-professional. He looks for his architect, attorney, ophthalmologist or pharmacist within his own city. And that is where he looks for his film producer. Of course, if he has limited confidence in the creativity reserve of his home town, the glitter of New York or Los Angeles may draw him away.

Promotional Techniques

Promotion comprises another road to business by invitation. Some producers think promotion means space ads in trade publications like *Back Stage* or reprints of self-serving publicity stories in any publication. Well, it does, but that isn't the meat of it. Promotion covers delicately planned public relations programs, publicity, public appearances, paid advertising, direct mail, participation in trade shows, printed matter, sample reels and screenings.

Georges Pessis, our French producer friend in St. Cloud near Paris, has a unique promotional technique that is perhaps peculiarly French. He calls it, "Projections." That isn't a fancy way of saying screenings. Here is how he does it, in his own words:

> I get virtually all my business through projections. Once a year I invite all my clients and prospective clients to a fine hall in Paris. There we will have good things to eat, elegant atmosphere, but no crowd scene. These are intimate, quiet affairs where I can personally speak to each person I've invited. Then we show a few of my most recent films. After that my guests congratulate me and open right up. "I've been meaning to call you," one will say. "We're about ready to do another film about communications." And that is all there is to it.

It all sounds disarmingly simple, and it works for Georges Pessis. He stays quite busy all year, filming in many parts of the world. His offices are domiciled in a fine building into which are concentrated a laboratory and all kinds of production staff and facilities which he rents as required.

The Sample Reel

The sample reel is the most-used promotional tool of the non-theatrical film producer. It can take the form of many sequences from several productions spliced together, or simply a reel of the entire motion picture the producer thinks is his finest. It is best used when the producer's sales representative is present throughout its screening. Then the producer can prepare the audience with marketing and production details. He can follow it quickly with his own pitch, and answer questions about it. If he senses his prospect is restless or upset, he can switch off the projector early, before key people head for the hall.*

If the producer is not personally represented, the sample reel had better be a lulu. *All* audiences today are sophisticated. Little children can spot a bomb as quickly as their grandparents. Businessmen have seen thousands of films and commercials; they have been around since TV began. So unless the sample reel is a truly exciting or highly pertinent experience, it can lose prospects just as quickly as it can gain them.

* One salesman we know purposely switches off the projector as a dramatic sales technique. He has a special spot in his sample reel he knows is a gorgeous climax. Just as it appears on screen, he flicks the projector switch and leaves his audience gasping, putty in his hands.

Any sample reel by itself will outsell a sample reel carried in by a "bum." It is no less than surprising to see how many executives of New York and California production houses go around looking like sweaty gaffers when they make their calls on sponsors. At a time in history when books are written about "body talk" as a means of finding subtle ways to relate to another human being (e.g., tilting one's head at the same angle), some producers show up in a corporation conference room wearing beard, torn jeans, old shirt open to the waist and open-toed sneakers. And they wonder why they lost the contract.

Recently Kinney Shoe Corporation gave our firm the nod on a new image film. Our studio, 700 miles from New York City, won the contract over four in-town producers, some of whose prices were lower. The sponsor confided to us that he was stunned by the shabby appearance of more than one bidder who had big Manhattan reputations.

What motivates men to such self-destruction? I suspect it's their belief that they are building a mystique and that corporate squares will stand in awe before these 16mm gurus. A great advertising agency art director at one time went around wearing octagonal shades, much hair and funny clothes. He said, when account executives brought their clients in to see the art director, that's what they expected to find, so he obliged them.

If producers want to sell sponsored films to corporations, they must do everything in their power to make a personality match that is sharper than a computer dating service. This is just elementary salesmanship, but so few follow its tenets. Tilting your head in the same direction as the prospect's is unimportant. Seeing eye to eye on industry politics is very important. Appreciating each corporate concern is essential. A sponsor wants to be at once impressed with the dynamic success of the sponsored film and the static rock-like stability of its producer. The old, gray American Arbitration Association awarded us three film contracts not because we have pretty blue eyes, but because their previous New York City producer pulled the string and left the sponsor with his negatives enmeshed in legal barbed wire. Industry, organizations and government do not want to be burned. Can you blame them? So their first requirement of a prospective film producer is dependability. Professionalism comes *second*.

Professionalism is what they hope to see in the sample reel. Too often they see arty, cosmic footage that is foreign to their communications needs. That upsets sponsors rather than impresses them. Certainly a prospective buyer of sponsored films does not wish to be sent off to snoreland during the sample showing. He wants to be moved, emotionally caught up in the film story. But that story must be reasonably related to the prospect's immediate concerns.

That is why we recommend the showing of one sample film in its entirety. There is a better opportunity to catch the sponsor's heart and mind in one simple presentation than in a fireworks display of cinematographic state-of-the-art *coups*.

The Mighty Questionnaire

Let us look into some of the other ways of inviting invitations. Public appearances, for example. Producers should be visible and audible. There is no better master of this art than Graeme Fraser, the sprightly smoothie who helps Budge Crawley operate Canada's superb Crawley Productions.

Fraser conceived and writes the studio's clever house organ, *Crawley Commentary*, which is readable and memorable. You'd hardly notice its strong self-serving undertone as you snap your neck laughing at the closing pun paragraph. He also conceived and wrote the questionnaire* form he uses on his sales calls. Graeme is always the gentleman, wherever he goes and whatever he does, so he doesn't have to prepare himself or rehearse before he enters the deep-carpeted chambers of a great Canadian office. He brings only his formidable questionnaire on the first call.

"I want to give you a very beautiful motion picture at a very attractive price," he will say, "and to do so I will need your help in answering a few questions. First, could you tell me the market you will be wanting to reach?" He will go on from there, getting the facts quietly, the way a seasoned courtroom solicitor will build his case. By the time the questions and interview are over, Fraser and his prospect are talking the same language.

But he does not press. He takes the form he completed in the presence of the prospective sponsor and does his homework. He figures costs and schedules, production and distribution precisely. Then he returns to the scene of his earlier session. The sponsor is presented with a proposal and bid not so much of Fraser's concoction as the sponsor's. For it was the sponsor's answers that comprised the specifications for his proposal. Neat.

The almost mystical power of Graeme Fraser's questionnaire can be confirmed in his story about the Patent and Trade Mark Association of Canada. The chairman of that association, an unpaid volunteer, phoned Graeme one day and asked if a film could be made. Fraser told him he came to the right place, but that he was leaving on a trip for a few days and would get back with him in about a week. Before leaving, he mailed the volunteer the marvelous questionnaire and some literature about the Crawley capability.

When he returned, the volunteer came to his office with the questionnaire filled out with everything but the budget. "What does a film with specifications like these cost?" the man asked, confessing his association had no money at all. Fraser responded that he was in the awesome area of $40,000. The volunteer gulped and said nothing for a moment. "I'll go see

* See Appendix B

if I can raise it," he finally said, put his hat on, and walked out. That, Fraser said philosophically to himself, is the last I shall ever see of him.

Three months passed. Then came a phone call. "Well, I have the $40,000," the volunteer was saying to an open-mouthed Fraser. "Come up and see." The man had put the arm on such giants as General Electric, General Motors, Northern Electric and other Canadian corporations genuinely concerned with lawful protection through trade marks and patents of their equipment, emblems, devices and processes. The list looked like the Canadian Community Chest. "When can we start?" beamed the volunteer.

Fraser stuffed some tobacco into his pipe. "I must confess I am shocked by what you've done. I really never dreamed you'd do it. When I quoted you $40,000, I believed that would be the last I'd see of you. I failed to tell you that a film must not only be produced but distributed, and additional funds would be needed for prints and distribution services to make it a success," he said.

The volunteer replied with a simple, Oh. Two more weeks passed before he called and said simply, "We're all set." The man had this time gone to the Canadian Patent Office and other federal government agencies. They had quickly promised support by committing to print purchases and assuring him they would see that the National Film Board of Canada would use them. This is something akin to being kissed by the Pope.

This Is My Invention became a national success. It was translated into Spanish, French, Japanese and Swedish. And it all began with Fraser's questionnaire being sent out in the mail to do its own selling.

Graeme Fraser's appearances are hardly limited to client offices. He is a formidable public speaker. He entertains in taste with his charming wife. He is active in various trade associations. He writes abundantly. While Budge Crawley is doing what he loves most, shooting in the wilderness for Silva or some other outdoors sponsor, Fraser is busy all over southern Canada, stirring the business fires.

Print Promotion

Direct mail is another stimulus. Producers are rather astute in this area, mailing their mininews bulletins, copies of laudatory sponsor letters, brochures and photos of their crews filming celebrities. They simply build a mailing list from among prospects they have contacted in the past who showed a little life. The cost is free of waste and results are often measurable. Producers who do this are aware that films are often one to three years in the fruition.

Trade ads are often trade offs. The publication announces a "special issue" and asks for tie-in space from producers and trade suppliers. He assures all that pertinent news stories will be carried on the same pages, and welcomes input from the very same advertisers. The U.S. Postal Service has no objection, so long as the free puff is carefully delineated from the paid puff. Producers believe that the combination of news and advertising space on the same page will be worthwhile as direct mail reprints even if there is no measurable pulling power in the publication's circulation.

Many producers will buy cards in prestigious publications just to be in the right company, again without any illusions about results. If occasionally a prospect will say to such a producer, "Oh, yes, I've heard of you," he's happy with his paid advertising ventures.

Some few producers will run hard-sell, large-space ads to attract business. Most of these push the personalities of the producer staff. They are pictured as inspired creative minds able to work a million mm miracles on 16mm film. This is often effective in the TV commercial area, where agencies are continually searching for the next Hot Shoppe before the crowd finds it.

Not too often a producer will make the sad and entirely unnecessary error of averring in print that all other producers are crooked. "Are you being film-flammed?" reads one disgraceful ad headline. The copy goes on in holier-than-thou tones to state that the advertiser will help clients escape the clutches of the overpriced, underbrained city producers. Happily, the sponsored film industry sees no future in dirtying themselves by dirtying others.

Press publicity is a favorite promotional device of sponsored film producers. It starts not from any innate lust for one's name in print, but from seeing another producer getting good press for something that seems pretty ordinary to the producer reading it. "Look at this guy. He's got a whole feature story on shooting atop Mount Katahdin," he'll tell his buddy. "Hell, I've shot all over that bump and nobody ever wrote me up." So the typewriters start humming and rarely stop. Every new film contract calls for a news release. Every new person hired calls for another story. (Did you ever read an article announcing their quitting or getting fired?) Each time a producer shoots into a distorted mirror he announces he's applying for patents on an entirely "new innovation" in cinema history. And so the game goes. Few read these handouts beyond the headlines, but they're harmless and all part of the game of establishing identity as a larger wave in a great sea.

Drip, Drip, Drip

Patience and persistence are companion sales qualities that most film producers don't employ. But they are invaluable stones in the sales wall. The St. John's Ambulance sale that Crawley Films made in Canada involved $200,000 for a series of first aid films totalling 90 minutes in showing time. *That contract took 16 years to mature.*

A film called *Number One Bush*, that Jack Hennessy produced for Crown Zellerbach, was 11 years in evolution. The initial contact brought nothing. Five years later that first contact brought about *Canadian Portrait*, and six years later still Crown Zellerbach's 100th anniversary film. So many valuable sponsors are slow to say Yes, but very quick to remember the qualities and details of a sales presentation.

PHP

Of course this chapter would not be realistic if we did not mention PHP. Knowing People in High Places has never injured any businessman. Joining the right club and buying drinks for potential sponsors will probably and deservedly stimulate no business at all. Working a lifetime with good people who are fortunate to attain great heights—that often helps. A close friend of mine of many years' good memory called the other day and asked me to contact his college roommate of 30 years ago. The roommate is now in high influence in Washington and is quite interested in an arrangement with a producer.

Giving away your services is good for the soul, the profession and sometimes creates business as well. Our firm has donated about a quarter-million dollars in films to various charitable organizations for which we have an affection. We try to do a new free film every year or so. Producers may joke that they already do too many free films, alluding to non-payment by once-trusted sponsors. But a well-run production house should always have room for charitable work, just as it has room to give vacations to its employees. The donated film must be every bit as good as anything else that comes out of your studio, because you want to be proud of it and because it can be used to measure your quality some day. Donated films should best not be identified with the producer's name— not so much for the aura of anonymity as to avoid anyone seeing the film to misunderstand and think your house has profited by selling the film to that charitable organization.

Competitive Presentations

Competitive presentations are sometimes involved in the sales of sponsored films. The sponsor will call in several producers to offer their thoughts in person to back up the written presentation each has drawn up. This may occur at one sitting, or may be spread out over several days. When the selection committee is made up of several people from different areas, the arrangement finds several producers waiting together for their chance at bat.

It would be my counsel to the producers facing such a schedule to enter the premises without introducing himself to anyone until called upon. I offer this because of the occasion of my bidding on the film for the Commercial Rose Growers Association some years ago. The trade association executives met in a midwest hotel. I arrived at the appointed time and sat down in the lobby after learning I was within earshot of the meeting room. Minding my own business which is my custom, I opened a magazine and perused.

A few minutes later I found myself listening to a loudly whispered conversation between two men not far from me. My head was putting the words together to make them irresistibly listenable. (I was eavesdropping, is what I was doing.) They were discussing their presentation to the Commercial Rose Growers Association. One person was obviously a member of the committee. The other was evidently his favored producer. The committee member was thrusting last-minute advice to his friend, based on the producer presentations that had already been made. The information was priceless. Quotations of my competitors came out in exact figures. Their promises and their ideas were explicitly conveyed. It was all privileged information that the producer was hearing, quite improperly, from a contact within. And I was taking it all deliciously in, perhaps even innocently.

Would it dumbfound the reader if I stated that I walked away with the contract that day? I did indeed, and the overheard conversation sharpened me into a winning position. I also walked away with some fine new friends with whom I was privileged to work for some years. To this day none knows about the eavesdropping accident.

Replacements

One of the most simple and comfortable avenues for sponsored film sales lies in replacements. Most films worth their salt are worth replacing in a few years. There are many obstacles, of course, but generally it works. Yet I talk with producers continually who talk about a paucity of business in their house but who rarely, if ever, go back through their own films to contact their sponsors about replacements.

I've contracted with one television station owner who came back on his own, six years after his first film, for an up-to-date interpretation of the earlier public image film. A highway association has been our sponsor on three successive films in 12 years. Some of our multiple-sponsored films gave birth years later to others bearing the same title plus a roman numeral II or III.

This may not be dazzling news to the producer who just hung out his shingle last year and has no list of sponsors or films to look back on. But any producer who has been turning out sponsored films for three years or more has a source of business in his own records. Of course, the producer's friends at the sponsor's office may have long since left for new jobs. Or time may have cooled the sponsor's interest in any replacement. But often things are just as they were and the door is open to the producer for replacement of a good film that paid back its investment of labor and funds.

Likewise, there is a source in other people's records of old sponsored films. Catalogs of government, industry and organization films usually list the years of release. The astute salesperson of sponsored films has only to curl up with such catalogs and contact some of the likeliest sponsors to remind them that their *"Story of Buff Orpingtons"* is still in circulation and badly needs replacement. That could lead to the sleepy sponsor waking up and stopping circulation at once, or it could just as well open the door to a logical sale.

MULTIPLE SPONSORSHIP

One phenomenon in the sponsored film field is the multiple-sponsored motion picture.

Having been told that our firm is the leading American practitioner in this specialized area, I am happy to share what I know about it, and even what some others know about it.

Simply put, a multiple-sponsored film is a sponsored film whose costs are shared by two or more sources. The idea is anything but new. Shared underwriting of promotion has been occurring ever since the first periodical took advertising from several business firms. Many if not most network and local television shows are spot vehicles for several non-competitive advertisers. Non-commercial shows on public television often list several firms which provided the total grant to make the project possible. The consortium concept is alive in many large-scale industry and government projects, such as petroleum development.

The shared sponsorship approach appears to be a practical way to finance a sponsored film that otherwise would not be successful. That is not always the case, but it usually is. It can give birth to a failure or success; it is neither an inevitable can of worms nor an automatic winner.

A multiple-sponsor film can originate with either the first sponsor or the producer. It is nothing short of clever for a corporation to approach a known producer and say, "We would like to see a sponsored film produced about hospitals and the good things that are going on in them. We are tired of all the hospital scandals and troubles that are so widely publicized, and it hurts our hospital product business. So we think such a film is needed. But we are not in a position to underwrite the entire cost, nor do we have a long and complex story to tell about our hospital-related products. So we'd like you to look into producing such a film. If you can put the project together attractively and professionally, we'd consider underwriting one share of it—let's say one fifth."

That is what he says to the producer. Now here is what he leaves unsaid: "This idea of mine puts the dirty work entirely on your shoulders. You must go to the trouble and expense of soliciting and signing four other sponsors. They must all be agreeable and non-competitive to my corporation. You must do this promptly and successfully. If you fail to get the fifth sponsor—which represents much of your profit—I won't make up the shortage. I will have full editorial and distribution control even though my firm will pay only 20% of the tab. You must also please the other four sponsors in the same way you please me; otherwise the project will fail. You must protect me legally from any claims by the other sponsors, or from public claims against the four co-sponsors. If you fail anywhere along the way, you cannot charge me, and if the project dies, I pay you nothing at all.''

He does tell the producer that he will help him research the script, find suitable shooting locations and get the service of a leading hospital expert to appear in the film for an interview.

You might assume that any but the hungriest producer would tell such a corporation to join the next parade of lemmings into the sea. It may seem very unfair, unattractive and unnecessary. But there are merits. It gives the producer a chance at some business. With one of the five sponsors in his pocket and a viable concept, he at least has a head start instead of a cold proposal. If he fails, he has lost some pump-priming money, but not his reputation. If he handles things well, he may have a long-term customer in his stable. In fact, he may have five.

When the producer conceives the project, it works out pretty much the same. The producer uses his knowledge and wisdom to divine a subject and editorial approach that will be at once appealing to five sponsors and to the viewing public. Here is where the men and boys are separated. If the public finds hospital hardware a nebulous bore, no amount of expert production will turn it around. For the film must be successfully distributed as well as produced, and if the distributor can't stimulate showings, all is lost.

Conversely, if the film is one the public will delight in watching but there are no substantial public relations opportunities for five sponsors, the producer has bought himself a failure.

There are other ramifications. Let us assume the hospital project gets off the ground. The producer signs makers of hospital furniture, floor covering, conveyor systems, communications systems and disposables. Or he may bring in food services, management services or designers in the service sector. He then sits down with each of the five sponsors and researches his script. Sometimes he will find sponsors at odds with one another. He may even discover competition among them that the sponsors did not realize when they signed the contract. Sometimes he will find areas of high compatibility where he can meld the interests of two or more sponsors in one effective sequence.

Further complicating the project is the entry of trade associations, professional organizations or sanctioning officials into the picture. The sponsors may insist they be brought in to lend authenticity and to obtain their later distribution favors. Such groups can be the most difficult to please with the script. Indeed, they can even call for limitation or elimination of commercial values of the very sponsors who recommended their participation. When this happens, the producer figures the only constructive thing he can do is commit suicide.

But we will assume that the producer handles all this very beautifully and comes up with an intelligent, balanced, valuable script. Each of the five sponsors has equal treatment. (If ad agency people get into the act, as sponsors sometimes permit, one may well demand equal *time*, right to the second.) Locations are acceptable to all. This is not a simple thing, since one location may be the ideal one for Sponsor #1 and also the prime competition of Sponsor #4. The Assistant Surgeon General has agreed to appear, and everyone likes that provided he doesn't say anything controversial or inimical to the sponsors.

The film goes into production, perhaps two months late. Since it probably took many weeks to line up all five sponsors, the ones who signed first could by now be angry at the delays associated with those who signed last.

With a multiple-sponsored film, the producer finds his cameras grind exceedingly slow. Everything usually involved in film production suddenly seems multiplied by five—except the fee. Travel multiplies if it does not quintuple. So do script changes. Sponsor vacations. Label changes. Government squabbles with the clients.

The producer gets the film in the can. He starts cutting, faithful to the script which is still getting word changes from the legal department of two of the sponsors. (Each time the script is changed, all sponsors must be copied in for approval.) Now one sponsor wants to see dailies before they are cut, while another doesn't even want to show up until answer print stage. The producer must take a firm stand and often advise the sponsors that This Is the Way We Are Doing It.

Interlock time is something else. One sponsor will inevitably come armed with the script and spend much of his time checking the track against the script as if he were proofreading a manuscript instead of witnessing an interlock showing of a new motion picture. Another will spend his time trying to spot breaches in safety, anachronisms and disconcerting hairdos on incidental talent. Still another will play poker with everyone else, remaining silent until he's heard what everybody else has and then showing his hand. Sponsors will occasionally bring a crowd without advance warning. If five folks show up from the sponsor, that could give them the balance of power in the discussions if the producer isn't alert. And sometimes one sponsor doesn't show up, only to arrive a day later to point out that his interests were neglected at the earlier interlock.

There are compensations, though. More often than not a consortium of sponsors fully realizes the situation and all parties work to sustain a team attitude. Such sponsors know they can not be sustained in all matters and accept compromise in good spirit. After all, they are good corporate types, meeting often with their own people and well versed in the need to get along with each other. Under such circumstances the producer finds himself with measurably more power than he has with one sponsor. He can be like the mayor at a council meeting, where the group turns to him for the tie-breaking vote.

I remember once we had not five but 12 sponsors, all utility companies. We were wrapping up the interlock and things had been going rather well. We got to the very end of the showing. In the approved script, all sponsors had gone along with our windup where we tell the audience that the problems haven't been solved but the electric and gas industries had their collective sleeves rolled up and were doing their best. Suddenly one sponsor howled his disapproval.

"We've never taken a negative attitude like this in our promotion. It's weak. We leave ourselves open to public criticism. Let's tell the viewers that we have indeed solved the problems and are ready for the next challenge." Well, the other 11 trounced him. They suggested he was all wet, got him smiling again, and the whole crowd got on their respective planes satisfied. We never had to say a word. We had 11 sponsors working for us to turn the 12th around.

The job is far from over after the interlock. When the five-sponsor hospital film is corrected, the originals conformed and sent off to the lab, the producer has to consider ordering up to five prints for the sponsors to check rather than one answer print. One takes too long to circulate and drop-shipping from sponsor to sponsor is impossible. We did that only once. It kept getting lost and the picture was months late getting released.

Again, five sponsors offering answer-print corrections can come up with five times as many changes. Or they may all say, "Let 'er go!" (One sponsor recently wrote us, "Print That! God, I've always wanted to say that to somebody and now I've done it.")

Chapter Four

Making Sponsored Films

As the professor confided to his class, those who took this course earlier and are simply refreshing may skip today's lecture. However, those who have not tread this path before should study it most carefully. For to understand all that follows it is quite necessary to understand the life story of one sponsored film. From birth to death we shall now examine academically the lift of *Eggmagination*. That title and all identities mentioned here are justifiably fictitious.

A CASE STUDY

In the summer of 1971 the two-man staff of the Egg Marketers Association in a midwest state was planning its promotional materials for the coming year. They noted that their printed materials were embarrassingly outdated and needed radical revision. They agreed they had to budget new promotional flyers, publicity feature stories, convention handouts, and a fresh annual statement.

As they detailed their thinking, one of them suggested making a film for the association. He had experience with the use of films at the trade association where he'd previously worked, and saw the absence of an Egg Marketing Association film as a handicap. The two men agreed on the spot to begin planning a promotional film for budget approval by their board two months later. One phoned a friend with another trade association in Chicago to get a suggestion for a suitable producer. Three names were quickly offered.

Letters went off to all three, outlining what the EMA had in mind. Within a week all three producers called or visited the association. Out of those contacts the film plan matured in scope and detail. The producers asked good questions: What is the purpose of this film? What is the market? What are the budget constrictions? What is its projected life span? What message do you want to convey? Have you any ideas of your own how you'd like to do it? What do you want to avoid?

The two association professionals replied that the EMA needed sympathetic ears among the entire American public to the problems of egg production and marketing. They did not care about having an introspective film talking about the functions of the EMA itself, or of its members. As for budget, the EMA did not have anything like the $25,000 to $50,000 that their Chicago friends spent, so the EMA would have to find some way to raise it from among its membership. They said they would hope the film would perform for five years. They suggested that a display of egg dishes was a generally accepted, non-controversial way to attract the public eye and a narrator could offer EMA-slanted editorial material while the dishes were shown.

With that, all three producers agreed to type up formal proposals. One said he'd include a treatment, so the association could appreciate his firm's creativity and perception of its public relations challenges. The two association men didn't wait; they would proceed with their own script treatment.

A few days later one producer hand-delivered his bid and proposal and got the opportunity to talk again with the two association staffers. The other two bids came quickly by mail. Their prices were not a surprise: $28,500, $31,000 and $38,000. Each bid contained a rationale for its costing—production crew, talent, travel, lab costs, optical effects, script, sound tracks, editing, materials, studio, equipment, lighting, props—all the important essentials for any film production. Happily, the $31,000 bidder included substantial extras with its production services. He volunteered to include 50 quarter-hour color prints, print maintenance service, and updating of the originals for five years. It was that same bidder who had offered a free treatment, although the EMA staff decided to use their own instead.

The $31,000 bid was the subject of an immediate phone talk between the association professionals and their elected president. That officer listened carefully and agreed to come to visit the association's men the following week to discuss funding the film and the proposed new printed matter.

On his arrival the EMA president told his paid professionals that $31,000 seemed beyond reach for their limited trade group. He asked his men if they thought they could raise that additional sum from among only 54 members. They replied affirmatively, saying they could pro-rate the total according to each member's three-year gross, much as previous assessments had been arranged.

They pointed out to their president that there was more than $31,000 involved. They would need money every year for five years to distribute the new film. How much? $5,000 a year, they estimated.

The president asked more about the projected film, to be sure his professionals knew what they were talking about. The three brainstormed for about an hour. One mentioned that in theory an egg PR film had to be a safe, positive investment. "Engineers will like it because it respects the finest piece of engineering in nature," he smiled. "Psychiatrists will like it because it honors the motherhood symbol. Artists will go for it because eggs are a favorite subject for painting. And cooks will go for it because eggs taste great." The president suggested that it might be time for his employee to take a much-needed vacation.

They got into details of how egg dishes would be prepared on camera, and how reprints of recipes seen in the film could be offered on a self-liquidating basis in the closing titles of the film.

The president finally gave his men permission to contact the membership about funding the film program. He knew he was going out of office at the end of the current year, and did not want his peers accusing him of poor judgment in a few years.

By the time the annual board meeting began, the film program was a *fait accompli*. The board members were among the total 54 egg producers and marketers who had already agreed in principle to the assessment that would get the film project off the ground. $6,000 for new printed matter was approved with the copy and comprehensives for each piece. Raises for the two professionals were gently turned down due to industry conditions.

The producer who bid $31,000 got the news by phone that he'd won the contract. "We like it all," he was told. "Your price wasn't the lowest but we think we'll get the most for our money with you, so bring us your contract form to sign. At the same time, we want to give you our outline, which is more on target with our association objectives than yours."

The producer brought the contract, a standard trade form used by the sponsored film industry,* two days later. Before the association men signed it, they talked carefully about it with the producer. They went over the projected production schedule. They talked about the crew—whether they would be staff or free-lancers. They discussed the concept: a display of more than a hundred fresh ways to prepare eggs as a lunch or dinner star. Their working title would be *Eggmagination*. The association's consulting home economist would be called in to help prepare and dress up the dishes to be filmed. The producer would pay her expenses but no fee, since she was already on retainer with the association.

The producer worked on the script with his own people for a month.

* See Appendix A.

When it arrived at the association, it looked so good that the few changes that were made were done so mostly to show everyone involved that they'd played some part in it. Copies were mailed to each member of the board with a recommendation it be approved with minimum change.

It took the producer the better part of a week to work out the pre-production aspects of the assignment. That meant setting up a kitchen as a studio or a studio as a kitchen. It meant assembling a distracting variety of everyday and fine china, flatware, silver, linen and table decor items. It meant planning with the home economist so that recipes could be transformed to attractive dishes at the proper pace for photography.

When pre-production was behind him, the producer was able to put his crew to work and get the bulk of *Eggmagination* in the can—completed on film—in four long shooting days. His production house had an important TV commercial deadline to meet, so the editing of the association film was put off about three weeks.

The producer's editor got back from the lab the workprint of all the print takes—the best scenes they'd noted at the time of shooting. He began to cut the workprint to match the script and in a few days was showing a silent rough cut to the producer, who liked what he saw but made several suggestions for tightening up the picture from 20 minutes to the 14 needed for free television exposure. The editor complied.

Soon the producer's sound man was building music, narration and sound effects tracks to create the sound dimension for the film. It was easy work because in this case there was little lip sync material in the film. But it was also a creative challenge and the sound man spent three nights working out some ear surprises.

The producer called the association professionals. "We've got your film in shape for you both to look at. Can you come over to see it at our studios?" The two men were there the next day to see their new baby. They spotted some scenes that were too blue, the eggs looked gooey in one shot, and one recipe went by too fast to appreciate. But all in all the film had visual excitement, bright and changing music, acting scenes that were valid and entertaining, and a lively pace. On the second showing they found a few more things they'd missed earlier. The session lasted only two hours.

Two weeks later three board members and the two professionals were in the producer's studios for the formal interlock and acceptance of *Eggmagination*. It was a contest to see who was happiest. The producer was handed his third and final check in exchange for a promise that the answer print would be in the client's hands within three weeks, after which the 50 release prints would be made for national distribution.

When the answer print was approved in the association office, it was immediately returned to the producer who in turn forwarded it to the lab to use as a control for the making of the release prints. Then it was forwarded at association instruction to the distribution house in New York. There the distributor viewed the new release. He found *Eggmagination* to be a rather attractive "cooking" film that could follow successfully the long line of kitchen-oriented films his firm had booked for many years. He could see how TV stations would program it adjacent to women's shows and how women's clubs and schools could become interested in showing it. He was particularly gratified to see a new trade association coming into the fold, because that could mean several more films following in later years.

The distributor called the association at once, and told them they had a winner. He asked to have all 50 release prints sent to him as soon as possible so distribution could begin. He had them in two weeks.

Six weeks later the association had its first computer printout confirming national showings. That printout showed that *Eggmagination* held real promise as a success on television and among schools, churches and women's groups. More than 300,000 people had already seen the picture and the film stock was still green.

*   *   *

It's five years later and we see some changes at the Egg Marketers Association. One of the two staff members has moved on to become executive secretary of a medium-sized trade association in Washington. The remaining man is now the only professional, but he has three employees working for him.

The new EMA president is scanning five years of distribution printouts with the association professional. Together they are pleased to see a handsome case history fully evolved and worthy to show the board at next month's annual meeting. They hold confirmation of 17 million people having seen their film, and not a single known refusal from a television station. The president expresses his opinion that the association's expenditure of $56,000 had brought it millions of dollars in reputation and public confidence.

With that they kill the film.

Eggmagination is interred in dignity by reason of senility. The actors in the film had been looking dated, the music style wasn't current any more, and just about everyone in the industry had seen the film many times. The producer's offer to update the film had been invoked twice during the five years, but now it was beyond updating. It was time for the association film to retire to that great silver screen in the sky.

A letter goes to the distributor to return the 34 prints of the original 50 that are still in use.

By the time the two big boxes arrive at the association's office, the executive secretary is typing the outline of a *new* EMA sponsored film.

Birth, life, death. There we have the simple account of one sponsored film, told in normal sequence and not too far from daily fact.

IN-HOUSE PRODUCTION

The pattern of industry is rather clear. Early in its corporate life, industry does a lot of subcontracting. It buys products and services broadly rather than involve itself in the strange intricacies and trade problems of each sub-industry that feeds it. The fledgling boat manufacturer will subcontract its windshields, communications equipment, running lights and brass fittings. It will then concentrate on fiberglass forming as its prime function.

But as the years skitter by, the manufacturer sees the economic advantages of involving himself in the supplies that make his manufacturing and assembly costs soar. So he buys into his chief suppliers, or buys them out, or goes into competition with them.

Some of these practices can restrain trade and there are federal statutes to prevent or limit them. But usually such conduct represents American free enterprise happily at work.

This evolutionary process can take many years. After it has settled out, industry starts looking around to further effect economies and efficiencies. It fingers through its ledgers and stops at those $40,000 film production fees. Aha, murmurs the executive vice president, I could set up a modest production facility within the company and staff it for *that* kind of money. The first film we turned out would pay the bills and the succeeding films would cost us next to nothing.

And so begins a secondary pattern of industry: the in-house filmmaking capability. It's all too familiar to the producer of sponsored films who witnesses his customers going into competition with him. The independent producer becomes very defensive when it comes to in-house production. The producer jeers at the kindergarten approach industry often takes in setting up shop. The producer aches to criticize the academic nature of the end product. And he is almost eager to look at the in-house cost breakdown to show that the low production costs flouted by industry do not reveal the salaries, waste and real estate that may not appear on the cost analysis.

In actual practice, industry has performed rather well in supplying itself with films from within. True, companies tend to overequip and understaff for a few years, and the results are temporarily disastrous. Or they may try to expand a still photography capability into a motion picture facility. ("Hey, we've already got the studio and all those lights!")

But eventually a solidly run corporation creates a valuable film facility to turn out training, sales and technical films of very satisfactory merit and at reasonable cost. Most important, the company believes it is in close liaison with its own production facility, closer than it would be with an "outside" producer. Too, the in-house facility is there solely for the company's work, and has no other assignments to divert its thinking and performance.

Some in-house capabilities are enormous, lavishly equipped, handsomely staffed and quite able to produce extraordinary creative films. Many of them dwarf the very independent producers who were issuing the "Bronx cheers" a few years before. An example would be the Audiovisual Services of the Standard Oil and Amoco companies in Chicago. Willard Thomas manages the total operation. Tom Richter supervises the production section. Victor Johnson manages the art and graphic services. Don Beyer supervises the photographic section. Byron Houston is supervisor of the television section. Walter Smorowski heads the meeting and distribution section. Reprographic services are supervised by Paul Vandehey. Erdis Staggs directs technical illustrations. Jim Fortney leads the art services group.

Did you count? That totals nine supervisory personnel. That is more than many independent producers have on their entire staff. But wait. The goodies are yet to come. Listen to the petroleum giants' own inter-office report:

Audiovisual Services provides a wide range of internal communication support to Standard Oil and the Amoco companies in the new building. For example, if a manager needed to tell others about how our new building supports the functioning of the corporation, he or she could:

Have a film, videotape or audiotape written, produced and directed without leaving the 25th floor.

Have a booklet designed, typeset and illustrated by the Art Services group on the 25th floor and printed in the reprographics shop on Lower Level 3.

Have pictures taken, developed and printed on the 25th floor.

Have one of the 34 meeting rooms scheduled, equipped and set up.

Have technical drawings produced by the technical illustrations group on the 47th floor.

In other words, all a manager needs to create, prepare, produce, distribute and present a message is right here in the building at cost effective rates.

We are proud of the products we produce, the facilities and equipment available and the speedy, economical service. As you visit each of the sections, the following data will help you appreciate the effort. . . .

Now, read what this one in-house facility delivered during the year 1974:

10 motion pictures
35 videotaped programs

```
       15  audiotaped programs
       12  filmstrip programs
       20  slide/audio programs
       15  graphics support programs
   80,000  slides
   18,000  black and white prints
    7,000  color prints
    3,000  identification photographs
    5,000  still photographs
    1,600  videotapes processed
      400  audiotapes processed
   12,000  meetings scheduled
   15,000  programs distributed
      500  graphic design projects, including publications
    1,250  presentation designs (24,720 slides)
    2,100  exploration drawings and maps
      150  engineering drawings and maps
45,700,000  pages printed
 1,900,000  square feet of blueprints and maps
  180,000  booklets printed
```

Your everyday film producer would take one look at that laundry list and start singing "I Surrender, Dear." How can I ever hope to compete with the creative army that one client can field? But hold on. The same corporate entity that turned out all that in-house audiovisual work gave our firm two sponsored film contracts and I feel sure several more to other independent producers. It becomes plain that corporate mammoths have no interest in depriving independent AV people of their livelihood. They simply must create their own source for the immense load that otherwise might tie up hundreds of contractors. But by and large, in-house production services are limited by their superiors and must work just as hard for annual budget allocations as the advertising or printing departments of the same corporation. These in-house film production facilities are usually asked to produce as many films as possible each year, and on as diverse a basis as possible. The vice president in charge, after all, does not want to be accused of putting the film facility heavily in the hands of one department at the expense of others, or of tying itself up with someone's pet film *tour de force* at the expense of a half-dozen training films urgently needed in manufacturing.

So the independent producer, more often than not, is called in to perform the more difficult, intricate, creative, publicly-shown films.

Sponsored Films–In-House or Industry Production?

The overwhelming majority of sponsored films are created by the specialists and not by in-house facilities. The reasons are varied. They are at once valid and imaginary, objective and subjective.

First, industry is often self-conscious, almost embarrassed to father its own lofty self-image films. It would much prefer to take circuitous routes to influence the public. A securities analyst is watching championship tennis matches on television. He sees Jimmy Connors winning with a Wilson racquet. Then he waits while a Dunlop commercial runs its half-minute life. Which stock is he going to be more interested in watching the next morning? Wilson, of course.

That's how industry presidents and public relations professionals reason. So they wince as they imagine the title credits in their own in-house sponsored film: "How to Pick the Right Service Station. . . . Written, Directed and Produced by Exxon's Own Motion Picture Facility as an Impartial Service-to-Mankind Educational Feature." No. That won't work. Better to read the credits of a well-known independent producer in the titles, and reduce Exxon's exposure to a "made possible through a grant from Exxon." Yes. That's better. Then the Exxon story can be told more persuasively within the film's body.

Second, industry isn't convinced its own in-plant filmmakers have the breadth and imagination to bring off a successful sponsored film project. "What have we taught our people about distribution? Did we ever hire a heavyweight theatrical film producer for our staff? Have we got a crew with the guts to write and produce a real chunk of show biz? Are our in-house people a nice bunch of yes-men who will simply turn out a bore and blame it on us higher echelon guys?" The confidence in their own capability in the face of national public opinion doesn't seem to be there.

Third, industry realizes it needs an *angle* for a winning sponsored film program. Industry finds itself short of angles and goes out into the marketplace to find them. Independent film producers have the angles. So do TV networks. They may have exclusive rights to tie the corporation's products or services to a famed personality, organization, event, movement or mystique. It's a lot simpler to tie in with the producer who has the sole film rights to the Olympic Games than to try to negotiate them individually for the corporation, just so the corporation can produce its own sponsored film.

Fourth, industry executives fear, correctly, that they will find themselves in the untenable position of motion picture producer if they assign sponsored films to their own crews. The breadlines are filled with former public relations vice presidents who played film producer once too often. When something went wrong, they got the blame and had no one to pass it to. In the public relations profession they had been trained never to say "I don't know" and suddenly as momentary film producers they were saying "I don't know" several times a day. No sooner did a cameraman ask the PR vp, "Should I send this off for an A-wind or B-wind track?" than the PR vp moans, "I know I should have hired a specialist to do this."

Some strong executives can handle the realities artfully and resource-fully. But they can't stomach the jibes at lunch and at home. "How's old C.B. DeMille doing with the corporate epic?" "Did you have a long day in the director's folding campstool today?"

Just as untenable is the budget. Training films can be budgeted rather easily, based on precedent. But a sponsored film full of interviews of senators and costumed historic reenactments? That, to borrow a plumber's term, is no lead-pipe cinch. No executive wants to flush himself down the drain by misjudging costs of a nebulous, one-time project.

Sixth, sponsored film projects appear to be a testy interruption of the work flow of the in-house film operation. No sooner does management announce that the in-plant crew will make the new sponsored film dealing with unfair foreign competition than the film department head is in the office, red of face, shouting, "Just how am I supposed to complete your new employee orientation film by March 10 when you drive this B-747 through my schedule?" Before an answer can be assembled, the filmmaker is reminding management about recording an original musical score, the cast of thousands and dealing with trade unions. It all looks very black to the in-plant film professional and he makes it known rather lucidly.

So, for the time being, sponsored films seem to be safely outside the realm of in-house film production facilities and in the hands of independent professionals who dedicate their careers to the specialty.

Distribution

Strangely, so does the distribution of sponsored films. I say strangely, because distribution is the type of capability that American industry could take on much more successfully than film production. The distribu-tion business is a highly mechanical function. Any corporation with the motivation could establish an efficient film distribution office in a few months. Staff is clerical, with minimal training. The functions of repairing and cleaning prints, handling mail requests, shipping and receiving prints, and producing print-out reports comprise the type of work most execu-tives understand very well from their experience in other management areas. There is very little mystery or trade jargon that the sponsored film distribution business has developed. Opportunities for making serious mistakes are small. Distribution is a matter of efficiency and logistics, but it is not a whipper of good men.

The principal reason industry doesn't set up shop more often in the distribution of sponsored films is that the motivation just isn't there.

Houses like Association Films and Modern charge fair prices for showings and deliver businesslike, readable, accurate reports of their work. Industry pays for each showing, no more, no less. Why should a film sponsor roll his own cigarettes when American and Liggett & Myers are out there making good ones by the billions?

Well, economy is a worthwhile reason. The one-time cost of capital equipment wouldn't scare most industry sponsors. Nor would the personnel or office space. With Modern or Association Films charging $15 to $20 per confirmed television showing and $4 to $6 per public group showing, a corporate could—*and does*—spend $35,000 a year distributing just one sponsored film. (That's right up there in the region of production costs. But who is to say that distribution of a film isn't just as valuable, or more valuable, than the production costs? After all, an ad agency may commit $250,000 to production of two new TV commercials and another $11 million to TV networks or stations for their transmission.)

But economy isn't a valid factor if the sponsoring corporation isn't making a regular annual thing of sponsored films. It doesn't look too attractive, bottom-line-wise as the adman might say, to set up an in-house distribution facility to service a spotty flow of corporate films. Most sponsored films are made to fill an individual need. They are not usually part of a five- or ten-year plan, or a lingering series. They are planned and budgeted as needed. Corporate executives looking back at the records find that their firm may have sponsored eight films in the past ten years, some of them bunched up in two years, and several years without any film issued. A record like that doesn't send experts off excited about saving distribution dollars by setting up an in-plant office.

Another reason industry doesn't dip its toes into film distribution waters is that they've already been frostbitten.

Thousands of corporations are *slightly* involved with circulating prints of their sponsored films. I don't think you'd find many of them ready to claim they enjoy it and think they are doing it well. Most often they admit all too freely that they are months behind on bookings, can't find many prints, don't have proper print inspection and repair facilities, and their records are handled capriciously by clerks who think a white leader is a KKK Dragon.

The thought of upgrading such a process would be anathema to many sound-of-mind middle executives.

So again the independent specialist gets the business, and there is no trend visible other than the continued expansion of private distribution houses to service the dynamics of sponsored film distribution.

BY-PRODUCTS

TV Commercials

TV commercials are often made as a by-product of sponsored films. But sponsored films are rarely made as a by-product of TV commercials. That's an interesting commentary on what sponsors and their agencies consider the more important.

And it's a little weird, too. Because TV commercials often cost more than sponsored films. Not long ago John Burgess in our studio was assigned to produce a quarter-hour sponsored film. In New York his brother Tom was simultaneously assigned to produce a TV commercial package for the same sponsor. The parallel work was a fluke and the sponsor was unaware of the brother thing.

Tom and John both worked several months to complete their creative and production work. When both finished, John's quarter-hour sponsored film came in at under $40,000. Brother Tom's TV announcement package, not including station time, cost the same client $250,000.

Now that is not an unusual comparison. Sponsored film budgeting generally takes a back seat to TV commercial production budgets. And yet we often encounter ad agencies coming into the picture early in production of a sponsored film asking, "Can you overshoot on this job and give us some specific shots for a couple of new 30's we're planning?" We oblige. So do hundreds of other sponsored film producers. The sponsor or agency may get footage fresh out of the camera, or a completed TV commercial, or anything in between. Whatever, they are getting TV spots as a by-product of sponsored films.

Elsewhere we pointed out how one sponsor took up an uncommonly large portion of his house publication to proclaim the advent of his new sponsored film. Other pages in that publication were devoted to media buys that cost many times more than the sponsored film, and yet the sponsored film got much bigger billing.

Quite often sponsors absent-mindedly ask their producers, "Now what's this costing us again? Is it $50,000 or what?" Once the contract is made, sponsor people tend to forget the bargain they are enjoying and devote just as much attention to the evolution of a $40,000 sponsored film as to a $5 million TV commercial campaign.

Sometimes the TV commercials cost less than the sponsored films and in that case it's easier to understand the making of spots as a by-product. For example, a national association or organization like 4-H or PTA needs new public service spots all the time, and if a sponsored film is being made for them, their people are quick to jump on the wagon and try to spin off a few public service announcements as efficiently and inexpensively as they can. Producers like to go along because they may profit by the expanded order and find more success being identified with a coordinated campaign involving two or more media.

Slidefilms and Stills

Slidefilms often are involved as by-products of sponsored film contracts. If the sponsor is alert and in good communication with all his departments, he may be able to come up with coordinated orders for slidefilms to match the production schedule of the new sponsored film. When that happens, the film producer can shoot hundreds of 35mm or larger transparencies of the subjects that have been carefully staged and lighted for the sponsored film. Those transparencies can become the bulk of the new slidefilms and save the sponsor a bundle. The sponsor who thinks of all this too late and who tries to elicit quality projection stills from single frames of his sponsored film will generally be disappointed. The blowup quality of 16mm action frames rarely pleases anyone when they are compared to carefully photographed stills.

Similarly, stills can often be shot for the sponsor's advertising agency during production of the sponsored film to give the agency attractive and timely illustrations for its client's print campaigns. If the lights are hot, the talent still fresh, the props in hand, the sponsored film scenes safely in the can and no one is too anxious to break for dinner, it's a good time to get several 8 × 10 transparencies for next season's magazine schedule. Quite often the agency is represented on the set anyway, and there is no trouble switching attention from motion pictures to stills. No sponsor or agency person ever doubts the professionalism of the sponsored film producer or his capability of shooting fine stills. The film stock is more often than not the same, because a low color contrast film is required both for sponsored film originals and for illustrations that are headed for four-color separations.

WORKING WITH ORGANIZATIONS

"The Americans of all ages, all conditions and all dispositions constantly form associations. They have not only commercial and manufacturing companies in which all take part but associations of a thousand other kinds, religious, moral, serious, futile, restricted, enormous, or diminutive. The Americans make associations to give entertainments, to found establishments for education, to send missionaries to the antipodes. Wherever at the head of some new undertaking you see the government of France or a man of rank in England, in the United States you will be sure to find an association."—Alexis de Tocqueville, 1805-1859.

*   *   *

Organizations and associations are responsible for germinating thousands of sponsored films. They are also responsible for putting film producers out of business, bringing agony into their lives and sending the industry racing backwards toward the 19th century.

Yes, organizations and associations are at once a blessing and a damnation to the sponsored film producer. Here are some memorable examples:

A certain national organization with immense female power kindly worked with a reputable producer to turn out four colorful motion pictures. One was their organizational story. The other three were club program films on subjects related to the group's work. Organization and producer got along famously throughout production of the four pictures. The organization chose to distribute the prints of the films, which were sponsored by four different prestigious firms. The only connection the producer had with the organization, once the print libraries were made up, was when a print needed repairs. Then the organization would ship a damaged print to the producer for a few splices, new leaders and a thorough cleaning.

After a year or so of this, the producer suddenly woke up one day and realized not a single print had come in from the organization for repairs in several months. Something's up, he figured, and got on the phone. He called the executive secretary, the cliché that stands for the one reigning paid professional. The operator said she wasn't there and immediately the president of the organization, an unpaid volunteer, was on the phone. The producer asked how distribution of their four sponsored films was coming along.

She replied that she dreaded this moment. She was afraid that the producer or one of the four sponsors would call one day to ask about use of their films. The concerned producer asked what she was talking about.

She then confessed that her executive secretary of many years' trusted responsibility had been embezzling funds from the organization. The producer, polite to a fault, commiserated with her. Then he asked what this scandal had to do with distribution of sponsored films.

"She's *in* every one of them," answered the distraught president. The errant lady was the one wearing that awful hat made of illegal bluejay feathers, she said, adding that her organization was too embarrassed ever to show any of the films again. So they had quietly stored them away with the old books.

This time it was the producer who paused. Oh, boy, he thought, one woman with long fingers has just made white elephants out of four of my best films. How can I tell the sponsors who dropped upwards of $150,000 on them? Should I tell them at all? What time is the next flight to New Delhi?

"Fear not," he heard himself saying. "Simply gather up all those prints and ship them off to us at once. We will buy a sharp pair of nippers and scissor every scene in which your former friend appears, and return them all to you ready to show again."

The president was disbelieving; she'd never thought of that. She agreed to send the prints that very day.

The offer the producer made was not easy to fulfill. It took days to keep those flashing scissors and splicers working to complete the revision of 200 half-hour prints. But it was done and the prints returned to resume years of wholesome distribution. The cuts in them just looked like normal wear-and-tear repairs, and nary a word was ever again uttered about them. Where the lady with the bluejay-feather hat ended up, I do not know. Running through a lava flow, I hope.

*　　　*　　　*

Another organization was without funds for a film but was willing to work with a producer to find an industry sponsor to tell a vital humane story to the public. The producer signed up a leading pet food packer who had sponsored a previous film for the same organization. The president of the organization was pleased with the arrangement and production began. A few months later, when production was almost complete, the organization president called the producer.

"The sponsor of our film is running misleading advertising," he reported. "They are making nutritional claims for their pet food that we cannot accept." The producer took profound interest when the caller added that their organization did not wish to be associated with the sponsor in their new film so long as they continued advertising in that manner.

The organization then asked the producer to intercede to stop the advertising campaign altogether. The producer could not believe his ears. So the request, complete with implied threat, was repeated. The producer felt a box being nailed about him. He was being openly used by the organization to sandbag the sponsor into scrapping a costly ad campaign because the organization found it misleading.

The sponsor then asked the officer what his private pet society had to do with advertising claims, since that is rightly the aegis of the U.S. Federal Trade Commission. The response was that the organization was deeply committed to ethical conduct of anyone associated with pets—a *non sequitur*, at least to the producer.

The producer then asked why the organization had not approached the sponsor directly. The frank reply was that the producer knew the sponsor better and was the one who stood to lose the most if the film were not completed.

It didn't take the badgered producer long to call the sponsor. He felt much better when the sponsor informed him that the campaign under fire had already been stopped and that a new theme was already in production.

Quickly returning to the pet society, he passed along the good news. But a week later the society president was back on Line One. "Your sponsor is still running those ads with those unacceptable claims," he said glumly. With that the producer felt he'd had it. He bluntly told the organization officer that he was a sponsored film producer, not a guardian of ethics, not a battler of giant corporations, not a judge of ad copy and most certainly not an arbiter of disputes between organization and sponsor that were unrelated to film. He told the pet society gentleman never to threaten his contract or livelihood again, and never to bring up that matter again. With that the call—and the story—ended happily.

*   *   *

Two other organizations fought bitterly with their producers over rights to prints. The producers made fine films for these organizations and all seemed serene until the organizations got around to ordering additional prints.

Let us examine Case #1 first. The organization was the sponsor. It had paid for its film out of its own funds. When the time came to order prints, the producer quoted the price that was stated on their signed contract form. Strangely, the organization then balked and said they could get them cheaper elsewhere. Undoubtedly they could, since the producer was depending on print sales markups for part of his income on the job. The organization then demanded that the producer turn over to them the originals and negatives so the organization could go directly to a lab and save the producer's markup. The producer, who was then president of our trade association, stood firm. He pointed out that if this technique was to be employed, the matter should have come up before the parties agreed in writing to sell and buy prints at a given price. The organization responded that they read the contract differently—that the prices quoted were merely offers in case the organization wished to patronize the producer for prints.

So it all went to court a couple of years later. There a gavel rap sounded the news for the producer: the organization was required to buy all prints at the contract price from the producer, and the producer had no obligation to turn over the originals and negatives to the organization, even if such material were their property. That decision established important precedent for the sponsored film industry.

In Case #2, colossal nerve was the memorable characteristic. The organization did not fund that film; the producer came up with a benefactor to pay all costs of production and the first 100 prints. The film was a roaring success. National demand quickly exceeded the print library's capacity. So the organization, in the health field, asked the producer what the price would be on a number of additional prints.

The producer, happy to share in the success, quoted a reasonable price that included a normal markup. "I think we can do better on our own," the executive secretary phoned. "Send us the negatives and we'll get our own lab to make them up."

"Why, sir, that just isn't done," the producer responded. "We have the right to make a reasonable profit on print sales, and it isn't proper for you to ask for the negatives and roll your own."

Things grew colder about that time. "May I remind you that this is *our* motion picture? The contract calls for you to give us—"

The producer interrupted. "—just the prints. Go read it. I wrote it; I ought to know. The contract also states that the motion picture is the property of its purchaser—the sponsor. And may I remind you that you are the beneficiary of our outright gift? That we secured 100 per cent of the funds for this project? That we did all the work? That all you did was OK the script and accept a gift of $8,000 worth of prints? And you have the gall to demand that we turn over our negatives so you can deny us our profit? You must have popped your toupé."

Whereupon the executive secretary hung up and called the sponsor, asking that the boom be lowered promptly on the producer. The sponsor then did a strange and wonderful thing. He said it was none of his affair and he didn't want to get involved.

And the producer? He went to his storage area, pulled out the negatives of the film, put them in a metal waste basket, took them outdoors, poured gasoline over them and threw in a lighted match. The terrible smell was the sweetest he'd enjoyed in many a moon.

*   *   *

Jack Hennessy, President of IQ, tells the one about the three gentlemen from the Piano Technicians Guild who approached him, letter of authority in hand, to produce their trade association film. One of them was a member of Mrs. Hennessy's church. They needed the film to advance American interest in the piano and in caring for it through the good people who tune instruments. Jack took a proper interest until he read the letter, which appropriated all of $8,000 for the project, including the cost of 10 prints.

Hennessy, like any sensible producer, said no way. He told them the financial facts of life and that what they were asking for should correctly cost $30- to $40,000. The three men were crushed. They were even more trampled when Jack, as gently as he could, pointed out that their wish to demonstrate all the technical steps of piano tuning in the film would probably attract a total world audience of three persons and a cat.

All this took the better part of two hours in Jack's home. By the time he'd finished educating the three piano tuners, he'd sold himself on his charitable obligation to do the film rather than sending these men out into the world to get ripped off by a sleazy source eager to grab their $8,000.

So Jack said yes and the men were jubilant. *The Music of Sound* was filmed mostly in Jack's huge living room, to save money. (The professionals found Jack's piano so out of tune they had to bring it back in stages over a period of weeks.) Jack had his way with the script, and he shot for a broad audience. He hit the target so beautifully the film sold 160 prints, won the ASAF award and brought in a fine profit for Jack.

Hennessy admits the stories aren't all rosy when it comes to organizations and associations. He would like to forget one of the worst films he ever did: something he made in collaboration with Charles ("Cap") Palmer of Parthenon Pictures in Los Angeles for what is perhaps the nation's largest and most powerful association. Hennessy found them impossible to work with in producing this theatrical-style film, and cites the example of casting. "Every time we suggested another person to appear in the film, the association would send out telegrams to their huge film advisory committee, asking them to vote. The telegrams might say:

WATCH SIX MILLION DOLLAR MAN SUNDAY NIGHT

PARTICULARLY ACTOR WHO PLAYS CROOKED COP.

HE IS UNDER CONSIDERATION FOR PART IN

SPONSORED FILM. ADVISE YOUR EVALUATION BY

RETURN WIRE."

Hennessy and Palmer would then wait in agony while 50 committee members would criticize each suggested member of the cast by telegram. Never again, vows Jack.

Chapter Five

Putting Sponsored Films to Work

In the life cycle of the sponsored film, its birthday is the day it is completed. It might be appropriate and wise for producers to cut a cake just after the answer print is approved by the sponsor, to remind all present that this is in fact a day of birth and not the day of retirement of the sponsored film.

The way some sponsors treat their issue, you would think the sponsored film should be presented with a retirement gold watch on its release. Completion should certainly be a time for celebration, after all the months of study, work, cooperation and commitment by sponsor and producer. But any tendency to deprive the film of its full life-span after that by putting it out of mind should be defeated. Turning the prints over to the distributor is not equivalent to filing in the vault or archives. It is the beginning of a long life. If the sponsor team and the producer are no longer to be its parents, then surrogates should be appointed to see that its life is healthy.

MARKETING SPONSORED FILMS

Marketing the sponsored film is a developing art that should be documented in some detail. New sponsored films deserve and often receive special marketing attention before the mechanics of distribution take over. Marketing aspects include:

Premieres	Award entries
Press and TV releases	Mail announcements
Convention introductions	Publication of literature
Issuance of special prints	Catalog listings
Indoctrination of sponsor personnel	

The premiere should be orchestrated to match the tone of the fledgling film. Let us look at a film called *Beauty Is* . . . a few days after its birthday. The film documents the professional work of five very different women leaders. One is a high executive in the United Nations. Another is an elderly black woman who turned her dying home-town into a model community. A third is a widow successful in business. The fourth has led the nation's garden clubs and the fifth presided over America's women's clubs. The sponsor is Avon, the maker and marketer of cosmetics.

The premiere of *Beauty Is* . . . took place in the Avon theater and social hall in Avon's highrise headquarters in midtown Manhattan. The five personalities appearing in the film were brought in to attend the affair which lasted a little more than one hour. Press, radio and TV were invited to witness the first formal showing of the sponsored film and meet the five ladies who starred in it. Avon supplied beautiful people—their own executives—to host. The producer was quietly present. Professionals behind the scenes saw that everything ran elegantly. Food and drink were not overdone. (In New York City, the success of a business social is measured not by the abundance of food and drink but by its modesty.) Resulting newspaper, magazine and TV coverage was reasonably good and included work done by writers and editors who couldn't be there. The five ladies enjoyed the attention. Avon did everything in good style.

When its garden films are first publicly shown, the National Council of State Garden Clubs sets up a special time on its national convention program to introduce them. Sponsor and producer attend—the sponsor to make a self-serving speech, the producer to see that the sound problems of the big hall can be overcome in projection of the new film. The president graciously accepts the first symbolic print of the new film from the sponsor in full view of a thousand or so organization leaders. The event is duly chronicled in the convention program and in the next following issue of the official publication.

Variations on that theme occur daily. When National PTA premiered *People Taking Action*, sponsor Field Enterprises was all over the St. Louis convention with its promotional literature, and on the dais as several thousand PTA leaders stood to applaud their new official film. American Bakeries saw to it that a large number of the executives of the General Federation of Women's Clubs not only enjoyed their new sponsored film at their national convention, but received gift boxes of American Bakeries' four brands of cakes and cookies.

It may look like gilding gold to send out TV news releases on a new sponsored film, but it is actually effective marketing. One or two minutes of excerpts from the new title are made into a handout for TV stations and shipped with narration copy to hundreds of stations for free air time. About 20 per cent can be expected to carry the material, which makes it well worth the modest investment in footage, script duplication and shipping.

Press releases can take the form of news and feature stories already written, ready for typesetting, or factsheets containing the bare bones data in list form, so the recipients can create their own stories from it. And they will contain black-and-white 4 x 5 or 8 x 10 glossies of production scenes with some representation of the sponsor's interests. Press releases are sent to daily newspapers, general readership magazines, trade journals, special audience periodicals, organizations publishing their own journals, government offices, radio stations heavy on public interest material and trade associations. Whenever possible, personal telephone calls to important publications precede the mailings, to herald the shipment and warm up the writers.

Press material should contain ample material about production of the film. Many writers get caught up more quickly in production anecdotes than in the substance of the film. If some adoring fan came to David Janssen's lunch table and told him what room she was in during production of an Anaconda Aluminum sponsored film on home safety, you can bet some writers would make hay with that knowledge.

A limited but vital number of prints should be made up to disseminate among key people. First go the proper courtesy prints, as a matter of social grace, to the sponsor, organizations supplying script and production help, star of the film and director (his prints are all he has to rise professionally and his career depends on them). Then go the prints given for the publicity of having given them rather than their ultimate effect: The White House has welcomed more than a dozen of our sponsored films over a period of four administrations. Finally, one sends out the prints that may well prove to be the most effective part of the marketing program: the prints that go Where It Counts. These take various forms, from presidents of professional societies to chairpersons of Senate committees, from the Library of Congress to president of a TV network.

When we made *Mother and Child* for LaLeche League International, we found that three of the most ardent champions of breastfeeding were Natalie Wood, Princess Grace and Susan Saint James. Ms. Wood and Ms. Saint James appeared in the film to promote the natural feeding concept. We shipped gift prints to all three. The one going to the former Grace Kelly had the shortest address in our memory, just one word: Princess Grace Rainier, Monaco. It got there.

Preparation for award entries is usually made before birth of the sponsored film, so it can be exposed to judges as early in its life as possible. Many a festival fee has been returned or forfeited because producers didn't get a print in time for the deadline after weeks of effort to make it. Awards are substantially important in the successful marketing of a sponsored film and their entries should be taken seriously. If there is no surfeit of trophies, less formal commendations can be employed. "Your new film, *The Story of Tennis Elbow*, is the most remarkable treatment on this subject we have ever seen", a tennis expert might write the sponsor, and such a quotation could enhance publicity, literature and catalog listings.

Mailings announcing the release of a new sponsored film help achieve stature for it. While costly prints cannot be given away to every present and past officer of the organizations and trade associations connected to the new film, all can and should receive letters from the sponsor telling of its release. Government agencies, professional societies and the academic community should be notified. The sooner all important people know about the release of the new sponsored film, the less likely they will be to participate in any effort by another sponsor to make a similar film that would water down the first film's value.

Should literature be published describing the new sponsored film? Some argue that a sponsored film is its own medium and does not require published material as a crutch. But backup literature is only sensible in the due marketing of the sponsored film. It is useful for the distributor, for mail inquiries, to send to catalog publishers and internally by the sponsor. Many sponsors publish envelope stuffers that contain tear-off return cards to order the new sponsored film on free-loan.

The sponsor's own people comprise a potent force in the successful marketing of the sponsored film. Whether he employs 2,000 or 100,000, the sponsor has a controllable population that can work for the good of the new motion picture. A sponsor cannot demand *esprit de corps* from his vast team any more than a bank can tell the public that it's a safe bank. But the promotion-minded sponsor can develop employee morale by factual displays of its feats in the marketplace. Employees are very amendable to stories of new company-sponsored films.

Kinney Shoe Corporation's internal organ is *What's Happening*, published bi-monthly. One four-page, three-color issue took 1½ pages to describe the company's sponsorship of a Thanksgiving network TV special, *An Evening with Walt Disney*. One page went to the announcement of Kinney's sponsoring its first public service film. Half-page writeups were devoted to Kinney's newspaper campaign showing the public the locations of its stores in each area, to subsidiary Susie's Casuals' radio campaign and to the company's seasonal magazine schedule in *McCall's* and *Good Housekeeping*. The manufacturer, in giving double play to a sponsored film over its more costly investments in print and radio, betrayed his excitement with what is a new medium to him over the more mundane media.

The sponsored film in-house promotion reads, in part, like this:

> Millions of teenagers are *babysitters*. And when the National Safety Council and Camp Fire Girls informed our Communications Department of

the need for an instructional film on child care, the time was right for Kinney to delve into a new aspect of public relations—the *public service film.*

That's the story behind *Parent for Tonight*. This fifteen-minute, full-color motion picture is geared to teenage audiences and treats the subject of child care with an informative, upbeat and sometimes humorous style. It is officially—and visually—endorsed by the National Safety Council and the Camp Fire Girls and Kinney is prominently credited as sponsor at the beginning and close of the movie. Tasteful yet effective references to Kinney are also included throughout the film. . .

Kinney's film is now being promoted and syndicated *free of charge* to commercial and cable television stations, schools, movie theatres and organization . . . all over the nation. Prints of the film will be syndicated continuously for the next ten years. As a special promotional project, the Camp Fire Girls will officially introduce *Parent for Tonight* to groups attending their annual conference this November.

The film is available for loan to any Kinney employee who wishes to make it available to a local group or organization. Simply write (distributor) and request a print of the film. (Be sure to mention that you are a Kinney employee!) Special prints of *Parent for Tonight* have been developed for use by employees of the Susie's Casuals Division. Within these films Susie's is credited as sponsor . . .

After this opening barrage, the distribution begins—by the sponsor, producer or distribution house—or all three. Many a sponsor carries on a formal or informal hybrid distribution system and it can flourish without conflict. Duplication of effort in offering the film enhances its success and confuses no one.

Marketing should continue throughout the active life of the sponsored film and not end with its distribution sendoff. At least annually the distribution figures should be promoted by the sponsor internally and externally. As Prudential Insurance Company announced release of *Ahead of the Crowd*, it proclaimed that previous sponsored films in its sports series has achieved showings to 200 million viewers. From time to time the sponsor should re-announce and repromote his film with enthusiasm, remembering that the first time a viewer sees a fine sponsored film, he is starry-eyed about it even if the picture is four years old.

THE DISTRIBUTORS

The history of sponsored films can be traced through distributors as well as producers. The undisputed daddy of all the distribution firms is Association Films, Inc. In 1911 the International Committee of the Young Men's Christian Association started the YMCA Motion Picture Bureau. The Bureau functioned until 1949 as part of the YMCA, when it was incorporated as an independent enterprise under the name Association Films.

A. L. Fredrick and J. R. Bingham had long held management

positions in the YMCA Motion Picture Bureau—Fredrick since 1917 and Bingham since 1911. The two became owners of the new company and shepherded it until their retirement in 1967 and 1968. Robert D. Mitchell had joined the firm in 1958 and took over the presidency in 1963 from Bingham. He's still top man.

Sterling Movies was founded by Charles F. Dolan, a Cleveland man who served previously as sports editor for Telenews. He joined Sterling Television Company in 1954 to form an industrial film distribution division which was named Sterling Movies U.S.A. Dolan bought the division from Sterling Television in 1956 and formed an independent company that he renamed Sterling Movies, Inc. In 1960 Dolan set up Sterling Communications, a broad-based company with interests in CATV systems and CATV hardware development. In 1968 Roger Cahaney was promoted from executive vice president to president of Sterling Movies and held that post until the merger with Association Films in 1970.

Association Films, Inc.

The two companies were made one that year when Macmillan, Inc., the book publishing giant, acquired Sterling Movies. Association Films had previously been sold to Macmillan in 1968 after Fredrick and Bingham retired. Mitchell was named president of the merged entity and Cahaney executive vice president.

It became clear immediately, from within Association Films, Inc. and from without, that the best buds of both firms would bloom together. Association Films had created a network of company owned-and-operated film centers around the country. They had developed a full range of distribution services to a broad range of audiences. Its AF-35 theatrical distribution service had made bold strides in the 1950's and was responsible for much of the acceptance sponsored films won from theater-going audiences. Its film centers made it possible for Association Films to expand sponsor services to include printed matter, premiums and other materials sponsors wanted to put in audience hands when they saw their films. Association Films' On-Campus film distribution program pioneered the effort to reach college students in and out of the classroom with sponsored films. Like Modern, it also invested in a form of distribution to airports called Travel Cinema. But Association had the wisdom to cash in those chips after five years. They could see the physical changes taking place in air terminal construction and design and the decrease in air travel that would make their investment eventually sour.

Sterling, on the other hand, brought to the 1970 merger a background in creating new formats for sponsored communications. Since 1955 Sterling had packaged news and featurette clips to send out to TV news editors. Through the years it has produced several hundred business-oriented TV programs using such well-known personalities as Jim Bishop and the late Bob Considine as interviewers. In 1967, when the theater newsreel finally faded from American theater screens, Sterling Movies created a similar concept called *Theatre Cavalcade*. That format offered industry and organizations the opportunity to "report" important developments in a news-like fashion to theater audiences. Each *Cavalcade* episode incorporated four or five short reports, much like the old newsreel, in a single 10- to 14-minute show. The program proved an immediate success and today it remains an important part of the combined Association-Sterling sales package.

The merger of the two distribution firms made it the most diversified company in its field. Its rental division, Association Instructional Films, had operated with growing success out of Association Films' film centers since 1960. Today it's responsible for 20 per cent of the company's income. Recently that division has added entertainment films to its rental library. Volume increases 15 per cent annually, according to President Mitchell.

Today the company works to expand its distribution services. It continues to offer help to sponsors with special communications needs, especially those of a short-range, high-impact nature which can't be solved by production of a conventional, standard-length sponsored film.

Its creative staff has been grouped in an operating division called Creative Programming Services. It includes writers and specialists in film, videotape, radio, slide and filmstrip preparation. Together they are equipped to plan and oversee production of almost any type of audiovisual message. The services that division provides at one time were seen to have their greatest promise in opening doors for film distribution contracts. While this is still true, the division's volume has increased every year since 1970 and it is standing on its own as a profitable enterprise.

Association Films pioneers and experiments with new distribution services. Their VIP service, begun at Sterling Movies in the early 1960s, is an example. The VIP idea is to reach top businessmen, educators, government officials and other highly influential people with important sponsored film messages. It's a prestige kind of distribution. Minimum annual retainer fee is $5,000 and Association Films guarantees its performance.

A spinoff from the VIP program is Association Film's specialization in sponsor request and physical handling programs. That phase now accounts for almost 30 per cent of the overall volume of the company. Simply put, the sponsor in this case promotes his own showings. Association Films does all the mechanics: booking, shipping, and servicing prints in its 10 distribution centers. The program works primarily with highly specialized audiences like the staff and administrators at hospitals, textbook adoptive committees at colleges and high-level corporate executives who gather not for diversion but learning. The sponsors are usually suppliers of professional, educational and technological software. Association Films promotes the sponsor's image by imprinting his trade mark on film cases, booking forms and film leader. Thousands of prints are handled this way in the Professional Services library. These are not the films you would find in general interest catalogs and promotion.

It is obvious to the sponsored film industry and to Macmillan, its parent company, that Association Films, Inc. is in capable hands. R. D. Mitchell, G. Roger Cahaney, Bob Finehout (an old fellow-journalism student at Chapel Hill) and the others are giving their enterprise breadth and depth. We posed several questions to Association Films' top management and thought you'd like to share the answers.

Q. It's no secret that most sponsored films are not distributed by you, Modern and other professional houses but by the sponsors themselves—industry, organizations and government. Is there a trend away from that practice and toward the retention of professional help?

A. We believe it is clear that there is. After years of trying, we distributors finally got through to industry that the cost of maintaining distribution facilities—if they considered *all* cost factors including overhead items usually overlooked—was higher than the distributors' service fees. We think this is generally accepted today.

Q. Which is the larger and older firm—you or Modern?

A. AF is the oldest distributor. It is difficult to know which company is the largest. Neither publishes dollar volume of business. It is safe to assume that we are fairly equal in number of clients.

Q. What is the future of sponsored films as they are presently structured?

A. Your question is relevant to many participants in the industry, from film producers to reel manufacturers. Possibly it presses down on the distributor a bit more than other supplier components since the apparent direction of most ongoing technology seems to be the creation of a product that would have a single-trip distribution life. For example, the new videodisc would likely be shipped once to a school or library and be placed on the shelf for repeat use. The distributor would provide highly specialized marketing services, including promotion to desirable groups, reports on usage, demographic analysis and other A-V services.

Q. What about the videodisc? How do you as distributors plan for this new delivery system and other technological changes as they loom in the future?

A. The videodisc still appears to us to be on a distant horizon. Yet it's a development that might affect the future of the now 50-year-old 16mm film as an instrument that business and organizations have used to communicate visually with their publics. But at the moment, at least, we film distributors are inclined to shrug and say something to the effect that we've been through this sort of thing before.

One of the inhibiting factors has been the lack of compatibility between competing systems, leading to a diminution and fracturing of efforts. It's true. In the last 20 years a number of technological developments have threatened, or have been propheted, to put the old reliable 16mm film out of business. None developed into an effective threat to 16mm film, although all of them found a limited role in audio-visual communications.

To the distributor, the 16mm film is as much an income source as the sale of bicycles is to a bicycle dealer. The distributor markets a single free-loan print as many as 30 times a year to audiences of various kinds, and is paid each time it happens. He could do the same thing with 8mm prints, and likely would have done so if 8mm had caught on as a public communication product. At the time, many visionaries predicted that the difference in cost between 8mm and 16mm prints would induce many audiences (particularly schools) to buy 8mm prints for permanent use, thereby eliminating the middle role performed by the distributor.

But it didn't happen. Several factors intruded. The so-called public institutions had already invested millions of dollars in 16mm projectors and films and saw no justification for sizable capital expenditures in order to replace them with 8mm projectors, with admittedly inferior picture and sound reproduction. But the main reason it didn't happen is that the 16mm film still offers, after some 50 years, the ideal combination of flexibility, cost and visual image that has enabled it to bounce off all the technology that has come along.

Eight millimeter film never became a competitor as a device for reaching a broad base of American audiences mainly because the size of the picture it produced was so small it failed to attract the imagination. Economics was part of the situation, as already mentioned—the heavy investment in 16mm projectors that had been made over many years—but even if this had not been a factor, it is doubtful that the small picture produced by 8mm projection would have effectively bridged the gap between the sponsor's message and the viewer's absorption of it.

The VTR development of the 1960s, like some earlier developments, was destined to sound the death knell of the 16mm film, according to its developers. The hardware was compact, and by a simple attachment to the antenna leads of a television set, the program was projected.

The videocassette was seemingly the right product at the right time—a classic marketing situation. Except that the videocassette didn't make it. Today its use is limited to certain professional (hospitals have particularly found a use for it) and administrative (inter-company applications in sales, engineering, etc.) uses. After several years of intensive marketing, advertising and publicity, most American consumers would be hard pressed even to identify the videocassette.

Q. What's your prediction as to growth of sponsored film production and distribution in the future?

A. Nothing goes on forever. Our company is attuned to the inevitability of change. We don't see today an increasing growth rate of volume of production for pictures intended for broad-based audience exposure. But the use of the 16mm picture by special-interest groups is growing.

Q. What kind of special-interest groups?

A. More films are being made today by the marketing departments of middle-range companies than at any time in our experience. Organizations of many types whose *raison* extends from philanthropy to support of social causes are using the 16mm motion picture to get the story they want told across to smaller but significant—to them—audiences.

Q. How are sponsored films being used today most successfully?

A. Sponsored films are being used extensively today to create a special marketing relationship—rather than to sell directly—between the manufacturer and his professional market. In pharmaceuticals, for instance, they are used to a greater extent today than ever before. Book publishers use sponsored films in much the same way, to help establish acceptance for their textbook lines in the educational market and to offer educators a text-film classroom program. Government agencies also continue to be a major user of the 16mm motion picture to address audiences in all social sectors.

A decade ago major corporations produced "blockbuster" films with prints in quantities of up to 1,000. The frequency of production and distribution of such "blockbusters" has dropped off somewhat, but the slack has been picked up by other more short-range endeavors that are attuned to changing audience needs.

In a sense they serve as a recorder of our times, of the special-interest viewpoint, the audio-visual specialists with foresight and insight into our life styles whose ideas might otherwise not get exposed. The 16mm motion picture, with its peculiar ability to convey a message effectively in sight and sound, seems to us to have a future that, right now, *has no foreseeable limit*. And as long as that continues to hold, there is a firm role for the distributor.

Q. And what about Cable TV—is that part of your future and ours?

A. Cable TV distribution offers business a growing opportunity to reach audiences, and this outlet should continue to grow. Pay-TV will become a factor, but there should be a substantial place for sponsored films through cable for years to come.

Q. Finally, what are AF customers asking for that they haven't asked for in the past?

A. *Nothing*. They have thought of everything over the years! If there is a singular development, it grows out of the specialized distribution that is characteristic of much of the business we have today. Involved is the insistence by the sponsor for closer communications between himself and us. He feels a need for more feedback from the people who use his films, which means tighter and additional controls on our part.

Modern Talking Picture Service

Sharman Messard is a pretty young lady who is assistant manager of Modern's Washington, D.C. distribution office in the first basement of 2000 L Street, Northwest. I visited her and her five associates to see how a typical sponsored film distribution office works.

Her office handles about 500 sponsored film titles, plus another 300 to 400 "locals"—films that come to her for use in the Washington area and peculiar to Washington. These local films come from embassies whose governments want the U.S. mind suitably softened for their messages. The office is small, modestly furnished and quiet. A print cleaning machine was marked "out of order." She and another girl were posting booking records. A young man was handling prints. The others were out. Bob Kelley heads the Washington operation from a plush office on an upper floor.

Computer booking was gradually assuming many human duties and having its effect in reducing personnel and improving booking efficiency. The computer and administrative control are situated in New Hyde Park, New York. Each week Modern's offices receive a printout in the mail that gives each office its optimum status and a ten-day forecast. If all prints have been returned on time, then the printout correctly tells the Washington office that they will have three prints of the Bahama Tourist film next Friday and can therefore commit that number. Unfortunately, Ms. Messard says, people simply don't return prints to Modern on time, and she can't take the printout as being realistic when she is staring at empty print racks.

New Hyde Park also provides Modern offices with microfiche reports every other week which provide clerks with essential information like the audience restrictions on each film. For example, National Bankamericard may want *Think of It as Money* distributed among the nation's schools, but not to children in 7th grade and lower. So Modern offices would have continuous reminders to refuse all requests from schools asking for that title to be shown to younger children. There are also geographic, seasonal and audience quality restrictions put on film distribution by sponsors. All this makes things difficult for Sharman Messard and her peers. Restrictions like that are costlier to Modern, who would prefer free rein. Also costly to Modern and other distributors is the perennial shortage of prints. Sponsors tend to be miserly with prints and turn over far less than an ideal total to their distributor. Perhaps they think that whipping on Modern's back from time to time will comprise a businesslike substitute for a correct investment in prints, but it isn't. It takes Modern, Association and the others a lot of time and money to refuse requests. It's possible the day will soon come when distributors given inadequate print libraries will charge sponsors for each contact with the public where a booking had to be refused because no prints were available. It would only be fair.

Of Modern's 28 libraries in the U.S. and Canada, only six book prints to television stations. TV station prints should be kept separate from school prints, and they are. Stations have a way of returning prints so clean you have a difficult time determining if they were shown.* Schools have a way of returning prints so torn up you wonder why they bothered to return them.

Film libraries like that in Washington perform only the mechanical functions of circulating films and administering them. They do not handle promotional work to secure their bookings; that is done out of the home office. So is handling of money. There is almost no chance of cash being embezzled in the libraries. Virtually all of the local accounts in Washington arrange their own bookings and tell Modern when and where to send the prints. Their biggest such customer is the German embassy. Modern distributes feature films for them as well as sponsored films. The oldest feature film is a silent title dating from 1919. The oldest sponsored film is a German gem dating from 1959, black-and-white. But most of Modern's sponsored films don't go back more than five years.

Late returns are the distributor's nemesis. Not too much can be done about it. Modern does warn borrowers who have bad habits that they will not lend them more free films unless they change their errant ways. Reminder notices will be sent out when prints are late. Those usually do the trick. If it were not for them, borrowers might hold prints for months without pangs of conscience.

Ms. Messard found that inventory control is a traditional film-distribution weakness. Periodical inventory-taking puts regional libraries back in better shape, but the problem continues as a trade disease.

Print damage is so common that everyone takes it in a matter-of-fact way. Instructions to schools on good projection manners do not always get through. Since 70 per cent of Modern's volume is with schools, the damge factor follows the company like a shadow. Inspection machines help the library staff locate breaks and other abuse quickly, but the repair work is nevertheless a giant burden.

Loss of prints is accepted unemotionally by distribution offices. They do not pursue borrowers beyond the normal U.S. Postal Service tracing

---

*A time-honored way to tell if a print was shown is to put a small label over one of the spindle holes on the reel. If it comes back punched through, you know it was shown.

mechanics. Prints are not returned insured, so no insurance claims can be made when the prints do not show up. I got the feeling that the staff isn't too sure that "lost" prints are not actually the result of poor handling within the library, and so they are not too anxious to point accusing fingers at borrowers. This same situation is admitted among thousands of book libraries, who cannot take inventory to know where their books really are.

Of course, lost prints are not the property of Modern or any other distributor, and do not jeopardize profits. It is the sponsor who loses and either cheerfully or grudgingly pays for fresh prints to take care of "normal attrition." Another thing the sponsor obediently does is supply his distributor with replacement head and tail sections. Inasmuch as schools will do their greatest damage at the beginning and end of each print, those sections must be replaced often rather than junking the entire print. The Modern National Print Depot at New Hyde Park tries to stock head and tail sections so libraries can have new ones within a week or so of requesting them.

Some sponsors are outright nuisances. They call Modern or Association Films libraries to rush a print on short notice to an overseas location. They want one or two prints to make a noise like 20. They will use the distributor for free storage space for hundreds of prints and then not send Modern any orders to ship them, which is the only way Modern can profit. Distributors are not unaware of such shenanigans and try to impose a minimum $300 distribution charge per quarter.

Short notices are costly to the distributor. Offices like Ms. Messard's are caught in a dilemma: spend ten times the usual shipping fee to get it there on time, or cancel the booking and cost Modern the booking income. The library usually chooses to ship expensively rather than cancel.

Distribution offices rent and sell prints, too. The American Banking Association places their *Face of the Future: Banking 1985* with Modern for $25 rentals among American banks, using the funds to help pay for the cost of the film project. ABA also places free-loan films with Modern for public showings. Sales of prints are described as a small activity, only two a month in Washington. The library also derives income from print repairs, charging walk-in customers $4 or $5 for putting damaged 16mm prints in projection condition.

When one distributor office doesn't have a needed print, they contact another library to secure one. From their sustaining records, each office knows where prints are located throughout the U.S. and Canada. When a library needs special information, they use New York's 24-hour telephone service to get it.

I asked Sharman Messard if Modern ever recommended to sponsors that they retire a tired old sponsored film. She answered No. She said that as long as a sponsor believes there is life in a film, it's Modern's duty to distribute it. The reason I asked is that we made a film for Gulf Oil years ago about the Great Smoky Mountains National Park. They gave it to Association Films to distribute it. Association did a fine job for a decade, so fine that it became in time an embarrassment to us as producer, to the resorts in the area and to Association Films. For the content quickly dated and was superseded by new attractions, fashions—even roads. I jumped on Gulf Oil to give our film the *coup de grace* and finally they did. Outdated sponsored films should be updated or buried without benefit of clergy.

Distributors do provide hints of overage condition to sponsors by means of the report cards they provide. On these sponsors can read audience reactions good and bad. Distributor libraries keep in touch with one another through annual conventions attended by managers and sales staff, and through their quarterly house organ, *Modern Close-Up*.

Like most businesses, Modern keeps its library staffs on their toes with monthly reports on their relative performance in terms of revenue and print turnover.

Lost and Damaged Prints

Does it come as a total surprise to read that prints of sponsored films occasionally get lost?

Logic should tell you that print losses are to be expected. If presidents can lose tape recordings, armies can lose nuclear weapons and libraries can lose a million books a year, then sponsors and distributors can well take a philosophical attitude about the thousands of prints that are lost each year.

Print losses are not a popular subject around the water fountain. After all, corporations put out a lot of money to build print libraries for their sponsored films. They don't want to put those libraries in the hands of people who will go right out and lose them, at $80 a print or thereabouts. They don't argue with normal wear and tear, since there are few people so pure as not to have torn up at least one 16mm print in their lifetime.

So the stories about lost prints are told quietly, in the profession.

Like the used car dealer who called the distribution house from a deep-south city to report he had seven half-hour prints and wanted to know what to do with them. All of them had the distributor's label affixed. "What are you doing with seven of our prints?" the girl asked. "Well, a guy traded in a car here a few months back and today we busted open the locked trunk. There were these films. He musta been a salesman for the company that sponsored them. Whatdya want me to do with them?"

Or the letter we received from one of the two largest life insurance companies in America. The writer apologized for reporting earlier that a missing print wasn't there. It turned out an executive had just died and the print had been found in his personal effects. It was being returned—a little old and dusty, but still usable.

Once a half-hour print came back to us, courtesy of the U.S. Postal Service, after having suffered untold tortures. It was imbued with purple dye, fused to its melted reel, shrunk from intense heat, and twisted like Quasimodo. When you think back on all the valuable letters the postal folks never delivered to you, you had to smile a little as you contemplated this drippy mass of worthless plastic being delivered by America's finest postmen.

Those, of course, are stories about *found* films. Let us dwell a moment on the prints that were *never* found.

A common occurrence is the old switcheroo. The distributor gets the wrong film back from the school. What happened? The student projectionist (an officer in the school Cinema Club) played it cool and never rewound a film. He'd just hand prints back to the teacher, fresh off the back spindle. Then he'd take the empty reel off the front and use it for a take-up reel. That would put every print on the wrong reel. One student can perpetuate distribution errors like that indefinitely throughout the school.

Another delicious habit is switching cans or cases. Even though prints are rather well identified on the opening leader, many users look only to the label on the can or case to identify it. When two or more prints are shown at one time, chances are rather favorable for a mixup of identification. And again the film library gets back the wrong print. Usually the error is not discovered until the next order is filled, which may be weeks later. By then there is no way to match up the two or more prints that were shown together that afternoon back on February 8th in room 20B.

Thousands of prints are just plain lost. Lost? How do you lose pounds of film, inches in diameter? *In the postal service, that's how.* The U.S. Postal Service is somewhat sensitive over myriad complaints about losses in the mail which they believe to be subterfuges to cover personal embarrassments. That is understandable. What is not quite so understandable is the glut of sponsored film prints which the U.S. Postal Service readily admits to funneling to the junkpile.

Of course one must thank the U.S. Postal Service and Congress for permitting sponsored films to be circulated in the mails at bargain rates. Libraries are permitted to interchange books and films at special library rates. Thus, an average shipment of a 1,000-foot 16mm film print would cost 19 cents to ship anywhere in the States. If you equated that weight to first-class letter rates, the same print would cost $5.90 to ship. An upward shift of such favorable library rates would terrorize Association and Modern Talking Picture Service just the way increased mail costs threaten periodical publishers.

Countless films are lost because *they all seem to look alike.* A church office borrowing several films a week has trouble telling one from the other, and doesn't bother to count or log prints in and out. They are handed out like library books, and the loss statistics are closely related.

Often someone falls in love with a film after seeing it once and sidetracks it. Many times we hear of a television station employee who took a print from the station to show to his civic club. That's all very nice, except more often than not the print gets left at the restaurant and never does get back to the TV station and the distributor.

Embarrassment resulting from print damage causes many prints to get "lost." Projectionists not infrequently deboss a new set of perforations on a print by misloading the projector. Rather than let the word out about the damage, he or she will drop the damaged print in a waste basket and pretend it was duly returned.

More prints are damaged than are lost, and the process of restoring them occupies great bites of time and money. Many film libraries automatically order extra head and tail leaders when buying prints, knowing how borrowers abuse prints when putting them on and taking them off projectors. (A little extra leader would be much less expensive, but they never seem to think about that idea.) Repairs of prints are responsible for a large percentage of the labor cost at distribution houses.

All this activity on print repairs seems to cover the serious outright losses of prints. Millions of dollars of film prints are lost every year, second only to the larger scandal of library books not returned. In the case of library books, thousands of librarians call the loss *theft*. But no one in the sponsored film industry believes that their prints are *stolen*. "Why would anyone want to keep your films?" they ask, as if the concept were not logical.

Why, indeed. There is an enormous and growing underground in the field of 16mm motion picture prints. Prints are clandestinely obtained and shown. The activity appears to be hobby-like, but it has its commercial aspects. I know a physician in a large midwestern university whose hobby is obtaining and showing fine theatrical films of yesterday and today. He pays his own way to attend the Cannes Film Festival each year. He raises $15,000 from college students each year to support his print-buying activities. There is a question in my mind that these prints are obtained and used without authority or proper payment to the producers and distributors. And this is a fine young man, of impeccable reputation and family.

We might mention the reputable film laboratories whose staff are attracted to certain film subjects they are processing and who run off a few extra *sub rosa* for themselves. This practice is not restricted to pornographic films.

I have no doubt that a vast number of sponsored films are lost to such people who keep what they should return. We made a film on bear and boar hunting some years ago and it was hell getting those prints back, no matter who borrowed them. Those hunters felt that once they'd seen our film, it was theirs, like bagging an elk.

Is this stealing? Naw, it's just hotel ashtrays. That's what the thieves say. To the sponsor who paid for the print, the distributor who spends money trying to find it, the producer whose product isn't seen again, it's stealing all right, and the lowest kind.

DISTRIBUTOR OUTLETS

Theaters

Anyone who looks upon sponsored films as peripheral should sit in the audience as they receive Academy Awards.

It warmed my heart one evening not long ago when I watched our fellow IQ member in Yugoslavia, Zagreb Films, pick up an Academy Award for one of their clever animation productions with a voiceless track suitable for showing in all nations. *Why Man Creates*, sponsored by Kaiser Aluminum & Chemical Company, *Breaking the Water Barrier*, sponsored by Mobil Oil, and *Project Hope*, sponsored by Ex-Cell-O Corporation, have all won Academy Awards.

To do so, they had to appear in the nation's motion picture theaters. Thanks to the distribution industry, sponsored films have an illustrious past, present and future in theaters.

They entered by a unique door. If the reader is old enough, he can remember when the movie theater bill of fare included shorts. They took the form of animated cartoons, sports features, travel shows (who can forget *Fitzpatrick's Traveltalks*), comedy trifles (Lew Lehr and Pete Smith) and news films (*The March of Time*)? No self-respecting theater would fail to have at least one short to flesh out its program of two features, newsreel, previews, audience notices ("Ladies Please Remove Your Hats") and giving out the free dishes. Officially theaters paid rental fees for those shorts, but often they were thrown in by the distributor to sweeten the deal in which the features were rented.

Time passed, production costs went cloudward and today shorts are in short supply. Animated cartoons are ridiculously expensive to market. Newsreels long ago bit the dust left by television real-time reporting. Thus the theater door opened to sponsored films. Wide.

Theater managers greet colorful sponsored films at the rate of more than 32,000 bookings a year, via Modern Talking Picture Service. Every one is free to the theater. Audiences enjoy them, in sharp contrast to their resentment over theatrical commercials that remind them of the Tube. Sponsors surely enjoy them, if only because theater presentation is light years ahead of conditions in the corner cafeteria where the Central Lions Club is showing the same film from a shaky serving table. In the hard-top theater, the sponsor gets full measure of quality: wall-to-wall curved screens, plush seats, 35mm xenon-lamp projection, sound reminiscent of a World's Fair presentation, and an audience captured in a darkened auditorium. Drive-ins give formidable showings, too, with big bright-white pictures, and portable speakers and air conditioners in each car.

Sponsors who once looked upon motion picture theaters as a dying vestige of quaint Americana gave them a double take. After a period of closing of thousands of theaters when television displayed its young muscle, a dramatic wave of new construction is now a matter of record. Shopping centers are seeing twin and triplet theaters open to shoppers happy to sit down in movie boutique theaters with a fine selection of first-run fare.

The motion picture audience is a selective, high-quality one. To obviate any misapprehension that theater crowds are composed mostly of post-diaper-aged idiots with heads made of buttered popcorn, the Motion Picture Association of America surveyed the market and found 75 per cent of the audience to be 18 or over. That figure appears correct, although the survey somehow puts 100 per cent of the yearly admissions and population in the 12-to old-age brackets, leaving not a single child under 12 in all America accounted for in a movie theater. This, of course, is a switch worked by the fact that under-12 youngsters don't pay to get in, and therefore do not exist statistically.

Modern claims to service over 10,000 of the nation's 17,000 motion picture theaters with sponsored films. Happily, sponsored films are matched up with first-quality current theatrical films, and sometimes there is a careful subject match as well. Sponsors are counseled to prepare their films to succeed on the motion picture screen just as carefully as for the TV or community screen.

That means the running time should be 10 minutes, the old one-reeler rule, the most economical length to produce and distribute. Sponsors often make up a 10-minute theater version of a longer sponsored film used elsewhere. The subject must be appropriate. Quality must be excellent to appear in the best of Hollywood film company. Prints must be prepared in 35mm form, which means shooting the original on 35mm stock rather than 16mm. Lively sports, nature and historic 16mm footage can be success-fully blown up and used on wide screens of modern theaters. Labs use liquid gate optical printing to get the finest possible results. But shooting the short on 35 mm color stock makes the best sense. Still, most of Modern's theatrical business involves poorer quality blowups from 16mm originals.

Commercial values in a theatrical short should follow the dictates of taste used in producing sponsored films for television. Audiences will readily accept commercial exposure for the sponsor when it is tastefully, refreshingly, pleasantly and informatively done.

Modern Talking Picture Service uses regular theatrical distribution channels to effect its program rather than its own network of libraries. 35mm prints are stored, trucked, inspected and shown by theatrical specialists in those fields. Modern negotiates showings of sponsored films with chains and circuits. It puts a lot of stock in personal contacts to arrange for successful use of sponsored films in theaters. And it backs up these contacts with promotion—fliers on each release, catalogs of current titles for theater use, premieres, posters, publicity, space advertising and special mailings.

Sponsors get their regular monthly computer printout on theatrical showings, just as they do for other forms of sponsored film distribution. Sponsors are billed only when the distributor has a report card in hand for each booking. They are shown the name and address of the theater, playdates, number of times shown and total audience. Each booking period is seven days. There is no charge for extra showings within that period. Each additional week—or part of a week— is charged as an additional booking. Long-run bookings are much to be desired because the finest theaters are involved and the sponsored film can ride along for the full run of the successful feature. Sponsors get advance written notice of theater bookings, so sponsors may feel free to check up on their success personally. Finally, Modern provides cumulative totals of all booking facts so the sponsor can readily know the up-to-minute results of his theater distribution investment.

Modern does not do all this gratis. As their Jack Lusk likes to say, "There is no such thing as a free lunch." So Modern invoices sponsors $10 per booking for one-reelers (films up to 10 minutes' running time), $12.50 for films 11 to 15 minutes, $15 for films 16 to 20 minutes, $17.50 for films 21 to 25 minutes and $20 for films 26 to 30 minutes in length. A typical Modern *booking* includes about 10 *showings*. For example, a 100-print program of a 10-minute film might reach 2,000 bookings a year at a total fee of $20,000 for distribution. Modern then rationalizes its cost-per-thousand thus:

If the total audience, as we estimate, were 3,000,000, the cost would be 67% of 1 cent. That's $6.70 a thousand.

What Modern does not say is that the above figures do not include the cost of the 100 35mm prints, which would add about 50% to the above costs. Not only that, $6.70 cost-per-thousand is an unattractive figure to a seasoned space and time buyer.

Videocassettes

Modern has jumped into a new distribution market with free-loan videocassettes. They boast an "outstanding collection" of ¾-inch U-Matic (Sony) videocassette titles on the same basis as 16mm film format. Sony's videocassette mode has been the far-and-away best-promoted of VTR formats, though the promotion outdistances the purchase of the hardware, which cannot be considered anything like widespread. Still Modern cannot be accused of being caught short in this area and has jumped in with both feet, hoping it can become viable and profitable. With increasing numbers of governments, industries and institutions investing in videocassette hardware, Modern may well bring it off.

Resorts

Still another market for sponsored films is another field exploited by Modern Talking Picture Service: resort and campground cinema. Modern claims almost a quarter million bookings in this market, and increasing somewhat each year. It's a summer-month activity, though Modern hopes to develop a winter season in Florida and ski resorts in the future.

About 1,500 resort hotels, motels and family campgrounds in U.S. and Canadian vacation areas are involved in the Resort Cinema program. The resorts show a different sponsored film program several evenings a week as part of their recreational activities. Modern supplies everything. Modern hires teachers and students to circulate prints and projectors on some 61 circuits throughout the summer vacation season. They tote the projectors and films to the resorts, show them, put away the hardware each night, get it all back safely to Modern at the end of the season and make some spending money for some no-sweat responsibility.

The distributor even thinks of notices in guest rooms about the evening's program, so guests can be enticed away from TV, night swims and shuffleboard. Resort owners go along because Resort Cinema is a free service they can promote, and the details are all let out to Modern's vacationing teachers and students.

Modern merchandises the audiences as a peg above the national norm (". . . a third higher than the national average.") They tout the attitude of the viewers as especially favorable. ("The resort audience is a homogeneous group, having similar tastes, interests and backgrounds. They enjoy traveling and sports and are interested in films on these subjects as well as films of general interest. The relaxed and friendly atmosphere at resorts is conducive to good reception of sponsored films and the relative absence of advertising exposures during vacation gives a unique impact opportunity to the film sponsor.")

Of course the same rationale could be applied to the merits of *sleep*. "The relaxed and friendly atmosphere at resorts is conducive to good sleep. . ." But no matter. Communications people know all too well that newspapers containing costly ads are used to wrap garbage, the TV set is used for children's parlor games, and car radios are switched off as soon as the commercial starts. No medium is as effective as its promoter would like us to believe.

Modern figures average resort audiences at 55 persons. Prints are circulated at about 2½ bookings weekly. So 50 prints circulated during a 10-week summer season could develop 1,500 showings and 75,000 viewers "from Squaw Valley to Cape Cod."

Colleges

Modern Talking Picture Service can take credit for developing many markets for sponsored films almost single-handedly.

One of those is College Cinema, a network of free campus movie lounges created as a means of reaching three million college viewers every year.

Modern ingeniously sets up these movie lounges in such popular meeting places as student unions and dormitory social centers. Modern sets up rear-screen projection units, delivers and picks up films to and from the lounges, and arranges things to attract the largest possible audiences. Modern's regional people line up students on campuses; each is responsible for about ten colleges in his area.

Two to four hours of daily programming are prepared on long-play reels. Student representatives are given posters, handbills, ad proofs for college newspapers and a publicity manual to get campus interest bubbling. One might wonder what a setup like this in a student lounge has to offer over the countless TV sets stashed in campus corners. If you were to listen to Modern, the TV stations would be showing the same sponsored films anyway.

There are subtle, important differences—differences enough to increase the campus audiences for College Cinema by a dramatic 50 per cent since the end of the Vietnam war. Modern does it with carefully selected programs from its sponsored film catalog, something it failed to do successfully in the case of Airport Cinema. Modern picks films about science, technology, business and industry, sports, travel, national and international problems. "More and more," Modern says, "young people are being exposed to highly creative and sophisticated movies, and they react best to sponsored films that are fast-moving and imaginative." That must be something of an understatement when you think about the millions of college students jaded by overexposure to porn, pot, the underground press, comic books and the tube.

The fact is that the condition that sets college students up to watch College Cinema is *boredom*. It is akin to the boredom that besets women at home and sends them to watch the soapers. Contrary to rumor among parents, press and public, college students do not rush from kick to kick. They have many adult attributes, among which is laziness. Students most likely drift from textbooks to bullsessions to beer. A cool hour or two in front of College Cinema fits that lifestyle rather nicely.

The showing pattern offered for a price to film sponsors involves one print playing daily from one week at each campus in a circuit. The circuit, arranged like Resort Cinema, takes 10 to 15 weeks. Then the print repeats the circuit in a new college semester. The whole season lasts about 30 weeks, varying from campus to campus. Average audience, according to Modern, is 25 students. Average number of weekly bookings is four. So one print can reach 100 students weekly and 3,000 per season. If the sponsor turns 10 prints over to Modern, they could deliver 30,000 students in one season. That number could be equalled in a single, hefty major-market TV showing with far less distribution effort, of course.

Modern charges around $4 per showing, the same type of charge that their regular community showings cost.

Other film promotions flourish on college campuses which, in one way, compete with Modern's concept, and in another way, enhance it. Student organizations book 16mm theatrical films for small charges, so that college students can see "In" films like *The Boob Tube*, great old Bogart flicks and film masterpieces like *Sounder*. Such programs can draw audiences away from *The Story of Pneumatic Drills*. But they can also be part of a campus-wide habit of watching 16mm screens instead of drifting downtown to watch the parking meters rust.

Cable TV Networks

The motion picture craft was never more effective than in the American Broadcasting Network special about fires. In that controversial film show, a building material was shown being tested in a horizontal position, as its manufacturer wanted.

Fire was applied to it, and the flame dutifully went out, implying the material was fire-resistant. Then the material was turned to a vertical position and the fire applied once again. This time flames whipped up and consumed the panel in a furious, quick *whoosh*.

Changing the angle made all the difference.

Changing the angle of sponsored film exposure also makes a profound difference. In November, 1973, Les Biederman and his son Ross put American Cable Network on line in the modest community of Traverse City, Michigan. They had suffered through three years of research into what type of programming the expanding cable television systems needed and wanted, what types of equipment were needed and available, and what programming was available.

The enterprise sprang out of the loins of Midwestern Broadcasting Company, which operates two television stations, five AM radio stations and three FM radio stations in Northern Michigan, all NBC affiliates. In 1965 Midwestern Broadcasting invested in CATV in Traverse City and called it Midwestern Cablevision.

The concept was simple and dynamic: sell the cable stations package programming in the form of ¾-inch videocassettes so the stations could originate local programming at negligible cost and build a vehicle for local advertising. To make out financially, the American Cable Network had to come up with a monthly fee that was low enough to attract hundreds of customers. There was only one way to turn: *sponsored films*.

The Biedermans did their homework beautifully. They approached myriad industries, producers, organizations and government agencies to get free films. The offer was almost irresistible. ACN wanted only to borrow indefinitely a clean print of their sponsored film. ACN would transfer the image to videotape and circulate the videocassettes to a growing national network of cable systems hungry for material to fill their own channels. The sponsor would get important additional exposure of his film at the next-to-nothing cost of a good print. And that print would even come back to him in time.

From the beginning, ACN had taste. They did not accept junk, even in their pioneer moments. If a sponsored film were boring, distorted, tasteless, unfair or introspective, ACN politely sent the print back. They still do. Our own firm sent them a fine, sensitive new film about infant nutrition that ACN rejected because it dealt with breastfeeding, even though no breast stood out. Though we hardly agreed, we respected their editorial integrity. ACN also rejects dirty prints, no matter how good the subject.

Within two years, ACN grew from one to 60 systems. They anticipate that figure going to 120 within another year. Those are important numbers. After a little over a year in service, ACN was in 26 states covering 400,000 paid cable subscribers. It would not take much vision to project this to one million. And then ACN would be in the big time.

Those words "paid" and "subscriber" must be analyzed carefully. Your everyday TV set owner is a peg above the radio owner, who is above the owner of no communications equipment at all. Each higher level in the pecking order commands additional respect as a more lucrative and selective market. When you add the dimension of paid service to the TV set owner, you arrive at a new plateau. For if the TV set owner is willing to separate himself from upwards of $80 a year to pick up more stations and a clearer, uniform signal, we must acknowledge that he is something special. And the work "subscriber" understates the market, because subscriber is a singular word whereas it represents more than two persons per household. True, some cable households contain two or more TV sets and thus reduce the number of persons viewing on each set. Nevertheless, statistically speaking, cable subscribers are like newspapers and magazines: more than one person is looking. And one survey finds cable households are responsible for 11 per cent more viewing than non-cable.

"Survey information for cablecasters is just about unavailable," states Ross Biederman, but one can safely assume that gap will soon be filled. One ACN affiliate, GE Cablevision in Wyoming, Michigan, near

Grand Rapids, conducted a survey of their own that set quite a few jaws ajar. On that community's five-channel cable service, locally originated programs were second in popularity, surpassed only by the weather channel. The American Cable Network tape programs chalked up a combined total percentage of cable homes watching of 94 per cent. The weather channel was first with 96 per cent, and the others had 86 per cent, 80 per cent and 68 per cent. This is something of an indication that sponsored films not only are *available* to 400,000 ACN viewers, but they are *watched* in an active, wholesome manner.

The same survey also examined specific programs to determine audience interest. Part of the ACN pattern is to strip-program sponsored films of similar content, such as winter sports films and automotive films. Those strips are given generic titles on the cable system schedules, for quick identification. Thus, ACN's strip of fishing films is called *Fishing Unlimited* and that appears on the schedule next to the *Smothers Brothers* and *Country & Western U.S.A.* Well, the Grand Rapids survey showed that the programs in first, third, fourth and fifth place were ACN shows. That appears to be a credit both to sponsored film quality and ACN's ability to pick winners from among the thousands offered them.

Ross Biederman thinks the most interesting aspect of the survey is the wealth of suggestions viewers volunteered for program ideas. Read a few:

"More country and western programs! Travelogues!"

"Give us legal advice such as wills, divorce, social security, individual rights, taxation, personal property seizure, etc."

"What is wrong with Channel 10 programming all day on Saturday and Sunday?"

"Please show different inexpensive crafts."

"More sports programs of all types."

"Animal films for children."

"Teach ballroom dancing on cable TV"

"We like nature pictures."

"As senior citizens, we enjoy Channel 10, most especially travel pictures. Keep them coming."

"I would like to see a program on fixing bikes."

"Photography. More cultural programs (ballet, opera, symphony)." "A program on the best food buys of the week."

"Cable TV is good!"

Biederman studied these responses and concluded ACN was on the right track.

Some of the most abundant sources of sponsored films for the network are Shell Oil films, Canadian travel films, Pan American World Airways travel films, Schlitz sports films, NASA, and the National Forest Service. They pick up many films from state and local governments—100 alone from the State of Florida. ACN visits embassies and foreign tourist offices for good material. "In all," he reports, "we have better than 3,000 films at our disposal for the cable network. And more come in daily."

What they require are good quality films, prints in good physical condition, cleared for television use, and the right to hold prints on a long-term basis. ACN will not schedule a film unless it's there on their shelves.

Insofar as fresh material is concerned, ACN's track record is far better than tape syndicates that feed FM stations. For ACN repeats its films two to six times a year, depending on their age, content and print condition. That is really very little repetition and compare favorably with repeats of network and off-network shows on commercial TV stations.

Indeed, repeats are often more excitingly watched than the first performance. In the Naples, Florida *Star* of October 4, 1974, General Manager William J. Ryan of Radio-Television Center's CableVision-2 is quoted, "We quite often get requests for repeats of certain programs. One example that comes immediately to mind was a feature called, *Fighting Fire with Science*. Not only did the professional firefighters groups ask for advance notification of its repeat showing, but an entire elementary school class wrote individual letters to us asking for another showing. We're very pleased at this sort of response."*

ACN printouts list the week of showing, city and state of the cable system, number of homes (paid subscribers), number of times run and total audience projection. The bottom line might show 464,500 homes and a total of 671,900 in the audience for just one three-month period. Those happen to be the exact figures confirmed by ACN for the *Great Annual Bathtub Race* supplied by the Canadian travel office; a very happy office, we shall assume.

There is no unhappiness among the cable systems, either. While they are paying for all this, much to the gratification of the sponsors, they are profiting, too. CATV operators are not known for their timidity. They have quickly surfaced in daily newspapers, mail promotion and on their own stations with heavy promotion of their own cable network programming. They take paternal pride in their promotional ads. NOW: 28 HOURS A WEEK OF ADDITIONAL PROGRAMMING AVAILABLE

---

*So is the author, who happened to produce the film.

ONLY ON CABLE TV, reads one headline of a page ad on the cover of the Woburn, Massachusetts, newspaper TV supplement.

> Your cable TV system in Woburn and Burlington has joined the American Cable Network. Available now, and at NO additional cost to cable subscribers, the American Cable Network will have 28 more hours a week of professional color programming without commercial interruption.* It's a family channel; it's a sports channel; it's an educational channel; it's a channel that will entertain, educate and enthrall you and all the members of your family. It's the family entertainment channel that can save you money for admissions, gas, baby sitters, etc. About half of all programs are 'Education-Information', and the other half are about recreation, sports and travel. Many of these programs have NEVER been on broadcast television and never will be. They come from a collection of over 3,000 titles that will be shown over the course of the year. This unique programming is available ONLY TO CABLE TV SUBSCRIBERS on your own local Channel 13. If you are now on the cable, consider this notice as a new year's gift to you.

That ad brought in 300 new Boston-area subscribers.

That is called merchandising. Woburn, Massachusetts, is not alone. A four-page special issued in Evergreen, Colorado, shouts EVERGREEN AND ITTREDGE JOIN AMERICAN CABLE NETWORK! A Homestead, Pennsylvania, bulk mail piece regales local citizens with 28 MORE HOURS A WEEK ON YOUR LOCAL CHANNEL 8 . . . IN COLOR . . . NO EXTRA CHARGES . . . TOP QUALITY—TOP FLIGHT—ENTERTAINMENT.

CATV operators are made aware of the cost savings in the mechanics of transmitting ACN material. Videocassette equipment costs 25 to 30 cents per hour to operate, they are reminded, whereas a color film chain costs at least $3 per hour, plus the cost of a projectionist. "A standard broadcast station has a film chain operation cost that is closer to $10 an hour," ACN relates. But the CATV operator need only have one unskilled hand available once an hour to change cassettes. Anyone in the office can do it. ACN uses quality equipment to transfer film images to tape: RCA color camera, Eastman projectors, and 900 series IVC one-inch videotape equipment with TBC.

Finally and most important economically, ACN tells prospective systems that their 28 weekly hours of duck-soup programming provides a splendid vehicle for local spot sales. Every break between quarter- and half-hour sponsored films is saleable on a local basis. To sweeten the pot, ACN will even help systems get set up for local origination if they aren't already, promising to do so with a starting investment of only $1,000.

About half the 60 systems which subscribe to ACN are selling local spots in the approximate five minutes per hour that are open to sell

*ACN makes an interesting distinction. They do carry commercials, but all are placed between programs and never within them.

commercials. This is all very good news to suburban cable systems committed to local origination that they cannot afford. Woburn's marketing manager, Don Mathison, calls ACN "the perfect saviour."

The ACN markets include some vital ones: Boston, Salt Lake City, Knoxville, Des Moines, Grand Rapids, Cocoa Beach, Baton Rouge, Buffalo, Syracuse, Tulsa and Columbus among others. And with every new one the fledgling network adds, sponsored films *automatically* earn audience dividends and a broader base for the future.

The Modern Cable Network is out to prove that CATV is a workable and successful distribution channel for sponsored films. Modern likes to group its sponsored films under shelters with appropriate titles, to give some form to an otherwise formless list of films. The titles include *Cable Journal, Modern Home Digest* and *Sports and Travel World.* Each series comprises 27 one-hour assemblies of two to four individual sponsored films, transferred to a master videocassette. They add introductory and closing strips with hosts to hold them all together.

Cable systems get them all free. In doing so, they must agree to schedule the series on a regular basis, to make it worth Modern's effort to supply films. Knowing how few research data are available in the cable field, Modern commissioned Throckmorton/Satin Associates, Inc. to study audience impact of local origination programming, which includes sponsored films from Modern. The survey revealed that 26.1 per cent of responding homes recalled watching one or more of three weekly program series out of Modern. *Sports and Travel World,* predictably, was most successful with 17.1 per cent recall of one or more films within it. *Modern Home Digest* recall was 10.7 percent and *Cable Journal* got 10.1 per cent. The cable systems telecast the Modern strips 1.8 times per week. The survey was conducted by mail among subscribers to cable systems in Mankato, Minnesota; Reading, Pennsylvania; Muscle Shoals, Alabama; and West Palm Beach, Florida. Those are four of Modern's 50 cable affiliates.

Modern found much to be comfortable within the survey. "The sponsors are reaching the public," Fontaine Kincheloe said. "Cable operators are able to offer their subscribers a much wider variety of interesting and informative programming, and the subscribers seem to appreciate the shows. According to the survey, eight out of nine respondents who had seen the programs found them valuable and a similar percentage said they would continue to watch."

What Modern did not know was that in at least one of the surveyed systems, American Cable Network programming was running the week of the Modern survey. So the survey was as much to the credit of ACN as their competition, Modern.

Association Films is in there with the same technique. Their *Daytime* videocassette network is being circulated among 175 stations, 3½ times the number Modern has signed up. They claim one and a half million homes in their coverage. *Daytime* also boasts a regular hostess, visiting celebrities, recipe demonstrations and movie reviews as icing on the sponsored film cake.

Association Films and Modern giving away what the American Cable Network sells—how long can that last? Indefinitely, if all manage their shops well. For the sponsored film resources of Association Films and Modern are quite limited compared to the American Cable Network. AF and Modern have only a few hundred titles in their libraries at one time, whereas the ACN has the whole world to draw on—including, ironically, Modern's and Association's films. The giant throat of all American cable systems cannot be fed with a few hundred titles rerun many times a year. Enormous and continuous sources of program material are required to keep cable systems fed with local origination material they need to sustain themselves.

Modern and Association Films are equipped to feed cable systems only four hours or programming a week or so. ACN supplies 28. Modern and Association Films thus seem to whet the appetites of cable operators for ACN's longer tape programming.

It is attractive to CATV operators to take Modern's and Association Films' programming free. It is equally attractive to the sponsors to provide programming to ACN free, especially after seeing Modern's invoices for $5 per play per system. It is readily apparent that if ACN can continue to expand its paid service to cable systems, sponsors will swarm to American Cable Network like honeybees.

Schools

Brown elephants? After the herd flounders around in the lake waters for a while, all the elephants emerging from the wet turmoil are coated with muddy water that quickly dries on their great gray hides. From a distance newly arrived tourists get their first look at "brown elephants."

Then they can watch the herd working its way through the East African grass and trees* eating everything green in sight. It looks like closing day at the circus. Everything comes down. Everything goes. Elephants suck up so much foliage you wonder how nature can keep up with them.

When they've gone, you look around and see utter ruin. You ask yourself, can anything on earth equal this great animal's hunger and depredation?

Yes. American schools. They chew up about 11,000 16mm motion prints every school day. They are responsible for debossing new perforations in three million feet of prints every week. They lose, temporarily or forever, 2,100 film prints a week. American schools are the marauding

*Sorry, Tarzan fans; there are no jungles in East Africa.

elephants of the non-theatrical motion picture industry. Anyone with any sense tries his best to stay clear of their great heavy feet.

Not Les and Ross Biederman of Traverse City, Michigan. The father and son team is out taming elephants these days, talking with them about paying for the use of sponsored films instead of borrowing them from Modern and Association-Sterling and then eating them alive.

A fool's errand, you say. Perhaps. But Educators' Videocassette Service is off to an auspicious start and may take firm hold of the American public school discipline. "EVS makes sponsored and other films available on videocassettes to schools and libraries," the younger Biederman explains. "EVS gives sponsors free school and library distribution. Our charge to the schools and libraries for duplication is $5 for up to a half-hour film. So a half-hour film would cost $32—$27 for the tape, plus $5 for duplication. And they get new Sony videocassettes.

"For unsponsored films, we can pay the producer a royalty," Biederman continues. "Our initial mailing of our catalog includes every college in the United States. We also send catalogs to the regional media centers for public schools in 17 states, as well as to various libraries that have written us about material in videocassette format that might be available to them."

The founders of American Cable Network plans to make thousands of sponsored films available to schools and libraries through this unique marketing technique. EVS quickly signed up such eminent sponsored film sources as Dow Chemical, Georgia Pacific, Liberty Mutual, NASA, and the U.S. Coast Guard to fill its 37-page premiere catalog.

The Biedermans are proceeding with the knowledge of certain truths. Schools have an elephantine hunger for sponsored films that photographic film print technology cannot economically satisfy. In other words, there is no practical way to get sponsored films into all the classrooms that want to show them. As schools equip themselves with Sony videocassettes and other VTR formats, one begins to see the proverbial light at the end of the tunnel. For schools can borrow sponsored film prints and transfer them to tape for broad, cheap distribution.

But the schools must, if they are ethical, seek electronic reproduction rights, often at the rate of one film at a time. That is a forbidding task to put before any educator or librarian. Comes now before the bench of sanity one Ross Biederman who proclaims, "We will sell you thousands of fine sponsored films befitting your educational needs for little more than the cost of new blank videocassettes. These are already on tape, ready to play on your Sony. You have no transfer work to do, no rights to bargain for. You pay just once and the tape is yours."

The appeal may be there for the herd of elephants. It may be there for the sponsors and producers. EVS is yet another avenue for the distribution of sponsored films to broadening audiences.

Airports

If the sponsored film industry is to burgeon—and that appears to be the case—new markets must evolve for their use, and they must command increasing importance in existing markets. That is obvious.

What is not obvious is the identity of these "new markets." It is simple enough to envision fresh markets, but it is something else to exploit them and make them lasting and profitable. Modern Talking Picture Service found that out the hard way when they plunged into something they called "Skyport Cinema."

Modern's officers saw corporation executives sitting in airport waiting rooms waiting for planes. They were riffling through newspapers printed in cities away from home, quaffing too many vodka martinis at noisy airport bars, and staring at the same dreary old barometers and stuffed animals in the shops before their jets arrived. Picture a $36,000-a-year vice president pushing quarters into a computer ping pong machine for 40 minutes and you can understand Modern's enthusiasm for the Skyport Cinema concept. Businessmen with free time were an attractive market indeed.

Modern worked hard and arranged leased space in a number of large-city airports for the installation of a projector, a stack of sponsored films and a few seats. They were modest, functional arrangements. The projector had a wide-angle lens aimed at a rear screen mounted on a simple wall facing the audience, Punch-and-Judy style. Simple legends on the wall described the action. Signs on the wall identified the title of the currently running sponsored film. The pictures were shown "segue," so people in the airport could spot the screen almost any time from a distance and stop by, sit down and rest their aching backs while watching *California Prunes,* sponsored by the California Prune Advisory Board. (That name challenges the intellect. Does a board of people advise prunes, or does a board of prunes advise people?)

True, the audiences were not large, but that never frightened the distribution houses who were used to small audiences per showing and had learned how to tout selective audiences to their prospects. "Air travelers are undoubtedly the most articulate, successful, active and alert group of people that populate America today," Modern quoted pollster Lou Harris, a college-days friend of mine, in their promotion material. "And these are the people we reach," Modern stentoriously added.

Modern went on, "Because there's a constantly changing audience, a film can show for several years on a daily basis before repetition poses a problem. Short films give you the best opportunity for frequent showings and are also advantageous with an audience that may have to leave at any moment." (Did you notice a crack open up there?)

Skyport Cinema was rationalized as a proper opportunity for airport types to put their waiting time to good use by watching informative films.

"Shorts about business and industry, science and technology, and important social documentaries are excellent for these viewers," Modern pointed out. "And when it comes to entertainment, they are the kind of active individuals who can be counted on to take a special interest in sports and travel subjects." Fair enough. Modern added that their experience showed that any film that is informative and entertaining is well-received by this audience. "However," they openly warned, "holding their interest is important, for the viewer can come and go as he pleases."

Modern worked out a ratecard for Skyport Cinema that looked attractive enough to customers and prospects. Price-per-showing ranged from $2.50 to $5.00 for films ranging in length from five minutes or less to 26 minutes or longer. Medium price before discount was $3.50 per showing of a quarter-hour sponsored film. To be sure the sponsor was never dissatisfied or doubtful about dwindling audiences at off hours, Modern promised a prorata discount if audiences totalled fewer than 20. If only 10 souls were present, the sponsor would pay only 50 per cent of the rate—$1.75 in this case.

Modern would throw in collateral costs of preparing promo slides or signs to identify the film titles to those who sat down after the opening titles ran.

All this sounds machine-smooth but it wasn't. "A projectionist is on duty at all times." That statement indicates what led Skyport Cinema to its grave. Troubles began to besiege the concept-in-action from the very beginning. Continuous-operating projectors, even with projectionists at hand, didn't function long without some kind of problem. Two projectors cost twice as much as one, so Modern tried to work one long-playing projector as hard as it could, swapping large reels infrequently. The machines got hot, tired and cranky. They would tear up prints in spite of manufacturers' solemn promises. Projectionists turned out to be projectionists and not projector repairmen, so hours might go by with a dark screen facing passing crowds.

I watched many Skyport Cinema lounges in action and enjoyed passing many hours there. My heart would go out to Modern when I saw films identified by the wrong title, the projectionist shuffling in and out of his booth not quite able to keep up with his duties and down-time, and audiences bored to sleep. Yes, I could turn around and count the sleeping travelers in the Skyport Cinema and wonder if the projectionist was dutifully counting all heads, awake or asleep, as "audited accounts of actual viewers."

Sponsors didn't help Modern too much with the titles they chose. The incredible and absolute dullness of some sponsored films was never more embarrassingly evident than in Skyport Cinema. If Modern had been more selective and more careful in which titles they solicited, audiences would surely have been more responsive and grateful. Yet some titles were superb and a showcase for the industry. Unfortunately, viewers had no channel dials to switch. It was watch, read, sleep or move on. Most viewers did some of each. If a sponsor ever stopped at a Skyport Cinema to audit his investment, he would lose confidence first time out. He would see most of the seats empty. Those that were occupied often had newspapers and magazines before them, heads hidden from the screen. (Modern had not counted on airport seat scarcity when they added their mini-theaters.) Viewers who entered did so idly, aimlessly—hardly the brand of a consumer intent on buying products seen on screen. Those who witnessed the films would frequently look away—at watches, other viewers, magazines, and the terminal. Attentiveness was something less than superb. "According to a recent survey of the Skyport audience. . . 10 per cent are business owners or corporate officers and another 54 per cent hold professional, managerial, technical or sales positions. The average family income is $16,035. Seven out of ten own their own homes and two out of three own stocks and bonds," offered Modern. But when a sponsor stopped in to check up, he didn't see these market claims. He saw a miniature waiting room with a movie up front and hardly anyone paying the kind of attention a TV set gets.

TV is what finally broke the back of Skyport Cinema. Franchise operators got rights to install small black-and-white TV sets locked to chairs in unused corners of airports several years ago, and the quarters have never stopped flowing into them. Airport administrations enjoyed their slice of the action, more dynamic than the rent Modern paid for more space. The airport waiting room crowd could now watch a screen and see familiar shows, perhaps catch a favorite show they thought they'd miss during the trip. The screen had a dial the viewer could switch, so his quarter wouldn't be wasted on a bomb. The public didn't realize their quarters would tumble into the slots fast, since it would take fancy planning to prevent the set going off some time during the first quarter's investment.

Sponsored films continued to be seen in airports—on the screens of those little franchised TV sets. But all the screens of Skyport Cinema finally went black after Modern looked at the bottom line and saw red. The costs of projectionists, space rentals and equipment repairs exceeded the unenthusiastic income from sponsors, and there didn't seem to be any improvement trend. Modern realized that closing Skyport Cinema wouldn't endanger their good business with the same sponsors in other markets. So Skyport Cinema died, the only large-scale failure ever to stain the sponsored film field.

Television

As mentioned elsewhere, Association Films had the good sense to pull out of airport showings of sponsored films five years after they took the plunge. Several of the distribution areas where Modern is strong and successful are also the domain of Association. AF is just as heavily committed to educational distribution, general adult audience distribution (Modern's "community distribution"), television distribution and theater distribution. A sponsor could feel confident in assigning his film's distribution to either Modern or AF to reach such audiences, and of course there are other competent distributors who can deliver them, too.

AF calls its theatrical distribution service "Association-Sterling/35." It's operated out of theatrical booking offices in some 30 cities. Association, like Modern, supervises placement of sponsored short subjects in movie theaters, works with producers to blow up their 16mm titles to 35mm, promotes those films to the circuits, booking services and independent theaters, provides monthly exhibition reports and creates custom national and regional distribution programs. AF and Modern rates for theatrical distribution are *identical*, which may strike the reader as quite a coincidence.

School distribution services at AF include regular mailings to principals, teachers and department heads in such curricula as science, social studies, home economics, consumer education, health and safety, distributive education, mathematics, career guidance and business education—fields that provide the best audiences for sponsored films. Some specialized mailings go out to superintendents, school boards, school systems and audio-visual directors of school systems to keep requests coming in for specific titles listed by Association.

Television distribution is the hottest angle in sponsored film circulation to many sponsors. AF displays just as much originality as Modern in seeking out fresh approaches to TV stations for productive use of their sponsored materials. They develop series programs, special concepts and packages, and offer individual sponsored films to the nation's commercial, public and cable outlets. Television circulation at AF is handled by five regional TV centers which maintain daily telephone contact with stations and systems. Association's TV rates are $17.65 per confirmed telecast, $7.65 per cablecast and $3.80 per preview.

Modern's TV rates are almost the same: $17.50 for films over 7½ minutes' running time, plus $2.50 extra for the first five bookings confirmed each month, and $7.50 per cablecast.

Such rates seem to satisfy sponsors; at least hundreds of satisfied Association and Modern customers pay them. But they appear simplistic when compared to the ratecards of the 508 VHF and 192 UHF commercial TV stations on the air. Commercial ratecards break down station time availabilities into many categories relating to audience, time of day, special talent and programs, length of commercial announcement or sponsored show, frequency and volume of advertising. Yet the distributors charge the sponsor the same $17.65 or so (there are volume discounts, of course) whether his film ran on WNBC-TV in New York at 9

PM Thursday night or on KTVA in Anchorage at sign-on time Sunday morning.

Distributors are candid with their sponsor clients. They tell sponsors that they will get the bad with the good, and that over the years a good mix of audiences will result in a comprehensive TV distribution program. That is true enough, and considering the overriding commercial intent of sponsored films, and the fact that stations are running them free, the sponsor should be grateful and content. Still one would hope that distribution rates will evolve into a more complex and fairer system similar to station ratecards.

It would not be difficult for Association and Modern to work out such a rate schedule. They go to immense trouble to determine TV showings details and spend a substantial part of their fees in time and tolls contacting stations that fail to confirm details of showings of sponsored films.

A client of a professional distribution house gets his $17.65 worth. He knows it when he scans the monthly reports that come in confirming all showings that have accumulated. The sponsor can read an itemized list of the cities, call letters, network affiliation, time of showing, date of showing, time class, time value in dollars, number of TV homes in area (or CATV subscribers), and estimated viewers. Then he can see summary figures showing the number of billable telecasts, total telecasts, total time value, total estimated viewers, number of previews where there was no telecast, and activity totals for the month, year to date and from the beginning of the program.

Once in a while we hear a sponsor say, "I've made sponsored films and had them distributed in the past and I never could determine any results." This is pure poppycock. A single month's report from a reputable distributor is proof of results. That same sponsor is also busy telling his advertising agency that he is switching agencies because he couldn't "see any results." They have places for such clients; they are called hospitals for the blind.

Most sponsors are pleased with the long-term results and remain faithful clients. In one of their fact sheets, Modern says, "In any given year, Modern makes bookings to about 95% of all TV stations. And 30% of our bookings are in the largest 20% of the markets. Only 12% are in the smallest 20%. Films are telecast at favorable hours. In the overall averages, 16% are shown in the evening, 53% in the afternoon, 31% in the morning. Many of the daytime telecasts occur on weekends." This is heady information to a corporate PR manager anxious to get top-level approval for the sponsored film project he has proposed.

To add to his euphoria, Modern tells him the average audience per booking is 45,000 persons. At that rate, it takes only 25 bookings to reach well over a million viewers. "And most films get over 100 telecasts in a single year," Modern reports. "Many with very broad appeal frequently go over 200. Depending on your budget and acceptance of your film, 20 to 50 prints are adequate for most TV programs." Many stations hold sponsored films long enough to show a second time before returning them to the distributor. Modern says about 11 per cent of their bookings result in extra telecasts, and there is no extra charge for the bonus. Why would a TV station show the same film twice in a short period of time? Because their audiences are like crowds on a city street—constantly changing. A good sponsored film can be shown at 7 PM Monday and again at 3 PM Wednesday with little duplication of audience.

Distributors make friends and keep them at TV stations as part of their success pattern. A few TV libraries in major cities give personalized service to stations and cable systems. Each office covers only a limited number of stations. That makes it possible for them to become knowledgeable in the wishes and needs of each station, and to give them personal service on a day-to-day basis. These TV offices keep their own prints, separate from those used among schools and community audiences. All prints are kept in meticulously fine condition. They are marked with the exact running time to make programming easier for stations. Hundreds of stations subscribe to Association's and Modern's regular program series package.

Placement is accomplished through regular mailings of distributor catalogs, brochures on specific titles and newsletters. Stations respond with letters and phonecalls requesting sponsored films for specific play-dates, for audition, or for taping for later telecast.

TV Networks

One might judge from the variety of outlets sponsored films have found, from the closed-circuit TV network among the Alaska pipeline workers to college lounges, that sponsored films are seen everywhere.

That is not quite true. One noticeable gap can be found among the television networks. It is a great rarity when the CBS, NBC or ABC television network transmits a sponsored film without charge. Their pride alone prevents them touching films of this type. Each network has built news gathering staffs including good to superb film capabilities, and the intrusion of an independent film run as a public service is simply too much for them to bear.

One independent producer was so incensed about the network doors slammed in his face that he brought suit against them. But all the rest quietly accept the inevitable, and do not even submit their award-winning films to the network bosses.

When a sponsor comes along and puts up the ante to run one, the networks change masks. Ralston-Purina decided that their *It's A Dog's World* was appropriate for network showing—not once but twice. Since they were agreeable to picking up the tab, who was the network to say this CINE Golden Eagle winner wasn't suitable for its viewers? *It's A Dog's World* was a David Wolper production, and our sequence on dogs hunting bear and boar was part of it. Wolper started out on the road peddling syndicated TV films. He bought up rights to an old newsreel vault and started building films out of the old public-domain material, picking out footage of famous stars. Then he graduated to original works like the Cousteau undersea series for *National Geographic,* and then into theatrical features. For many years Wolper films have appeared on prime network time, which is saying something. Most of them have taken the form of sponsored specials for TV and for the aftermarket wherein prints are circulated as sponsored films.

The networks will pay sponsored film producers for footage quite frequently. When our crews went to East Africa to document the Safari Rally, both ABC and CBS networks welcomed some of our footage to run on their news and sports feature shows. Doing so was compromising for us as producers, since the networks soup-up the originals and start cutting the scenes they want without benefit of workprint.

The FCC squeeze on network time is an additional valid reason for networks discouraging the use of sponsored films. They pragmatically believe that the place for sponsored films on TV is in the form of locally-originated programming, which the FCC cherishes so dearly. And that is what happens. Thousands of sponsored films are transmitted annually by TV stations as locally-originated shows. The only thing local about them is that someone local-mounted the reels on the projector.

Libraries

Ambitious libraries are becoming increasingly important in the distribution of sponsored films. Most libraries, public and private, are so inundated with books, periodicals, paperwork, politics and labor scarcity that they do not have a single film of any kind in the house. Only 2,000 list an organized film section within their libraries. I visited the American Jewish Archives on the campus of Hebrew Union College in Cincinnati and asked 80-year-old Dr. Jacob Marcus where the films were. "Films?" he said. "We have none. I don't know how to keep them," he added. It is understandable that scholars think in terms of books and graphics. To them film is simply a modern delivery system for the same material, but one generation removed. A scholar works in the original Greek, Aramaic or Sanskrit and would not dream of accepting any translation as a true source. Film to him is a translation.

Those 2,000 libraries which have equipped themselves with films think differently. They often started their service in response to public demand for 16mm prints of Disney cartoons to entertain birthday party celebrants. Then they advanced to filmstrips and films on school subjects, to supplement public school studies. Today libraries often boast thousands of current and valuable 16mm titles, and many of them are sponsored films.

Some are bought on their own merit, side by side with educational films made for schools and libraries. Our own series of five on dog obedience training, sponsored by Alpo and with proper Alpo exposure in each, is a great favorite of libraries—and never has a word been said about Alpo's commercial exposure in them.

But most sponsored films are donated by sponsors to the libraries, which are usually short of funds and long on public requests for films. The proprietor of the Jefferson Parish Library in Louisiana has an interesting case. He, like many librarians, had vision. Instead of asking around the Parish for a few sponsored films here and there, he organized a writing campaign and papered America with requests for long-term loans of sponsored films.

Response was immediate and electric. Associations, organizations, industries, governments, producers and distributors fell all over themselves lending the Jefferson Parish Library prints of their sponsored films. Among them were Eastman Kodak, Dow, Exxon, GTE, GE, ADA, Alcoa, NRA, Lipton, NCR, Miller Brewing, Goodrich, GM, Kemper, Ford, Jack Daniel, Senator Allen J. Ellender, AFL-CIO, AMA, AGC, Carousel Films, Chinese Information Service, Coca-Cola, Johnson and Johnson, McDonnell Douglas, NAHB, NAM, Nestle, Newsweek, Philip Morris, P&G, Shell, Union Carbide, the U.S. Department of State, VW, USDA, and the U.S. Army.

Now, if the reader wants to make a quick buck, I suggest that he approach any of the above and give each of them one hour to find Jefferson Parish, Louisiana, on a map. Jules Bartels, the adventuresome librarian, was delighted at all the attention. But he was unable to cope. Prints he requested for long-term loan were sent back to their source after viewing instead of being held. Reports of showings were not forthcoming; they were a basic courtesy to the people who loaned the prints. Bartels would approach each of the co-sponsors of a multiple-sponsored film, not realizing he was asking each for the same film.

Still the plan was a good one and if the Jefferson Parish Library could manage the print flow a little better than Iran could handle its import glut, sponsors would eventually get satisfactory audiences for their investments.

Why do 213 such sponsors and others leap to lend prints on indefinite loan to an obscure Louisiana library? Because the offer presented fresh audiences without charge for films already paid for, and the donors had nothing to lose. I say *donors* because the good librarian knows better than anyone that once the prints are in hand, there is little chance they will be recalled, and his "indefinite loan" becomes a "gift."

What kind of film library did Jefferson Parish accumulate? Whatever balance or imbalance it has, the library is what it wants to be, because the titles were preselected by the librarian and solicited, film by film. It is more than conceivable that other enterprising libraries will follow suit, and print distribution plans will consider them as a market of their own.

State governments like those of Virginia and Minnesota have for many years built libraries of sponsored films for state-wide circulation, and they provide booking reports either voluntarily or on request, all without cost to the sponsor.

Adult Community Groups

Association Films lists 100,000 of them. Modern lists 200,000. Both consider them the cream of sponsored film distribution.

These are the community groups. Where schools bring distributors the quantity of requests, community groups offer the quality. No one disputes the contention that the doers, the joiners, the affluent, the interested and the influential make up the community groups that request sponsored films for their programs. It seems to be an ideal match of audience and medium; each gets the most out of the marriage. The civic club or church group is composed of optimum types the sponsor wants to watch his film. They watch under optimum conditions: darkened room, silent and respectful audience, introduction by a known, respected leader. Attitude of the audience is the best. There is no atmosphere of imposition as in the case of commercials interrupting a TV movie. Interruptions are virtually unknown. In fact, the club program director may be commended after the film showing for making such a fine program possible and a continuing series of pertinent sponsored films can lead to his reappointment for another year.

Association charges $4.35 per shipment; Modern $3.80, plus 35 cents each for the first 100 bookings per month. Sponsored films are shown to any adult group on a local basis, and this includes:

Colleges	Prisons
Civic clubs	Hospitals and other
Churches and religious groups	health care institutions
Fraternal orders	Homes for the aged
Women's clubs	Country clubs
Garden clubs	Cultural organizations
Social organizations	Educational organizations
Alumni organizations	Professional organizations
Adult camps	Labor unions
Sports organizations	Men's clubs
Armed forces	Farm organizations
Industries	Camps
Government offices	Investment clubs

Political organizations

Safety councils

Humane organizations

Veterans organizations

Historical groups

Science societies

Fine arts groups

Performing arts groups

Social service organizations

Hobby clubs

Modern claims 1,250,000 film bookings a year to such community groups, reaching 125 million persons annually—which figures to 100 persons at an average showing. It suggests to sponsors that such viewers are leaders rather than followers, key people who can and do influence countless others. Present at such showings, they say, are hard-to-reach business executives, club officers, government officials, ministers, teachers, businessmen, wage-earners, homemakers, parents. It is suggested that all such showings are followed by formal or informal discussions, which add immeasurably to the memory value of the sponsored films they saw.

Community groups hear about sponsored films from sponsors and distributors rather regularly. Direct mail promotions, publicity in organization journals and daily press, space advertising, convention exhibits and personal contacts are methods used by distributors to reach community groups on national and local levels.

The cost per thousand on community showings is dramatically higher than that of TV and school showings. But this does not frighten sponsors or distributors, because selective, quality audiences are the most productive and efficient. Sponsors are quite aware that hundreds of millions of people see the Martini name on racetrack and sports arena fences throughout the world, which must come close to the lowest cost per thousand of any promotion. But they also know such signs develop very few sales in relation to the numbers who see them. But sit a $35,000-a-year executive with his family at a Monday night Rotary social. Turn on the projector and show him and 100 others like him a film on how Rotarians throughout the world successfully raise funds for Rotary projects. Bang. You have attention. Motivation. Timing. A perfect match of sponsored film subject with audience interest. If, as the lights go on after the film, the fund chairman hands out boxes of official Rotary candy for fund-raising sales, you'd have 100 members ready to volunteer to raise funds and do it well, just as they saw in the sponsored film.

Small wonder the distributors call community audiences their primary audience market.

INFORFILM

The difference between a sponsored film and any other film is never more dramatically illustrated than in Inforfilm.

The International Association of Informational Film Distributors is no unholy alliance of disparate types. Rather it is a bright star in the sponsored film sky. Twenty-two distributors of non-theatrical films are intelligently banded together to circulate sponsored films on a global basis. As any international corporation can attest, such a concept is sophisticated. Distributing one title in one country may well seem academic. But try feeding prints, revoiced in each language, to a dozen countries. Try getting your prints back after each showing. Try paying the correct amounts to the best shipper for each shipment. Try reconciling all the audience information into a single monthly report. Try building a mailing list of the best markets for your film in all 12 of those countries.

Try all that and you would have a difficult time doing it better than Inforfilm. The General Secretariat is based at 16/108 Avenue J. Sibelius in Brussels, where Jan Botermans works as General Secretary.

The concept originated in 1958 there in Brussels with Botermans and G. F. Magnel. Botermans was Director of Distribution—among other things—at Sofedi-Films and Magnel was Director General then as he is today. The two filmmakers were in touch with people from Schweizer Schul- und Volkskino, Schmalfilm Zentrale of Switzerland. Each time they met they discussed how reasonable it would be to organize sponsored film distribution on an international basis.

So early in November, 1960, a first meeting was held in Brussels. It was attended by delegates of distribution houses in Belgium, Great Britain, Netherlands and Switzerland. The United States wasn't personally represented. But two months before the late Frank Arlinghaus, President of Modern Talking Picture Service, had gone to Europe to seek new markets. While there he contacted Sofedi-Films and learned of the plans for launching the new organization. He enthusiastically concurred.

In January, 1961, a second meeting took place in Bern. This time Arlinghaus was there in person, and France and Germany joined in. At that occasion a draft of the Inforfilm rules and regulations was drawn up and a formal vote to organize was taken. Officially Inforfilm was founded in The Hague in May, 1961.

Some in the industry wonder why a successful international organization would be inducting its 22nd member 14 years after its first seven members created Inforfilm. Jan Botermans quickly rises to explain that with the exception of two members in France, there is no competition among Inforfilm members, and there are very few sponsored film distributors in the world from which to select members. Their rules do allow for two members in one country in order to cover regions well, but the first member must permit the second to join so that everyone gets along together. Double membership, Botermans warns, has already proven a handicap to Inforfilm in the past.

The spark that began Inforfilm was the international distribution problem Sofedi-Films faced in 1958. Sofedi-Films had to produce a film about cotton fibers and its sponsor asked the producer to distribute it not only in Belgium but in Holland, Germany and France. Belgium was, of course, no problem since Sofedi was already active in national distribution of its products. But it took considerable research in the Netherlands to find someone willing to distribute their cotton fiber film there, and then they wanted the unreasonable price of $20 per booking, compared to $3 then current in the United States.

In Germany it was the same story. Sofedi-Films' sponsor was being charged $20 a booking just to offer its film free to an interested audience. And in France, Botermans couldn't find anyone to do the work at any price.

"If we, people in the film business, have so much trouble finding distributors abroad," Botermans asked himself, "what must it be like for outsiders?" That planted the seeds for Inforfilm. Let's try, they said in Brussels, to simplify the job for sponsors interested in distributing their films in other nations by putting at their disposal a network of reliable and specialized distribution organizations.

Inforfilm worked then and it works now. Each member promotes his fellow members within his own country. In the U.S., Modern Talking Picture Service remains the sole affiliate, and they actively distribute Inforfilm information among American industries, government offices, producers, associations and organizations. Collectively, Inforfilm publishes promotional literature that is distributed in each country through the members. Members pledge to speak about distribution possibilities abroad when they contact sponsors, and there is ample evidence that they do so.

Inforfilm participates at festivals of sponsored films throughout the world. Since 1962, Botermans and other executives have attended annually the International Industrial Film Festival organized by the European Council of Industrial Federations. Since 1965, they have used that forum to bestow an annual Inforfilm Award. Now they are extending their participation to other festivals: the International Tourist and Folklore Film Festival, and the International Agricultural Film Festival. At the tourist event in Brussels, the first Inforfilm Tourist Film Award was issued.

Botermans individually attends several national industrial film festivals each year as well. He makes goodwill trips to visit important international sponsors, spending several weeks a year in Germany, the Netherlands, Great Britain and France. All through the year he is mailing sales letters to sponsors all over the globe who might be interested in Inforfilm services.

Members meet once a year for four days to share their problems, experiences, technical innovations, new markets and trends. Inforfilm's executive committee meets twice annually. At first Inforfilm members tried to establish a uniform booking rate throughout the world, but with inflation, varying costs and monetary values, the unit rate had to be abandoned. Sponsors can, just the same, figure the average international rate to be $5 per booking and they would not be far from fact. "When you consider the average audience includes 60 persons," Inforfilm likes to suggest, "that means you pay for each viewer less than the cost of a postage stamp. When considered on this basis, a sponsored film is competitive with other promotional media, especially when you consider the average film length is 20 minutes and it is shown to a captive audience."*

Inforfilm's record is impressive. Since they opened their doors, they have distributed more than 40 million sponsored films to audiences nearing 2½ billion people. In the most recent single year for which they have figures, the total showings were 4,275,000 and the audience nearly 170 million. All these figures, Botermans assures, are certified by showings reports on record.

Inforfilm distributes more than 200,000 16mm prints in 20 countries. Of course these comprise the collective figures of Inforfilm's 22 member distributors, and should not mislead the reader into thinking Inforfilm has centralized computer-operated reports, billing and communications. They don't. Inforfilm is a simple, viable trade association in a highly specialized communications field.

Botermans notes that sponsored film audiences are tending to diminish in size but reveal a higher quality and more specialized nature. He feels tape and disc formats have been sluggish in their development, but whenever they mature, Inforfilm will distribute them. Evidently Inforfilm members have agreed that theirs is a software industry and they will go wherever the hardware goes.

"We are very keen to find new members in countries not yet covered," Botermans tells me. "But in fact they are very difficult to find and we accept only reliable and fully recommendable people.

"Membership," he continues, "does not imply that new members automatically receive the films of the other members to distribute. This is impossible. To the sponsor, each country is a different market where he may have his own subsidiary with its own promotion policy. That subsidiary reserves the right to make its own decisions about distribution of films coming from the home country. But quite often the local subsidiary receives recommendations from top executives at home that they would do well to deal with the Inforfilm member in their country in order to get trustworthy distribution." Talk like that recently brought in new Inforfilm members in Brazil and France.**

*Whenever someone feeds me that tricky term "captive audience," I remember the time a radio professional and I drove past a vast cemetery over which lorded an 800-foot radio transmission tower. My friend muttered, "Captive audience."
**See Membership roster, Appendix D.

Inforfilm literature is published in English, German and French, side-by-side. This practice has not led to dancing in the streets of the members whose languages include Japanese, Swedish, Portuguese, Turkish, Spanish, Danish, Finnish, Italian, Czech, Afrikaans, Bulgarian, Norwegian and Arabic. That hard fact led to the demise of *The Inforfilm Bulletin*, which could not be published simultaneously in many languages.

Language, though, is not a serious obstacle to the more vital worth of international distribution of sponsored films. World industry is quite used to paying for translation of their communications tools, and sponsors fully expect and quite readily agree to costs of special tracks for each additional language.

Sponsors who patronize Inforfilm include so many international giants that reading some of their names makes one wonder why such vast industrial and economic clout cannot be used to end all wars: DuPont, BASF, Unilever, Shell, Nestlé, IBM, General Motors, International Nickel, Mobil, Gulf, Kodak, Coca-Cola, Lloyd's, Ciba-Geigy, DeBeers, Nissan, International Harvester, US Steel, Sandoz, Procter & Gamble, Air France, Ford and BP.

There we have just a small section of the client list of Inforfilm. Collecting bills, we must assume, is not one of the association's problems.

The newest member of the Inforfilm team is Pedro Hatheyer in Sao Paulo. Pedro is a valued member of IQ in his operation of Helicon Film, a leading Brazilian production house. Recently he organized an affiliate, Difusao de Filmes S/C Ltda., to become the first sponsored film distribution service in his nation and reported:

> Sponsored films are a total novelty in Brazil. All we can say at this point, after only a few months of operation with Difusão, is that the idea is being very well received, enthusiastically even, by both sponsors and borrowers.
>
> To get the service started, we are relying mostly on affiliates of international companies who use the system elsewhere. Many are already clients of Inforfilm members in other countries. At the same time, we are starting an integrated Helicon-Difusão promotion campaign, offering prospective sponsors the idea of producing a film on an informative subject especially for free-loan distribution. This, too, is just getting started, but we feel it will be a success.
>
> Difusão is, of course, open to other producers as well. We are keeping it separate from Helicon both in name and address so as not to scare other producers away. This is also catching on slowly. We are confident that in the long run producers will see our point. After all, we are opening a new market for all producers in Brazil.

Difusão's first list of *Filmes Gratis* contained 24 titles. Pedro Hatheyer's sponsor customers included the Embassy of South Africa,

Goodyear, Merck Sharp & Dohme, Sandoz, Kodak, BASF, DuPont, Brasimet, Adventistas, and Carlo Erba.

It's a little funny to note that the first Inforfilm member, Sofedi in Brussels, and the latest, Helicon in Sao Paulo, are *producers* of sponsored films as well as distributors. The sole American member of Inforfilm, Modern Talking Picture Service, openly declares its unhappiness with the author because Walter J. Klein Company, Ltd., distributes the films it produces. Modern figures it suffers if producers don't patronize Modern and instead offer distribution service themselves. Yet, Modern works with our fellow producers overseas who are also in the distribution business.

THE PRODUCER AS DISTRIBUTOR

Cross-pollination between sponsored film producers and distributors is widespread. I would not want such a statement to offend anyone who might think it sounds improper. The practice harms no one and benefits all parties. It is proper and productive.

Most sponsored film producers include a plan for distribution in their proposals for production of new films. This may take the form of little more than a blue-sky paragraph thrown in to show the sponsor that the producer is thinking beyond the immediate. More often distribution takes an important and vital part of the proposal, and the concept may have distribution as its *sine qua non*. An outline of a new sponsored film instructing women on how to start and maintain their own investment programs might sound pretty ordinary. But sprinkle in the spice of guaranteed distribution among the 34 million members of America's women's clubs, and the package takes on the form of a savory dish. Especially to Merrill Lynch or Bache. Sales representatives of Association Films, Modern or other professional distribution houses are most willing to collaborate with producers who include detailed distribution programs in their proposals. Quite often proposals are made jointly by two salesmen, one representing the producer and the other representing the distributor, who have integrated their plans carefully.

The distributors offer this sales assistance to all producers without preference. They know they must remain impartial in their enthusiasm for encouraging producers to promote distribution as the essential success ingredient. The shared presentation can be quite impressive when the producer's time is spent on creative, subjective matters and the distributor follows with objective, factual matters. It compares with an advertising agency pitch for a new account when the art or creative director first reveals the graphic comps and copy themes and the media director follows with details of the media mix and tricks of time buying.

Now, turn over the coin. You have the distributors on the street working up business among the sponsors. Distributors can no more exist without films from sponsors and producers than sponsors and producers can market films without distribution. So one avenue of sales for the distributors takes them to sponsors and producers simply to find out what productions plans they have. Once they know the titles, subjects and release dates of new films, distributors can talk turkey. "Oh? So you are completing a film on hypertension with Lowell Wentworth at the Film Group? Great. Yeah, I know Lowell well. Great producer," the distributor sales rep might say to the sponsor. "You're going to want to reach a selective market of middle-aged men in particular, aren't you? Our community distribution program is just what you'll want as your anchor plan. Here, let me get out our community brochure. . . ."

Another sure-fire way for distributors to sell is to insinuate themselves where new films are being assembled: at awards festivals. It is no coincidence that the names G. Roger Cahaney and Carl Lenz appear on the trustees and advisory board of the Film Council of Greater Columbus, which annually dispenses the Chris awards. Cahaney heads Association and Lenz runs Modern. These gentlemen also serve as officials of CINE and other 16mm film festivals. It is a delicious sales experience for the two masters. Not only do the best of the new crop of sponsored films surface but so do their sponsors and producers. Lenz and Cahaney can do no wrong. They congratulate the winners and softly remind sponsors and producers not to keep the good news a secret, and that no better forum for telling the world is available than Association or Modern. In this manner, the distributors are assured that they have a chance at the very best products which will surely be easier to distribute and bring more success to the distributor than born losers. Even the publication of "Gold Camera Award Winner at U.S. Industrial Film Festival" in a distributor catalog will often be the deciding factor for a TV station to book a film. Presence of the distributor officials at awards festivals is also superb PR. Being around when good things happen to one's customers is an art. So here you find film industry cross-fertilization in its finest hour.

Quite often the distributor is in close touch with the sponsor before the producer knows a thing about plans for a new film. The distributor has been solid with a certain steel corporation for years, booking every film they ever turned out. The salesman makes his regular calls, knowing that when a new film is being considered, he's most likely the first to know. "Michael," the sponsor might well confide, "we're concerned about the aluminum industry reviving their pitch to the auto makers to convert bodies to aluminum to save weight and gas. We need a film to remind the auto guys and the public what steel really does to a car." This disclosure would naturally be followed by, "Who'd you suggest to do it for us? You come in contact with a lot of producers."

The cross-pollination now occurs. The distributor's sales representative is going to suggest one, two or three producers who work closely with that distributor on other sponsors and films. It's more than backscratching. The distributor cannot involve himself with anything but success if he is going to get a valuable new distribution contract. He will refer the sponsor to known winners. And again he will try to be fair, recommending different producers to different sponsors.

Cooperation among sponsor, producer and distributor, then, is a valuable if not priceless quality. (An Iranian student, new to the English language, once asked me if "price" and "value" had similar meanings. I said they did. Then he asked if "priceless" and "valueless" meant about the same. I could only smile and groan.) Elsewhere we discuss the sponsor as producer and the sponsor as distributor. Now we will look into the intriguing area of producer as distributor.

Why on earth should a producer elect, of his own free will and accord, to enter the distribution business as well? One need barely use his mental process to come up with sound reasons not to do so. The producer can point to the fact that no one has ever asked him to do it. So he might figure there is no natural demand. He need not look far to see exemplary distribution work already being done by Association, Modern and a long list of others in industry, government, education, and organizations which are deeply committed to distribution of 16mm films. And he need only look at his own daily troubles to ask himself, with due compassion, "Who needs more?"

The producer knows how often it becomes difficult to collect the final third of his production fee from a client fiscally equipped to bail out New York. So the producer can well imagine that he would not be paid that final third on delivery of prints, but that the sponsor would wait until some indeterminate future time when he became satisfied that the distribution program was a success. Another hole in the head.

The producer could feel squeamish about his not being at arm's length. He would picture himself making a fine sale of a new sponsored film to his client and then going back and trying to make an all-too-soon second sale to the same client for a distribution contract. The professional counselor never advises his client to patronize the counselor.

No, the producer reasons there is no sense in getting involved in distribution. And look what it takes, he tells himself. A computer is not for me. Only billionaires have computers to make printouts like Modern's. And film cleaning machines. Repairing splices. Lugging hundreds of prints to the post office and back. Keeping infinite records on who has which print and where it's going tomorrow night. Writing, printing and sending out thousands of promotional flyers on each title. Listening to some person on the phone in San Juan demanding a free-loan print by Tuesday morning or he's going to call the sponsor. Hiring a staff of people to handle the physical work. No. What kind of a job is that for a motion picture producer like me?

Of course, the producer is often already into a collateral, non-creative field when he takes the plunge with hardware. Quite a few sponsored film producers are sales representatives for Bell & Howell, Singer, Kodak, Sony and other manufacturers of film and tape equipment allied with their software. With such departments come the headaches: cash and space tied up with demonstrators, slow turnover and costly personal sales time involved with $600 instead of $40,000 sales. The discounts the producer enjoys by reason of having a special contract with Bell & Howell may not be worth all the agony of selling equipment as a professional dealer.

And a few producers are involved in their own laboratory business. The need to keep costly chemicals fresh and staff working demands that they solicit lab business from outside their own production—and that is painful indeed when they must get the trade from their direct competitors as well as regional schools, in-house industry facilities, government offices and overflow from other labs. Lab business, like hardware and distribution, is an easy thing to avoid.

So much for the rationalization. *Audiovisual Market Place: A Multimedia Guide,** 1974-75, lists 11 film producers who also distribute their films.

There is much to be said for the sponsored film producer going into the distribution business. He can approach it either as a profit-making allied business, distributing his own and any other titles he can attract, or as a free service to his sponsors alone.

In either situation, the producer must take the professional attitude that his customers deserve attention and service equal to that enjoyed with other distributors; he must be competitive. The producer asks himself what he can offer that the big houses can't. The obvious first rationale is the "small and personal" pitch—we can give your title lots more attention than the big guys; we can talk with TV stations and clubs on a personal basis and not through a computer. Such talk may be valid at times, but it can easily strike the sponsor as sour grapes, coming from a novice distributor ill-equipped to match the Modern and Association artillery.

No, the best competitive performance lies in superior delivery of bookings. Any producer wishing to establish himself in the distribution business has only to deliver the goods. Doing so delivers the money. The producer dares not forget that distribution is piece-work business. He is paid only for showings he confirms. There are no flat fees as in production, no cost-plus contracts, no contingencies with extra billing. "Show reasonable records that my print was projected before 34 persons in a particular church social hall last Saturday night, and I will pay you $5." That's it.

*R. R. Bowker Co., a Xerox Company, 1180 Avenue of the Americas, New York, N.Y. 10036.

The producer has a substantial start toward success in the distribution business if he already has a ready-made assortment of films suitable for free showings on television, and to schools (the majority of Modern's volume is among minors), churches, civic clubs, hospitals, prisons (why not?), industry, armed forces, camps, hotels, colleges, theater audiences, professional groups, women's clubs, fraternal organizations, youth groups and other selective audiences. The distribution house not associated with production has to pound the pavement to get titles to distribute. The producer who goes into the distribution business has an inside track on his own titles.

"Jerry? Tom. Yeah, fine. Yours? Great. When you going to tell me all the grim details of your ski trip? Oh, yeah? Don't worry. You'll be back playing tennis by summer. Listen. We're distributing our own sponsored films now. Yeah. Sure. So I thought we could take *The Story of Suppositories* and give you a whole fresh distribution program. Put it where it's never been seen before. No, the film, Jerry. Same price as everyone else charges. Yeah. What d'ya think? Yeah? Great. Be over after lunch. Or how about lunch? Dixon's? Better get there early. You know how bad it gets at the bar. Noon? Great. See ya then, Jerry."

Multiply that by 20 or 30 and the producer has established the most important part of his new business first: the income. The producer quickly writes down the potential and impresses himself with the bottom line. It looks considerably better than the 15 per cent commission he may be picking up from associating with a distribution house on some of his titles. Then he soberly examines the fact that *The Story of Suppositories* may not pack them in in Peoria. He goes over his list of past successes and picks titles more gingerly.

Next, he sets up the business. It takes him about three weeks to get equipped, staffed and operating. It takes him about three *years* to get into the black. He is going to win a few and lose a few. He is going to tremble at the traumatic slowness of the buildup of bookings on each title. He publishes leaflets (later to become catalogs) to promote his full list of free-loan films and mails them to lists bought from mailing-list houses of schools, libraries, TV stations and the like. Soon as he sees a school or cable system ordering several titles, he contacts them and suggests a regular weekly shipment as long as his inventory lasts. He turns out promotion pieces to go to sponsors to stimulate additional titles.

Does it work? Of course it works. Does it fail or succeed? It evolves like any other new business. It can go or falter, depending on the wind, the business acuity of the producer, and the time frame he has given himself to get into the black.

The producer who opts for going into the distribution business as a free service has the advantage of knowing he will always be in the red. If that constitutes a success, the world has more successes around than anyone imagined.

The friends of the producer who intentionally goes into a losing operation will figure he's lost his marbles. A strange man I knew in the Air Force used to say that all the time. "Aw, you've lost your marbles." He said it a hundred times a day, in operations, barracks, latrine—in his sleep. "You've lost your marbles." We all got up-to-here with it. One day during a training session, this bird opened up once too often with his, "You've lost your marbles." In the back of the room a dear friend of mine broke open a bag of one thousand immies, aggies, clearies, taws, glassies, monnies, shooters, mibs, ducks, miggs, commies and hoodles. They dropped at once onto the wood floor and bounced for over a minute. The cacophony was obscured by the laughing and crying of instructor and students. Only our strange man sat silent, turning his tongue over in his mouth. He never, never mentioned marbles again.

Pedro Hatheyer in Sao Paulo thought twice before he went into the distribution business on a paid basis. It would take considerable persuasion to bring him around to thinking he should do it all for free. And yet there are merits. If the producer can manage financially to price his film production attractively and still allow funds to distribute it, he has an edge over his competition, and a more attractive package to sell. Instead of offering basic production services, plus auxiliary paid distribution services from another source, he is willing to provide his sponsor client with a one-fee arrangement for *all* the work. To the sponsor it looks more than ever like a *medium* than a film.

Such a producer must watch his cost accounts carefully. He creates his own dilemma in that the more successful distribution he delivers to his sponsors, the more it costs him. It takes guts for him to beef up his distribution service, knowing that the more it performs, the deeper his expenses dig. If he plays good businessman and eases up on distribution, he is selling failure, an untenable situation.

UPDATING

"*Quan Luc Vnch Phan Cong* (The Vietnamese Armed Forces Offensive). This film, in black and white, shows the performance of the Vietnamese forces as they take the offensive against the invaders from the north. Available in Canada. 1972. 16mm. Sound. 20 min. Embassy of Viet-Nam."

That is an exact description of a film listed on page 347 of *Educators Guide to Free Films,* 34th annual edition, published by Educators Progress Service, Inc., in 1974.

I would hazard the guess that there will not be a single request for this film again in the entire future of mankind.

Now here's another:

"*Air Pollution in Perspective.* This film, in full color, gives a basic discussion of the role played by the automobile in air pollution. The picture discusses the significant progress made in reducing auto emissions, what direction future control systems might take to remove the auto as a source of air pollution, and shows some of the alternative sources of power that have been proposed for the automobile. Recommended for high school, college, and adult groups. Not available in Canada. Cleared for TV. 1971. 16mm. Sound. 25 min. General Motors Corporation.''

It doesn't take a doctoral degree in history for one to realize that here is a film with an important story to tell, but one that has become dated in the years since its release.

And one more:

"*Portrait of the Orient*. This film, in full color, presents the fascinating variety of the entire Orient, with comment on the life, peoples, and cultures that the travelers will see there. Visual coverage includes Japan, Korea, Taiwan, Hong Kong, the Philippines, Malaysia, Thailand, Singapore, and Indonesia. The film portrays why the Orient and its people are worth seeing and visiting. Available to adult groups only. 16mm. Sound. 28 min. Japan Air Lines.''

Here is a typical travel film you would see at a civic club or at 7 o'clock Sunday morning on television in Bat Cave, N.C.

What do these three films have in common? They are all sponsored films, 16mm, available through the good offices of their sponsors.

It's what is *dissimilar* about these three films that we should examine. The first might well have been hot stuff when released in 1972, but history caught up with it and wiped out its entire meaning, not to mention the Embassy of Viet-Nam which sponsored it. Today, it is an oddity of little value to anyone.

The second film, relating autos to air pollution, was thoughtfully made years ago on a subject that is still vital today. The chances of its showing old cars are good. Again here, history has probably dated some of the film's content, making it less viable today than in 1971.

Finally, we have what seems to be a pleasant, harmless, very general travel film that will probably be as effective to view in 2001 as today. It is not closely tied to current history, so its images transcend time.

From these three examples we can see that some films become dated quickly, some become dated slowly, and some not at all. This aging process is not related to the quality, length or sponsor of the film.

Books enjoy or suffer the same fate. Obscure religious tracts of the 16th to 19th centuries have only curiosity value today. A valuable reference on real estate tax advantages can remain valuable only if kept up to date. But Shakespeare remains timeless and should survive.

Investments in sponsored films are large and important. Therefore sponsors, producers and distributors should act to protect and enhance the life of each production. If a film is produced for short-term values and is put quietly to death after it has served its brief purpose, all well and good. But ordinarily everyone wants a sponsored film to be productive for as many years as practicable. There are more than a few films that have outlived their sponsors or their subjects, such as the Vietnamese film discussed earlier. But the real challenge is in keeping sponsored films from becoming white elephants before their time.

How do you do it? One way is not the best way: hedge as you script and shoot. Leave out all the statistics for fear of becoming dated. Don't show skirt lengths on any women; in fact, avoid all fashions. Show no cars at all. Avoid city skylines. Omit talking-head interviews of anyone likely to die or change positions in life. Avoid any current issues. Redline any present-day expressions. In short, take the life out of the film and make it a museum piece instead of an exciting treatise.

Another way is to choose a timeless subject. Now there's a trick. How does one go about making a timeless subject out of new developments in public transportation? Two of our films approach the timeless category: *The Garden of God,* which shows the flowers, plants and trees of the Bible, and *How Do You Explain Death to Children?*, whose wisdom and values don't change with the times. If the sponsor happens to have a subject, product, service or concern with timeless qualities, he can rejoice. If not, he must look for other ways to meet the challenge.

There is a third and correct way: *update the film.*

Now those three words electrify producers and distributors. They immediately see new income arriving with new film life. The producer received his fee in full some years ago and now dollar signs radiate from his eyeballs like star sapphires at the prospect of remaking large chunks of the same film. Likewise the distributor, who in recent months has been unable to generate fresh bookings even by rewriting the words in his monthly handouts, can hope for found money in a reissue that might be made to look like a new production. Let's not leave out the sponsor. The sponsor readily spots the good-business values in updating his white elephant. Officers would enjoy reading a memo about the salvaging of an almost-forgotten investment of five to ten years ago, with an investment of only a few thousand dollars.

Great. Everyone should do it. Right? Right. Do they? *No.*

No? They don't? Why? How do you put a shoulder shrug into words?

Perhaps sponsors look on the reissue of an old film as drudgery. Maybe they think it's like voting for a presidential candidate who lost the previous election. Maybe the prospect doesn't look important to a rising executive who wants to do important things. Maybe the sponsor contacted the producer and found out the industry is using a new film stock now, or that the originals or negative are in poor shape. The producer, possibly, is thinking that an entire new film will be in the offing for him if he discourages the remake job.

Or it is conceivable that the sponsor talked with the distributor and he, too, was thinking about a fresh, new film that would be more profitable than a reissue, as he discouraged the sponsor.

The fact remains that major remakes of old films are all but a rarity. It's a pity, because the work can be done deftly so as to blend the new scenes with the old. And the track can be re-narrated economically so as to give it the sound of Today.

Sponsors might rationalize that the few thousand dollars it might take to freshen up an old film could better be spent toward a new one. That is quite possible; it isn't arguable. But I would hope that such a decision would not be based on the sponsor's personal feeling that he is terribly tired of seeing that old film any more in any form. That just isn't good business.

There is still another alternative: update the film without paying a fee. Such a solution is possible when the original producer offers free updating services as part of his basic production contract. The sponsor can then come back months or years later and have his film updated and reissued, without the momentary trauma of facing an updating production charge.

Here is how it works. The sponsor and producer agree to make a film together. Their contract follows normal trade practices except that it includes an updating clause. This provides that at any time the sponsor wishes to update the motion picture, the producer will do so without charge for his services. The sponsor pays for the producer's out-of-pocket expenses to the laboratory, narrator and so on, but nothing for the producer's services. The contract limits the work to no more than one-third the total length of the film. It allows the sponsor to update the film one or more times within the contract period (five years, ten years, etc.). The total of these multiple updatings cannot exceed one-third the film's length.

The sponsor is the sole judge of whether and when to update. The matter is not one of discussion between producer and sponsor as to what is valid and important. If the producer were to share in the decision, there might be continual disputes as to whether those old cars are laughable, or whether the appearance of a man who has since died really detracts from the value of the motion picture.

Updating can thus be an important expense to the producer and he must prepare his original fee quotation gingerly. The service is not always used; it is more like a factory guarantee, where some financial cushion must be set up as a reserve, but certainly not the full amount that might be needed for an updating job. The producer self-insures, so to speak.

When a Sponsored Film Dies

Dying. Nobody likes to talk about it but everyone does it.

Sponsored films don't just fade away when they die. There is work to be done in wrapping up the life of a defunct sponsored film. It isn't as awesome as closing hundreds of A & P or Grant stores costing hundreds of millions of dollars. But there is, just the same, a list of details to be attended to by the disciplined team of sponsor, producer and distributor.

As we noted elsewhere, it is sometimes difficult to get a sponsor to say bye-bye to a pet sponsored film. I once viewed a new-car sales film from an auto maker of 12-year vintage. It was one of the funniest experiences of my life. There was this film star standing up there on the screen, in front of God and everybody, telling the audience straight-faced that this shiny bomb behind him was the all-time culmination of the auto designer's craft. He recited features that would frighten today's car buyers. If the sponsor had been present at the viewing of his old film, he would have taken the print in hand and torn it apart, frame by frame.

When sponsors recognize that rigor mortis has set in, they take action. First they notify the distribution people to discontinue as of a certain future date—at least one month's notice is preferred. The distributor can then notify all channels to stop using prints and to hasten return of those outstanding.

The sponsor should call in half a dozen prints in the best condition and stow them in corporate archives. One day a print may be needed in court, by researchers or an officer anxious to win a directors' election.

The producer should assure the sponsor that the negatives and originals remain in good condition for future use or adaptation, or ship them to the sponsor for archive storage.

All excess prints should be stripped from reels and destroyed. Reels, cans and cases should be disposed of as a sponsor asset and not absorbed by the distributor as his own property. The sponsor may wish to reuse the reels, cans and cases in-house, or donate them to a cinema school or public TV station.

All partners in the team notify all sources that were circulating the film or information about it that it is no longer available, to prevent requests dragging in for years, each requiring a costly individual reply.

Strangely, the activity associated with wrapping up a dead sponsored film can renew interest in it. Quite often a sponsor receives a fresh batch of requests for the film as word gets out of its impending rarity. The nicest thing that can come out of the demise of a sponsored film is the announcement of an up-to-date replacement, and very often the sponsor or producer makes one news release out of two. There is no better testimony of the wisdom of the sponsor when he invested in the first film than to proclaim production of its timely replacement.

Chapter Six

Business Management

Sponsored films, like babies, have to come from somewhere. Unlike babies, they come from several sources: industry, organizations, government—anyone with public relations or propaganda in his soul.

The immediate origin is that phenomenon called a producer. Now a producer is many different things and he takes many different forms. Producers have many things in common, of course. They have a talent mix involving photography, recording, lighting, writing, sales, editing and stagecraft. They are all essentially small businessmen working with small staffs and freelancers. Like printers, they tend to be long on equipment and short on cash. Few began as filmmakers. Most dearly love what they do, and like artists, they tend to involve themselves too deeply in the project at hand. Though their ranks are replete with oldtimers who once worked with nitrate film, most producers are beset with instability and their corporate entities change form almost as often as advertising agencies (if that is possible). No matter how they surround themselves with hardware, real estate and trophies, producers are in the service field and their fate vacillates with the personalities involved. Producers are professionals at a level of competence comparable to the architect, optometrist, attorney or engineer. But their education in that profession is rarely formally acquired, though they may in their time hire many with masters degrees in cinema. Yet their trade develops in them a surprising proficiency in many areas. I know producers who can repair their precision equipment, who understand double system accounting, who soup-up their color stills, who cut negatives, who can call a 5,000-cycle tone when they hear it, and who can notate a film score for six instruments.

I know several sponsored film producers who can drink in at least seven languages, and some who can even speak four. Some say producers are cameramen whose eyes fail or who can no longer lift light cases into the station wagon, and have to decide either to lead the pack or go into real estate. Whatever led them there, they are at once a group of intrepid, clever, sharp, creative and wonderful people.

But they are *lousy* businessmen.

RUNNING THE BUSINESS

That is one thing they have in common that doesn't earn them any gold stars. Tom Hope contacts more producers regularly than even their trade associations, and he nails the producers as poor businessmen. He saw that back in 1945 at General Mills. Producer budgeting was vague, hit-and-miss. Producers were not businesslike in their dealings. Blue-sky talk covered poor organization. At the early meetings of the Industrial Audio-Visual Association discussions centered around the fact that so many film producers were inept businessmen. "A few were unethical," Hope states. "Most were just untrained in business matters."

It continues. Eastman Kodak knows it. Their credit terms to producers are brutally strict because they have been burned so much. Many big-name producers are on a cash basis with Kodak. Producers go out of business frequently, surfacing with another firm soon enough. These transactions are covered with sugar and published as "progress" in the trade press, but you can bet many suppliers got caught with bad debts when the producers pulled the string. One man's name keeps appearing in full page ads in *Back Stage*. Every couple of years he's part of a new corporation. One time his firm was bought up by a top Hollywood feature producer. By the time the Hollywood owners realized what a bomb they had, they had dropped over a million dollars and couldn't even sell what was left—they just closed it down.

One cause of this "poor businessman" stigma is the fact that many producers are cameramen or filmmakers forced to run a small business. And they never passed high school mathematics. They mix personal money with business—forget to pay sales tax—don't watch the girl who opens the mail, pocketing the checks—rush low bids on government contracts without reading the costly small print—buy cameras they can't afford—are afraid to ask sponsors for payments when due.

The late, great Matt Farrell had a three-word philosophy that carried him through many years of relative peace of mind. He would utter them straight and hard. "Get the dough."

Sponsored film producers really should not have such a reputation. Their profit margins are right up there with attorneys, and they are pretty much in personal control of expenditures. Some are hybrid shops, doing graphics work as well as film, such as John Beck in Horsham, Pennsylvania. Men like Beck appreciate how difficult it is to thrive on 17.65 per cent markups on time and space and production materials. When you have a promotion, advertising or printing account, your little commission and modest fees comprise your *gross*. If your client fails or is slow pay, you can well get caught holding the bag for six times your gross. And that, to coin an equestrian term, ain't hay. But when you are producing sponsored films, fully 50 per cent of your fees can be your gross, and you have some fiscal freedom.

One small producer came to me for some business advice. The very act was an ego trip for me, suddenly thrust into father-to-son counseling. I dutifully looked at his firm's films, and they were good—better than some of our own. I looked at his books and they were models of bookkeeping prowess. I quizzed him about how he and his partner spent their days, how they worked with sponsors and agencies, what equipment they had, what their plans were, their volume and personnel. At first blush it all looked like a Walt Disney version of a sponsored film production house. Everything was cute, charming, four-fifths natural size, pure and promising.

"What's the problem?" I finally asked. "Not making any money," was the impatient retort. "Do you expect to be making a profit now, so soon after you've gone into business, before you've invested in all the equipment you need?" I asked.

"Expect? Man, we've got to *eat*," he answered, as if I should have realized. So there it was. Fine, creative minds pooling their miniscule resources, going into business like a teenage marriage. I pointed out that the average automobile service station represented an investment of $250,000, and most people looked upon service stations as very small business. This firm wanted too much too soon. Worse, they were selling films and running back to the shop to turn them out, then going out and selling again. They were like some football team, throwing the ball and running like hell down the field to catch it.

Another black mark was their books. "What's wrong?" my friend asked defensively. He knew his books sparkled. "Your books are much too good," I said, and he was crestfallen. "Who's posting the journal and ledger?" I said. "I am, of course," he said. "We can't afford a bookkeeper, even part-time."

"Doesn't that tell you anything?" I asked. "You are one of the principals of a business that depends on your personal sales and production hours to survive. And what are you doing with many of those hours? Bookkeeping. Three double letters in a row in that word, by the way. Did you know *Hawaiian* contains four vowels in a row?"

While I was talking word games, my fellow producer was waking up to reality. Today he is selling and producing more, and his books aren't so pretty.

Too many larger producers fall into the same trap of living almost hand-to-mouth. They sell a job of seeming major import and immediately involve themselves in its execution. By the time they are ready to deliver the answer print, there is little or no business waiting in the house. They understand very well the importance of a backlog, but they have little idea how to create and keep a running backlog of work to sustain staff and stomach. One reason is a built-in inability among some creative people to think about more than one sponsored film or commercial job at a time. If the producer-owner talks about concurrent work, the artist-type suggests one of the assignments be given someone else. That is pure, unwholesome garbage. Production houses must be so disciplined that they can handle tens, scores, even hundreds of jobs and keep them humming toward completion without confusion. This is hohum stuff to our largest producer friends, whose production status charts look like the schedule boards at O'Hare Airport. But elementary as it is, this truth is unknown to hundreds of sponsored film producers.

They are rather bad about shooting low on prices, too. They have this innate madness to bid low, work like hell and then tell masochistic stories about losing money on the deal. Some derive pleasure in bidding low just to cause several competitors to lose the job. Now there's a fiscal *non-sequitur*.

In the section on contracts we mention other whippings that producers bring on themselves. If a sponsor decides to postpone part or all of a film contract, the poor-businessman producer follows along like a three-month old Beagle. If a sponsor puts off payment for six months, the producer is more likely to slow his own payments to his lab than dare to ask his omnipotent client to pay up.

There just has to be a special place in heaven for folks like that. There surely is no place on the faculty of Wharton Business School.

PROBLEMS OF BIDDING

"Bidding on sponsored films, that's where." Ask producers where their greatest professional agony lies, and that would be their unanimous answer.

Ask a distributor of institutional kitchenware the same question, and he'd reply, "Bidding on kitchenware, that's where." Purveyors of nursery stock, architectural services, drilling bits and canned eggs can be expected to react the same. The bidding process is among the greatest groan-makers in the business world.

Sponsored film producers sometimes work for years to "rate" the state or federal bidders' list that may eventually bring them contracts from on high. Then, after they obtain these privileges, they often bite the hand that feeds them. Bidding competitively on a contract in the public or private sector is a poker game that makes all but the coolest characters

break out in the sweats. The sometimes overpowering volume of information to be supplied is enough to cause many bidders to quit at once. Others
take a powder as soon as they see that the sponsor is asking for a
"creative concept," "script outline," "description of scenario approach," or other wording for *free* script work.

Still others filter out of the bidding ratrace when they see that a
pre-bid conference has been scheduled in a distant city and that a costly
trip is needed just to keep up with information the other bidders will have.
And when bidders find out how many others are in there with them, some
figure they could get better odds entering the Irish Sweepstakes, and
excuse themselves.

All this is not lost on the sponsor or the bidders who stick in there.
They are poker players, too, and want to see the weak sisters drop out of
the game as soon as possible and leave the real competition to a strong
few. Of course the sponsor may see the finest producers dropping out at
the start, affronted by the parade of ethical breaches. Wealthy and
successful producers can well afford to do business only with those
sponsors who will talk with just one, two or three producers. Less
fortunate producers go along because it's "possible" business and they
must cooperate with the sponsor and his funny ways.

The pricing factor tears up producers. They know very well what
things cost, and can draw up a bill of particulars in rather short order. But
they do not know very well what is inside the sponsor's mind when he
writes a very brief "some animation" in the list of goodies to include in
the bid. "Some animation" can include anything from ten seconds of
kindergarten graphs to a minute or more of multiplane single-frame
animation complete with a cast of new cartoon characters the sponsor
plans to put on his consumer packaging. The producer quickly phones the
sponsor to get a better reading of the two words, and may well get this:

"Oh, yeah. I got several other calls about that. Well, we haven't
really nailed that down yet. This came from our marketing department
and I personally don't know animation from animal husbandry. Just put
down what you think it should be, you know, how you'd do it in your
script, and we'll take that into account when we look at all the proposals."

The producer takes that nebulous talk as a signal to include the most
basic animation description in order to keep his bid as attractively low as
possible. He cannot know that the marketing director at the sponsor's
firm expects the winning bidder to come up with a fresh concept in
animation and that this is his private test of the bidders.

Much soul-searching accompanies the producer's pricing of overhead, crew, travel, talent and script. Many producers bid low and pray for
every chance to inflate the billing with extras after they win the award.
Others are careful to price out every nuance of the free script outline that

accompanies the bid. Most hope that sponsors will go through all the bids to find the freshest and most workable concepts, filing the rest. That is generally what happens; the creative thinking of the bidder is respected far more than his ability to price equipment shipping costs between Chicago and Fairbanks. If the bidder commands the respect of the sponsor's film committee with his script approach, the details of costs are quickly worked out on the phone or in a preliminary meeting.

Producers have a built-in fear that the script outlines they submit gratis to the sponsor will be picked over for ideas that will be used with another producer, without income to the writer of the outline.

Sponsors generally avoid such conduct because of a possible legal mess and because they have before them a wealth of script outlines from many producers to choose from. If the script approach is the prime criterion for awarding the contract, it doesn't make too much sense for a sponsor to steal from rejected bids. Occasionally sponsors do "borrow" and when they face the originator, they will say that whatever concepts were submitted by producers became the sponsor's property when offered. That is why many producers correctly copyright their script outlines for a paltry $6, and carefully type the copyright notice at the top of the first page of the proffered outline, as due warning not to lift so much as a line of it that involves original thinking.

Even the most scrupulous sponsor cannot help but remember some of the clever ideas presented to him in the vast assortment of bids he summoned up. Then some of them may well surface in later print campaigns, TV commercials, or PR programs.

Sponsored film producers get uptight in bidding because of the costly time the process takes. The top person at the production house tries to delegate government and private bids to his accountant or others dependable on detail. But he is soon swept into the whirlpool and may chalk up a week or more of his time on one bid. The propriety of the system prevents undue communication with the sponsor at such a sensitive time, so the producer is prone to overkill—he covers every contingency that pops into his mind, and ends up submitting a 78-page proposal and bid. Some producers are known to squeeze three bids out of every one they submit. It's like getting three votes at the voting machine instead of one. They simply submit a bid for $42,000 on the basis of the specifications and then bid $38,000 as Alternate #1, whereby sponsor employees are used instead of paid actors, and $36,000, whereby an additional economy is effected by using stock shots instead of original shooting for scenes 13, 16, 17, 19, 23, 41, 42A, 67, 68, 69, 74, 81, 92, 101, 101A, 112, 113, 114, 116, 121 and 128.

Other producers use the building-block system of bidding when they are allowed to do so. They price each goody on its own. Then the sponsor may take any variety of goodies, smorgasbord-style, and make his own movie at the price he wants.

These practices are proper enough in themselves, but when the sponsor is confronted by a mixture of them, he is hard put to know which bid is the most equitable. Certainly the producer who submits a simple bid containing one price is operating at a disadvantage in such company.

Elsewhere, we discuss a federal agency that called for so many producers to bid on a new film that we figured more money was spent on the bids than on the film itself. A trade journal story once recounted how a producer invited to a bidders' conference got up and walked out when he saw 32 others in attendance. Just what is the right number for a sponsor to ask? How many producers should be invited to participate?

The sponsor has several considerations. He knows that the larger the number involved, the more work there is to be done and the longer it will take. If the film is a short, simple, inexpensive one, it is usual for the sponsor to call in a single favorite producer to get right into it, and forget the bidding process. If, however, the film is to be a blockbuster, a new-image thing for the entire corporation involving all divisions, the sponsor finds it wisest to involve a number of producers in a bidding contest. He then asks himself, how can I best serve my company? If I limit the bidding to a select few, I might pass up the opportunity to hear from a promising source who might well turn in the best film. If I keep the number down, I won't be making friends among the producer fraternity. But then I won't be making friends anyway, when I pick just one and tell everyone else he's a loser.

The Producer's View

Ask producers what they think the proper number is and you get many different answers. But by and large they feel that, as in any sport, winning or losing is not so important as the fair play. Producers would have sponsors introduce themselves to many producers over a period of years by looking at their work and their records. Then they should, on the basis of this carefully acquired intelligence, select no more than 10 producers to submit bids. Further, the sponsor should avoid putting producers to the expense of $3,000 to $6,000 per bid, which is often the amount of cash and time expense involved in important bids. He can do this by limiting the amount of custom preparation required of the bidder and put more stock in existing material. He can do it by simplifying his specifications and not trying to compete with IRS forms for complexity.

Most of all, the sponsor can make bidding fairer by supplying the bidders with all the research they will need to submit the bid. Most of the time a sponsor's bid specifications include only the most basic script information and *raison d'etre* for the proposed film. All that does is tease the bidder into spending days of research to catch up a little with the sponsor—to try to look into his head enough to come up with a script approach that is not just clever but, much more important, applicable.

Perhaps the single largest area of frustration in the bidding maze is the limiting of communication. Consider the countless film contracts that have gone bad even when sponsor and producer had every opportunity to talk with one another whenever they wished. Then contemplate the bidding experience, where 10 producers and one sponsor are in strictly limited communications, since fair play dictates that the same information be shared among all. The discipline fairly wipes out possibilities for real brainstorming, real interplay, real "vibes." It's sad, because no one wants it that way.

Occasionally the bidding business gets complicated by the presence of a consultant or an ad agency playing the part of transcendental angel in the wedding of producer and sponsor. In such cases, the producer may have two attitudes to please with his bid instead of one, and there may be a conflict. On one bid we were dealing both with the client and his Texas ad agency, which knew a lot about buying TV spots but nothing at all about sponsored film buying. The sponsor was open-minded about all matters. The agency wanted carefully structured bids on its TV spot bid forms, and no extraneous promotional materials from bidders. When a bidder is thus instructed to limit his bid to the simple facts and is not asked to include a script outline or self-serving puff, he might well celebrate the dawn of a new day. Or he might, on careful re-examination, feel trapped and unable to communicate.

Quite often there is a major change in the arrangement after the successful bidder has been awarded the contract. This change can be for better or worse. The producer may find that his one-hour film has been restructured as a half-hour film, and he may have to contend a bit to keep the sponsor from simply slicing his fee in half. Or he may just as easily learn that the project is to be expanded to include six TV commercials and a short version as well, all delivered to the winning bidder without further competition.

THE CONTRACT: A MEETING OF MINDS

Production and distribution of sponsored films call for a meeting of minds. Producer and sponsor must understand one another. Sponsor and distributor must spell out what their respective obligations are.

That means contracts—instruments recording these meetings of the mind so that in time no one will come up short of what he was due. While there is a buyer-and-seller arrangement involved, there is no master-servant relationship. The seller of production services cannot complete his contract without substantial performance by the sponsor. For example, the producer needs sample products to photograph. The sponsor must supply them, sometimes handmake or handpick them. The producer needs access to industrial plants and the sponsor has to arrange clearance. The producer needs footage that is in the sponsor's possession, such as Underwriters Laboratories test footage.

So there is a good deal of responsible performance by both parties in the production of a sponsored film, and these acts often need to be spelled out in specific detail.

A working relationship between sponsor and his producer or distributor is sublime when there is no contract paper at all. The parties can boast of their integrity and ethics that are so pure that no written contract need exist. That can ride along nicely so long as there is no trouble. It's like a nurse delivering a baby. She's quite capable of doing so, and often does, the mother not knowing that the obstetrician never arrived from his golf game in time for delivery. But, when there's a breech delivery, the doctor's presence is vitally necessary.

Producers and distributors, alas, all vendors, quake when it comes to asking for written contracts. They are not attorneys and do not appreciate the wisdom of legal instruments. They are business people who know how they can lose a good sale or a good friend with a contract imbedded on a desk by an angry fist. They remember the simple, good days when they made or distributed a film after a simple conversation, and there was no six-page agreement to refer to when something came up. Sponsored film producers and distributors tend to feel that while contracts do indeed protect them, they also cause work and strife *per se* that could have been avoided.

Not a few good film deals have been rendered asunder by delays while the corporate legal department picked its way through the film contract only to come up with changes that were untenable or unacceptable. Those legal-department time cushions often give management time for second thoughts, and a contract is lost.

So contract time is not happy time around the producer's or distributor's office. Nor is it in the sponsor's office, because when the sponsor gets to reading all the infamous fine print, he wonders whether he did the right thing after all. No one likes detail.

With all that, contracts are the base from which all motion picture successes operate. Talent arrangements are matters of exquisite detail involving billing, percentages and residuals. Can you imagine a Bob Hope appearing in a film on a handshake instead of a contract? Union labor won't start working without a contract. Large cities won't permit a camera crew to set up on the streets without a contract. Insurance underwriters won't provide protection to life and property without a contract. Films just don't happen without contracts.

What Should the Contract Include?

What's in them? Attorneys are sometimes nonplussed by clients who think the most important thing in contracts is legal gobbledygook. Form is quite important, but substance is supreme. No attorney can prepare a contract until the parties inform him of the conditions, terms, and specifications. No two contracts are alike, they say, and that is certainly true in the case of sponsored films.

How well I know. As the appointed chairperson of the contracts committee of our trade association, I was charged with developing a proper and acceptable standard contract form for our industry.

Why a standard form? Why not write a fresh one with each understanding?

One would like to feel that a standard contract would bring order out of chaos, gentlemanly qualities out of the wrestling arena. Parties to a contract are much more ready to accept established standards than to prepare their own. If accepted trade standards are interwoven into a standard contract form, there is an aura of tranquillity and goodwill. A sponsor fully expects his prints to be delivered on reels, ready to project. But a special contract might omit mentioning reels, cans or cases, and a producer might blithely deliver prints on cores, saving him some money, and setting the sponsor on fire. However, if it is a trade practice to deliver prints on reels, as indeed it is, and that is spelled out in a standard contract form, peace will reign.

All parties to contracts—especially attorneys—respect precedent. The widespread use of a standard trade form contract establishes precedent so respected that parties do not bother to argue. The contract speaks clearly for itself, therefore no interpretive conflict need arise.

Ah, but *writing* such a standard contract form; that's another matter altogether. To begin, I played the devil's advocate and submitted a sample contract to my peers for personal discussion. The reaction was, to understate it, lively. Suddenly we all realized that producers had directly opposite views on ownership of originals and negatives. There could be no right or wrong on that point, and there was trade precedent to back both sides.

Yet my fellow producers found unanimity on many paragraphs and a few suggestions even drew applause. I could see enthusiasm building for the concept, and no one has ever suggested that a standard trade contract would be unwise. They just said it would be *impossible*.

After all, it isn't a pushover to prepare a contract for use in 50 different countries involving many languages, forms of currency and laws. Nor is it easy to write a contract form for a spectrum of producers who sell and give away services in varying degrees. One producer charges *per diem* for trips, another includes reasonable travel. One producer will shorten a film without charge but another knows that's work and wants to charge for the contingency. How do you please them all?

Well, you *could* give everyone a blank piece of paper and tell them just to fill it out. I can't forget comedian Errol Garner, who once suggested how to end all crime. "Just make everything legal," he counseled.

The blank paper idea actually had some merit. I opted for including several paragraphs that called for blanks to be filled in by the parties. This gave them mandates to come to terms on each point, but left the details to the parties involved. Blanks cannot be left unfilled in a binding contract. So if there were no special agreement about talent, the parties simply would enter "none."

The final draft of the new trade contract contained blanks in the important areas of talent, music, ownership and possession of originals and negatives, prints, print sales, travel and accommodations, billing terms, locations and special arrangements peculiar to that agreement. It also left blanks for the dates of the production schedule to be inserted, as well as the names of the parties, price, date and place of the contract.

The remainder of the contract form had no blanks. It contained many paragraphs that constituted a bill of rights for sponsored films. That such protection was needed can be indicated by the long stream of abuses that had been suffered for many years.

Abuses Requiring Protection

Item: After location filming had begun, a sponsor decided the money could better be spent on another promotion project. He made no move to cancel the contract. He simply announced an indefinite delay because of other pressing commitments. The producer submissively stopped production to await later instructions to proceed. Months and years passed. The producer was left with his down payment, some useless footage, a script and a sour memory.

Item: A producer contracted with a sponsor to make a professional film in cooperation with a professional organization. He made a separate contract with the organization, which called for the funds to be paid by the sponsor to the organization for dispensation to the producer. The producer had no objection to the organization having this dole power, even though the organization was not putting up a cent of the fee. When the producer completed the script for approval of both sponsor and organization, the organization stalled for several months. Meanwhile the organization billed the sponsor for the entire film fee and the sponsor, in fear of offending the organization, paid. When interlock time came, the organization stalled several more months, saying they just couldn't get people together to look at the film. Even after the interlock, they stalled again, failing to approve the answer print for many weeks. By the time the film was accepted and released, the organization had successfully delayed production for over a year. Why? *To use the entire fee from the sponsor as an interest-free loan.*

Item: A producer was mid-way through a film production for a sponsor when he accidentally found out another producer had been given the same assignment and the first producer was being squeezed out without notice. The sponsor later announced the shift, saying the first producer had not done satisfactory work. The first producer was given no opportunity to correct his work nor did he collect for what he had done. He sued and lost.

Item: A producer was finishing up the script when the sponsor announced that the agreement between the parties was void because the person who signed it did not have authority to do so, and his superiors had rejected the film proposal.

Item: A financial institution contracted for production of a sponsored film with a producer, approved it and paid for it. The contract called for the originals to be shipped to the sponsor. A year later, the producer learned that the sponsor was selling rights to and prints of the same film to other financial institutions in other regions of the country. The producer asked for some income, since he had bid low for a regional film only to learn later that the sponsor had syndicated the film nationally. The sponsor won out because there had been no contractual stipulation about residual rights.

Item: A sponsor continually turned down the producer's scripts and revisions. Then the sponsor said he had a scriptwriter who could do the work satisfactorily, and if the producer didn't hire the writer to do the job, he would lose the contract. The producer had no choice but to come to immediate terms with the pet writer.

Item: Another sponsor continually turned down the producer's scripts for quite a different reason. The people at the sponsor's firm who had enthusiastically signed the contract for the film were no longer there, and their successors thought of all films as cursed. So they blithely rejected as inadequate every script the producer wrote, and the producer lost the ball game.

These are but a few of the abuses recounted to me by fellow producers in our trade association. Most occurred in the United States but some happened overseas. All are examples of injustice meted out by thick-skinned sponsors to thin-skinned producers. No doubt they are part of a pattern that some corporations follow in treating suppliers shabbily, using their purchasing power, reputation and trade clout to badger suppliers into submission.

What of injustices imposed by producers on their sponsor clients? There are many.

Item: A fine, struggling producer in a major city produced several excellent films for a grateful sponsor. The relationship was ideal. Then the producer went into bankruptcy. All his material possessions were frozen by the courts, including the originals of the sponsor's films. The sponsor could not get his hands on his own "masters" to make more prints, so he had to start over and produce new films at his expense.

Item: A producer hired a famous writer to prepare a script for his sponsor. The producer received a third of his fee in advance. The temperamental writer proceeded to argue irrationally with the sponsor, refusing to bend on essential script matters. The producer backed him up. The sponsor ended up by starting over, losing the one-third payment.

Item: A producer got careless during filming of his sponsor's work. A power cable that he ran along a public hallway caused a middle-aged woman to trip, fall and break her hip. The hip injury led to dangerous circulation problems for the victim. The producer was not worth as much as the sponsor, so when a judgment for $250,000 was announced by the jury against both parties, the sponsor ended up by paying off the judgment, while the producer just went out of business and started over under a new name. The sponsor never even got his film.

There are many others, usually relating to financial failure of the producer, leaving the sponsor holding the bag. Cases where producers are just plain crooked and bilk the sponsor are very rare. Nevertheless, the effect of producer irresponsibility is broadly felt and resented. A sponsor once burned by a film producer will not be shy about reciting florid details of the disaster, much to the detriment of all producers. Any effort to talk rationally with such a burned client, pointing out that the innocent should not be stained by the guilty, ordinarily falls on deaf ears.

Other Provisions in the Contract

The bill of rights of the new trade contract, therefore, serves both producer and sponsor, as it should. One blessing that helps both parties is the stipulation that one liaison representative be appointed by the sponsor to represent him in all matters relating to production of the film. This provision happily reduces to one the number of people to please at the sponsor end, so that things are not continually being put in committee or reviewed by troublesome later arrivals on the corporate scene.

The standard form calls for an agreement at the outset that the producer is professionally competent. This prevents any temptation to use incompetence as a dodge for aborting the contract. Rather, the sponsor must own up to the fact that if he has enough confidence in a producer to sign a contract with the producer, he should have enough confidence in him to permit a revision of the work without slamming the door on him.

Reselling a motion picture without reasonable payment is unfair, whether the offender is the producer or the sponsor. If the producer is paid in full by his sponsor for a new film, the producer has no right to resell it in its entirety or use great bites of it for profit without some equitable arrangement with the sponsor. Nor should the sponsor take his film and resell it to others without an equitable agreement with the producer. Some quickly jump up and say, "If a man buys something and pays for it, it's his property and he can damn well do what he wishes with it." That is simplistic and unreal. There are implicit as well as explicit values in contracts. A producer carefully considers the limitations and purpose of a film when he prices it. If his client dupes him and changes those limitations and purposes without paying more, he has done the producer wrong.

Of course, the stock-footage trade practice is well known and agreeable to all parties. The producer keeps outtakes from his various assignments and uses them to lace later productions, without getting special permission (unless principal talent is involved). The sponsor is satisfied with the practice since he also benefits in his film from outtakes from his producer's previous motion pictures. The producer who maintains well-filed and protected outtakes builds his value in the film marketplace.

The contract form clearly announces that the price is *net*. Can you believe that eminent advertising agencies shamelessly claim 15 per cent agency commissions on film production contracts unless that word is in there, even when they don't lift a finger to help in any way except pass along their client's checks?

Another blessing to both parties is the itemized listing of the projected production schedule. Sponsor and producer have specific dates to follow, to avoid delays, but are not held to them under penalty clauses. This provision tends to move approvals and work along at a businesslike pace.

Chapter Seven

Getting Along With Others

Visitors of one sort or another are continually popping into the offices and studios of sponsored film producers, and they are generally received with pride and pleasure. They are escorted through the facilities and their questions answered. Film production is not a complex business to understand or explain, especially since most Americans and many world citizens have seen sponsored films.

So many arts and crafts are melded into filmmaking that visitors quickly find common ground: stagecraft, music, recording, public speaking, makeup, interior design, fine art, still photography, creative writing, communications, television, optics, typesetting, layouts, modeling, acting. Visitors can identify with one or more of these pursuits rather quickly.

TRADE ASSOCIATIONS

When they see these things happening in producer studios, they often ask, "Do all other film producers have setups like this?" In years past most producers would have to confess they did not know. Their perspective on their own industry was limited, because there was little opportunity for producers to visit their fellow filmmakers, and there was often the aura of suspicion when a producer called on a competitor unexpectedly. Producers relied on trade suppliers to tell them what was happening at the competitor's premises. True, a producer often called on a fellow professional for help when working in his city, but then he might only see the crews he hired and miss getting a tour of the studio facilities.

Producers of sponsored films are not suspicious or jealous by nature.

They take pride and pleasure in helping another filmmaker in trouble. They welcome a chance to exchange stories, discuss new technology and chat about common friends in the profession. They are quick to admit their failures and weaknesses, ready to discuss vital business problems, and unhesitating about sharing hopes and dreams.

The International Quorum

Back in 1966 these truths gave birth to IQ—the International Quorum of Motion Picture Producers. Several trade associations had been organized in the area of non-theatrical film production with varying success and longevity. But at that time the field was wide open for organization of a society of 16mm film producers throughout the world.

Feverish organization work within the trade brought together a small film producer in Nairobi and a giant one in Tokyo, an old reliable firm in New York and a relatively new house in St. Louis. Producers, governments and manufacturers suggested the membership nucleus of IQ. Early presidents were Knut-Jørgen Erichsen of Centralfilm in Oslo, the author, Graeme Fraser of Crawley Films in Ottawa and Bill Legg of Paragon Productions in Washington. They and their officers and governors built the organization to a formidable membership of 118 production houses throughout the world. Many are the largest and most powerful in their countries. Virtually all turn out award-winning work.

Member producers meet at annual or semi-annual conferences, through the pages of their quarterly, *Quorum Quotes*, at awards festivals and by sharing work on sponsored film production. Their great "in" pleasure is showing their films to each other.

It's a truism that communicators suffer from lack of communication. People in the communications industries are most sensitive to breakdowns in communications, so it's natural that they are aware of this weakness and talk it out. One such forum is the trade association, such as IQ. Members relate to fellow producers and communicate with them. They are quick to say *that* is worth the price of membership alone. When they go out of their way to visit during vacation or business trips, what emerges seems priceless to them. Producers share woes as well as pleasures. When one producer confides that a sponsor never made his final payment because the film project was frozen by a new executive, he finds a little comfort in hearing that the same thing happened to a fellow producer 9,000 miles away.

Other Trade Associations

Not by any means is IQ the only trade or professional organization serving the sponsored film industry. Others relate and they should be examined. But none serves the same purpose as IQ, nor do any of them duplicate functions.

The Association of Cinema Laboratories in Alexandria, Virginia, works to improve lab quality, service and profits. The Association for Educational Communications and Technology in Washington studies learning resources—people, processes and media in educational settings. The Audio-Visual Service Committee of the Association of National Advertisers in New York concerns itself with practical matters of AV cost, production, and distribution. The Chicago Film Council promotes the use of film for commercial, informational and cultural purposes and to improve film production and distribution.

The Educational Film Library Association offers itself as a clearinghouse of information about use and distribution of 16mm films, though it tends to look down at sponsored films. The Farm Film Foundation distributes farming-related films, without charge, to rural America and offers consultation to sponsors and producers. The Film Producers Association of New York works to promote and improve all aspects of the film industry. The Industrial Audio-Visual Association in Waukegan, Illinois, studies and promotes all areas of audio-visual communications, including production and distribution.

Information Film Producers of America in Hollywood tries to advance the state of the art for industrial, documentary, educational, informational, promotional and government films. The International Film, TV and A-V Producers Association provides a forum for collecting new ideas on production, equipment and facilities and setting up international standards. The National Audio-Visual Association in Fairfax, Virginia, works to improve the professional status and business practices of the A-V industry.

The Society of Motion Picture and Television Engineers in Scarsdale, New York, sets technical standards for all motion pictures and provides the focus for broad research in the film and TV industries.

GOVERNMENT REGULATION

Americans weep when the government doesn't step in and protect them, and they weep when it does.

A proper balance in government regulation over its people has been an unfulfilled challenge ever since civilization began. Witnessing the struggle to achieve that balance puts a real sense of history into one's soul.

History has not caught up with sponsored films: *there is no specific government regulation over them.* Nor is there any trade regulation—no codes of practice or ethics.

What does that say to you? That here is a free-swinging, raw, undisciplined frontier field of creative endeavor that needs parental supervision? Not at all. It should say quite the opposite: that the sponsored film industry is so polite, so benign, so polished by client and producer care that it needs no outside regulation.

We must quickly admit that the same cast of industry-characters that worries over television commercials is usually involved with sponsored films. So the echo of tight regulation is still in their ears when they correct sponsored film scripts. There is a rub-off. But legally, there is no connection between what is shown as a paid commercial on television and what is shown as a public service, sponsored film.

The contrast between the two can be visualized quickly in the treatment of beer consumption. With all the lively openings of beer cans and bottles, bubbling and pouring of beer, one never sees a drop enter the virgin mouths of actors or actresses. Not in a TV commercial.

But in a sponsored film, a sponsor may display all the guzzling, swallowing, ingestion and gulping it wishes. And that film will be shown on the same television station at the same time of day as the commercial.

Silly? Not really. Commercial production is the front-line in a mighty capitalistic offensive on the public purse. The cleverest minds in advertising agencies, clients and attorneys' offices work on every nuance of thought that goes into commercials carried on the networks. Their messages are as powerful and convincing as regulations will permit. Taste has very little to say in such a *milieu*.

Sponsored films, in startling contrast, are not frantic or frenetic. To justify their existence they must be rational, reasonably correct, meaningful and in good taste. If they are to convey a commercial message, it must be sensibly integrated into the film's story. The sly "plugs" of yesteryear, when a viewer could spot a series of payola-style visualizations of industry products in a sponsored film, are—thank God—over.

Indeed some sponsors think the delicacy of sponsored film construction is an innate weakness. They rationalize that if you can't come out and say it in good, strong, selling words, what good is a sponsored film? They don't stop to think that what you transmit in a TV commercial and what the audience *receives and responds to* are two very different things. All the communication arts, from Soviet propaganda to Walt Disney nature films, are continually in a dynamic state as creative people strive to *make people believe* what they are saying.

I would quickly maintain that a sponsored film is a far stronger base from which to *make people believe* than any TV commercial. For one thing, the sponsored film usually has a quarter-hour or more to do its thing. The pressure to compress logic into high-speed encapsulated medicine isn't there at all. Have you ever witnessed a dramatic pause in a commercial? You never will. There's always an agency type sitting there with his stopwatch, telling you how much each millisecond of network time it costs.

But sponsored films run *free*. Their low-key messages are accepted by stations—and the Federal Communications Commission—as public service material. So stopwatches are put aside at the interlock showings, when sponsor and producer make final decisions as to what will be seen and heard in their newest sponsored film.

The pressure to overstate isn't there. The burden of shouting to be heard in a crowd isn't there. The plotting to snake through a plethora of regulations isn't there. This is, indeed, a freedom that is rare to savor, a nectar to sip that may not always be at hand.

The good sense of it all showed vividly in a film we made in the lake district of Chile. Our American fishermen trolled for and caught handsome rainbow trout and landlocked salmon. At sunset they cleaned and pan-fried them on shore. They enjoyed a hearty dinner of trout and good beer while we filmed. It was a wholesome, honest scene. It would have been idiotic to show each fisherman bringing a cold can to his lips and then cut. So we showed it all. The film was seen on hundreds of U.S. television stations, and never did a print come back with an editor's splice in it.

Common sense prevailed. When sponsors ask producers, "How much commercial exposure can we get in this film?" the only proper answer is, "As much as personal taste dictates."

The FCC Viewpoint

For those readers interested in chapter and verse, I am pleased to offer the words of William B. Ray, Chief of the Complaints and Compliance Division, Broadcast Bureau, of the Federal Communications Commission: *"The Commission has not adopted specific guidelines directed to televised films."*

In paragraph 6 of *The FCC and Broadcasting*, that federal agency says:

> The Commission is prohibited by Section 326 of the Communications Act from censoring broadcast matter and from taking any action which would interfere with the right of free speech by broadcasting. It should also be stated that the FCC is not the arbiter of taste. The licensee is responsible for the selection of programming based on what he learns about the problems and needs of his community of license. Thus, the Commission does not direct him to broadcast one program or cancel another, or as to the time of day when programs or announcements should be presented. . .

The FCC does call for sponsored films to identify their sponsors, as in normal title credits. In *Applicabiity of Sponsorship Identification Rules, Revision of May 6, 1963 Public Notice, as Modified by April 21, 1975 Public Notice*, the FCC offers Paragraph 2 as one of several illustrative interpretations of section 317 and the Commission's rules:

(a) A bus company prepares a scenic travel film which it furnishes free to broadcast stations. No mention is made in the film of the company or its buses. No announcement* is required because there is no payment other than the matter furnished for broadcast and there is no mention of the bus company.

(b) Same situation as in (a), except that a bus, clearly identifiable as that of the bus company which supplied the film, is shown fleetingly in highway views in a manner reasonably related to that travel program. No announcement is required.

(c) Same situation as in (a), except that the bus, clearly identifiable as that of the bus company which supplied the film, is shown to an extent disproportionate to the subject matter of the film. An announcement is required, because in this case by the use of the film the broadcaster has impliedly agreed to broadcast an identification beyond that reasonably related to the subject matter of the film.

The Television Code of The NAB

What the FCC does not regulate, the National Association of Broadcasters tries to do in its Television Code. That elegant instrument, voluntarily agreed to by television stations, reminds station management that television's relationship to the viewers is that between guest and host. It cautions stations in all matters of taste and warns them of their special responsibility toward children and community. Among General Program Standards of interest to film sponsors, producers and distributors are the following:

Program materials should enlarge the horizons of the viewer, provide him with wholesome entertainment, afford helpful stimulation, and remind him of the responsibilities which the citizen has towards his society.

No program shall be presented in a manner which through artifice or simulation would mislead the audience as to any material fact. . .

The use of the television medium to transmit information of any kind by the use of the process called "subliminal perception," or by the use of any similar technique whereby an attempt is made to convey information to the viewer by transmitted messages below the threshold of normal awareness, is not permitted.

Program content should be confined to those elements which entertain or inform the viewer and to the extent that titles. teasers and credits do not meet these criteria, they should be restricted or eliminated.

---

* The FCC states that the wording of such an announcement is to say that the matter transmitted is sponsored, paid for, or furnished, either in whole or in part, and by whom or on whose behalf such consideration was supplied.

Programs . . . should be broadcast with due regard to the composition of the audience. The highest degree of care should be exercised to preserve the integrity of such programs and to ensure that the selection of themes, their treatment and presentation are made in good faith upon the basis of true instructional and entertainment values, and not for the purposes of sensationalism, to shock or exploit the audience or to appeal to prurient interests or morbid curiosity.

INVESTIGATION AND THE LAW

A lady phoned me one warm afternoon, out of the blue.

"I'm from Sixty Minutes and we're planning part of an upcoming show on sponsored films," she announced. "We are concerned about industry getting to government agencies by crossing their palms with silver in the form of sponsored film funding."

There followed about two hours of give and take. I tried to be candid, all the time knowing in my innards that I was talking with a real honest-to-God muckraker. And she was messing with my own muck.

She was calling the right guy, I suppose. My firm produces films with private industry money for use by federal agencies, telling federal agency stories just the way those agencies wanted. The industries involved most certainly are deeply interested in the way those agencies act.

And here was a TV network reporter digging for evidence of influence buying in a new, insidious form. Was the sponsored film industry really part of it?

I laughed out loud. "You can't be serious. Do you really think our little films are the catalyst in industry plots to control government?" She allowed as how that was the premise of the story she was researching.

Then, while I was saying nothing and taking minutes doing it, I thought back on the innocuous picture we did for The American Legion and Pan American World Airways. It was mostly about death—how Legionnaires chipped in their dollars to light part of Arlington National Cemetery filled with American war dead. Why did an airline opt to accept our offer of sponsorship? Well, half of Congress and President Nixon were to be on hand for the button-pressing banquet that would officially light the Tomb of the Unknowns. Pan Am officials would be sitting on the dais with the President.

All this was at the critical time of decision when the trans-Pacific air routes were being considered. It was a hot political moment for Pan Am and they told us "yes." The film was made without one word of suggestion from Pan Am. Whatever the American Legion wanted was OK with the sponsor. It seemed that all Pan Am wanted was that positive exposure before the President and Congress. Everything went fine. Everyone was happy. The trans-Pacific route decision was not altered by the production of our film, but the sponsor completed a successful PR job.

· I told all this to the lady reporter. Then I asked, "Is this your idea of corruption? Surely you can do better."

Then I asked her to call Dr. Nicholas Vardac at the U.S. Bureau of Mines. "I talked to him yesterday for quite some time." "Did you learn much?" I asked. "Quite a bit."

How well I know. Dr. Vardac alone should have closed the book for this lady. His purity in handling sponsored films is legendary. For many years he has delicately arranged for the production of an entire library of films for the U.S. Bureau of Mines, all underwritten by industry (metals, mining, consumer products like borax and baking soda). The only tax money he's spent has involved his own modest salary and travel costs to oversee production. Vardac will not enter into a three-way contract among producer, industry and government. He insists that separate two-way instruments be executed. There can be no industry exposure in the film story, and only cursory mention of the donor in one title.

This fact was brought home to me memorably by Dick Ehlers, retired advertising manager of Agrico, the fertilizer giant. Vardac invited Agrico to sponsor a film on fertilizer and Agrico agreed. Ehlers found himself one day on location in the midwest, far from his New Jersey home, with Vardac. The script called for a long shot of a freight train carrying fertilizer across the plains. Ehlers tells it like this: "Here I was with Dr. Vardac, setting up this train shot for his film. Suddenly he says we can't show the corporate identity of all those freight cars. Not one of them mentioned Agrico, you understand. It was just one long, dreary exposure of Rock Island, Santa Fe and countless other railroad identifications. Vardac wanted me to arrange for all of them to be covered up. I told him to go to hell."

Here was this muckraker on the phone trying to show how industry controlled government through sponsored films and there was poor Dick Ehlers out there on the plains trying to figure ways to cover up a thousand freight cars in a film he was giving away to the government.

The unalterable fact is that federal agencies are entirely too savvy and too self-protective ever to allow their decisions to be influenced by sponsors of films they use.

A case in point: *My Nuclear Neighbors*. That was a self-serving film we did for the nuclear power industry in cooperation with the then U.S. Atomic Energy Commission. More than one sponsor company involved was in court with the AEC over rights to build additional nuclear power production plants at the very time we were shooting. Our sponsors made no overtures through us or our film to influence the AEC, and the AEC opened no doors to such overtures. The people were adults who clearly knew what *not* to do.

The *Sixty Minutes* effort was a failure if it was intended to alarm the public to a new ogre. Perhaps the real reason is economic. The median sponsored-film budget, at this writing, is around $40,000. That's important money, agreed, but not in the form of a public service film. Virtually every American is acquainted with more direct uses of cash among federal offices. As long as such corrupt practices continue, industry-sponsored government films will comprise picayune pickings for the likes of Ralph Nader.

PERSONAL ETHICS

Item: Midwest printers walk out, refusing to print two well-known "skin" periodicals because it's against their religious principles.

Item: New York ad agency resigns multi-million dollar consumer account after client asked agency to create ads full of lies and misrepresentations.

Item: Network fires top executive in payola scandal.

Lucky for the good guys, *ethics make important news*. There is hope for a world that can be stunned by a breach of ethics in the communications industry or in Parliament or in a Mobile, Alabama, bus. Whether humanity is properly attentive to its religious teachings is highly debatable. But you have to hand it to the public when they register sincere shock after hearing about a Central American official taking payoffs from U.S. industry. They know it happens every day, but they just won't accept it as right.

The pages of *Advertising Age*, the advertising trade journal, stay busy with questions about advertising ethics. Ad professionals write scathing letters to other ad professionals in the *Ad Age* columns, censuring them for ethical breaches. That's not bad for an industry that some have said is the "home of the lie."

No aspect of the communications field is more sensitive to ethical breaches than the public relations profession. It took years, but PR people finally convinced their superiors and their clients that covering up the dirt and telling lies are just about the dumbest thing to instruct PR counsel to do. Today a reporter with a tip can call an industry public information officer and get the straight story. He might also get a decent request to soften the wording, or to take time to get a quote representing the other side of the question. But the PR man won't lie.

The ethics of the American journalist are legendary in other parts of the world. Buying a reporter's soul to make him print untruths is as likely as Santa Claus shooting deer out of season. Julian Scheer was a solid writer for *The Charlotte News* before he went to Washington to head NASA public information. Once he covered the Lumbee Indians routing the Ku Klux Klan in Eastern North Carolina and he wrote that a T-shirt bore the inscription, "Souvenir of Chimney Rock." He did that as a favor to me, knowing the Chimney Rock folks were friends of mine. The T-shirt actually carried another innocuous legend. That was as big a detour around the truth I ever knew a pro to take.

Enter the sponsored film.

Here we have a dynamic new communications medium, growing in depth and breadth faster than its own professionals realize. Few of them ever stopped to ask about ethics. They may say they just haven't had time for a bath in the suds of philosophy. Or they may simply point out that nobody has complained—yet.

In all the years of meetings, informal and formal, of our trade association, no one has brought up the matter of ethics in sponsored films. Ott Coelln, one of the deans of the industrial film business, did remind us in one address of our preoccupation with film production technicalities when we should be examining loftier challenges. But even he failed to suggest we look into the mirrors of guilt and innocence.

Why should we? Well, I put it to the reader. I give you an essentially unregulated communications medium responsible for millions of annual viewings of films that are selfishly produced. Doesn't that alone beg the question?

Please do not drag any red herrings across the path, like saying that sponsored films are usually benign, educational, filled with valuable data, minimal in commercial exposure, and made by producers without a chip on their shoulders. All that may be true enough. But it does not answer the question: *Do sponsors, producers and distributors breach ethics enough to require regulation?*

Let us examine the possible breaches. During the intensity of the petroleum crisis in the United States, the majors tried to buy commercial TV program time to rebut the indictments the networks were running against them. The networks refused to carry such rebuttals. Yet those same petroleum giants are free to issue sponsored films containing the stories they wish to tell, and individual stations are free to show them gratis. If it is improper for the oil companies to tell their side of the issue in paid network programs, how is it proper for them to pay producers and distributors to do it free by means of sponsored films? Are the producers and distributors accepting such fees committing a breach of ethics?

An electric power company retains a producer and distributor to make and circulate a film about the company's ecological responsibility. Company spokesmen meet with the scriptwriter and feed him the best information they have, and omit the embarrassing matters that would not help the cause. The approved script calls for filming of many of the company's electric power production plants. When the dailies are viewed by the company, they howl at several shots revealing heavy smoke issuing from the stacks. The shots are ordered remade or removed. The producer complies. The film is successfully completed and distributed among tens of thousands of schools to show young people they have nothing to fear from the power company. Who, if anyone, is guilty of ignoring ethics?

A corporation that manufactures building materials specifies that part of its new sponsored film deals with fire safety. Its products have not yet received Underwriters Laboratories approval, and the corporation does not ask that the film imply any approval of fire rating. But it calls for filming a fire demonstration using low-temperature flame, such as from a match, to "prove" that the product has fire-resistant qualities. The film is produced and distributed. Millions see the sequence and assume that the building product is fire safe. Is there a hint of ethics being trampled here?

You can see from these examples that these are not questions of breaking public laws. No one involved is being so careless as to invite court action. It is not illegal in itself to serve one's own selfish interests. It is not illegal in itself to limit the amount of information you reveal and circulate.

But few film producers and distributors will say they have never in their careers had any pangs of conscience. They can rationalize that they were just following orders (familiar ring?) when they made or circulated a film they knew was a distortion of the truth, or that may be detrimental to the viewers.

So far, there has been no scandal. No one is known to have been badly hurt. No one has blown the whistle. They say someone has to be killed at a dangerous intersection before authorities will erect a stoplight. Perhaps that is what the sponsored film and distribution people are waiting for. Someone to get killed.

Or maybe ethical questions will begin to appear on the convention agendas and in the trade journals, and the professionals will one day prepare guidelines that they—and the sponsors—can live by.

Perry Powell, Director of the North Carolina Justice Academy dropped in recently and said he wanted us to make some training films and an image film for his new police academy—soon as he had the money. I told him I'd be pleased to do them, as we'd enjoyed a most pleasant relationship on two previous police films we produced for him.

He also mentioned he would like us to come over to Salemburg to lecture once in a while to his classes of police officers, attorneys, judges and other professionals involved in law enforcement. "What about?" I asked.

"Forensic photography," he replied.

Those two words open up a whole world of thought. As I rushed to agree to the lectures, I was thinking about the rapid advances law enforcement has made all over the United States with cameras of various types. Police pull out still cameras to document scene-of-the-crime evidence the moment they arrive. TV cameras, feeding portable videotape recorders, record the instability of a drunk driver. At meetings, police officers take one last look at the faces of wanted criminals on TV sets before going out on patrol. Defense and prosecuting attorneys set up screens in court to show to judge and jury motion picture details of the crime scene or evidence impossible to bring to the courtroom.

If you were a member of one of those juries, you would sooner or later wonder how honest were the images you were being shown on the screen. After all, you've seen *The Invisible Man* and a wealth of TV commercials displaying camera tricks no ordinary magician could work. It doesn't take a professional filmmaker or photographer to tell you that people can tell the truth with film, or tell lies with it.

What good are films, tapes and still pictures of vital evidence if one can't depend on them to be truthful? We can say the same about humanity: what value is a witness if one cannot believe his oath to tell the truth?

Let us say you are a photographer working for an attorney defending the driver of a car involved in a fatal auto accident. The attorney explains it is in his client's interest to show any way possible that he was driving slowly at the time of impact, and that his car did not go far after impact. The photographer might then go to the scene of the accident and take motion pictures, tapes or stills to influence judge and jury. Standing at an unusual distance and a switching to a telephoto lens, the photographer has no trouble showing the car very close to the point of impact in relation to other objects in the area. Were he trying to indicate the opposite, he would have only to switch to a wide-angle lens to show the car quite far from the point of impact. This is basic stuff.

There are subtler ways to "lie" with a camera. If a sponsored film producer has an assignment from a political candidate or party, he almost automatically films The Man from a slightly low angle. With the lens always looking up a little at the candidate, the viewer gets the gut feeling he is watching Abe Lincoln.

If an actor is to appear to be threatening and unappealing, the cameraman has only to position that actor close to the lens and facing away. If another actor is to appear to be threatened and appealing, he will be positioned at some distance and facing the camera. This is just simple motion picture craftsmanship as old as D. W. Griffith's work. Make-up, lighting, camera positions, actors' positions, dialog and other variables in the film field can be made to change the viewers' minds. Such resources are perfectly proper in theatrical work when one is dealing with fiction.

But apply those techniques to documentary films, forensic films and sponsored films, and the producer is breaking with reality, ethics and honesty. I have watched TV and film interviews that were, to me as a professional, obviously edited to show the person at his worst. A pair of scissors is all the editor needs to make or break a personality during an interview. When we do a "talking head" for a sponsored film, we shoot much more footage than we will use and take the best material from among it and use it for the final edit. Everyone does that. The effort in such a case is not to show a person better than reality, but simply to display him as effectively and professionally as possible. But the opposite effort is malicious. One can intentionally edit an interview to include false starts, errors, drifting in subject and unattractive photography. The result can be damaging and misleading—in short, it is untruthful. Why would anyone do that? Let us not be naive. If it serves someone's purpose to belittle or degrade another person, such as in a political campaign, you can be sure the matter will at least be considered. If cameramen can be paid to come up with unattractive footage of the opponent, it may well end up on screen.

The camera can mislead the public just as penetratingly by omission. Surely you can think of a President or a presidential candidate who spent most of his day hours in a wheelchair. Now go back in the archives and seek out motion picture footage and still photos and videotapes of such a President or candidate moving about in his wheelchair. Not too easy, I assure you. Great pains were taken to obscure the fact of the disability because it was feared the people could not accept a crippled national leader.

What American adult has not had the heart-rending experience of watching war atrocity films? It was relatively easy for us teenagers to volunteer in World War II after we saw Hitler's Stuka bombers leveling Rotterdam, and Japanese soldiers laughingly violating Chinese mothers and throwing their screaming babies into the air to be caught on the shafts of their bayonets. Were those films lies? No, we saw the truth. But the act of showing them to the public was as much a matter of propaganda as of reporting history. Selected films can condition the people. Adolf Hitler said as much, and had his cameras grinding out brainwashing films in awesome numbers.

The sponsored film producer of today would be less than honest if he did not admit to learning from the work of Leni Riefenstahl, who made unforgettable films for the Nazi cause. Through the decades, producers have become adept at cinematography, recording, editing and scriptwriting to tell a story precisely the way the sponsor wishes it told. Watch the next film sponsored by an airline, any airline. Listen for the sound of the jets. Beautiful! Like the sound of meadowlarks walking in a dewy meadow. Who could suspect from an airline-sponsored film that whole cities enact legislation to define jet flight patterns and engine speeds, just to lessen the cacophony?

When is the last time you saw a film sponsored by any medical organization that showed a physician saying "I don't know" about anything, anything at all? Have you ever seen a film sponsored by industry that included smokestacks billowing out their pollution? Or any government-sponsored film that freely discussed its agency's past or present inefficiencies? What's the last travel film you caught that showed the lost luggage, ripoff in currency exchange, beaches littered with metal and plastic, inflated hotel rates, impossible telephone service, hours-late planes and land "packages" impossible to cash in? You probably never saw such a film, sponsored by any aspect of the travel industry, and never will. It's too much to ask any industry, organization or government to be entirely frank about every subject in a quarter-hour or half-hour film. So the viewer is going to have to accept the inevitable fact that what he sees in a sponsored film may not be a lie, but it also may not be the whole truth. The rule of *caveat emptor* applies as much to sponsored films as to used cars.

Chapter Eight

Moving into Sponsored Films

". . .Friendships that are won by awards, and not by greatness and nobility of soul, although deserved, yet are not real, and cannot be depended upon in time of adversity."—Niccolo Machiavelli, 1469–1527

AWARDS

Walk down the corridors of Fred Niles' production house in Chicago and you will note that Fred doesn't give a fig for Machiavelli's famed quotation. The Niles' halls are literally papered with festival awards for his films. Fred will confide that some are hard-won and coveted and others aren't worth the holes in the wall they cover.

But it's Fred Niles' business to secure as many awards as possible for his firm, as part of the image-building process necessary to achieve production volume. Hundreds of sponsored film producers join in this continuing grab, like so many old-time merry-go-round riders who reach from their painted horses to pull a metal ring from the dispenser.

Awards festivals have suffered discrediting abuse by the pitchforkful. They have enjoyed the applause of presidents and kings. They have attracted thousands of glamour seekers and have played to scores of empty tables and chairs. Their judges have been called fraud and friend. Their fate flutters in the wind like the fashion shows of Paris couturiers, enduring the fickle fluctuations of the stock market. Yet no one doubts their impact on the world of films, or that they will endure.

CINE is that unique organization that methodically funnels the choicest of American films into world festivals and gives its own Golden Eagles and other awards in the process. Daryl Miller of the American

Dental Association is one of its functionaries who looks after entries in the professional fields. "CINE must reject many perfectly good sponsored films simply because they have little international validity," he states. "It is our concern to represent the United States as strongly as possible in world competition, and we just cannot do it with narrow-focus films."

Does it matter how much money the sponsor invests in the film? Not at all, avers Miller. Films are judged on merit and not financial fat. "And subject," he quickly adds. Last year, he will volunteer, he was inundated with films about venereal disease, which, I suppose, has to be one of the dangers of being a CINE judge. This year? "None."

Sponsored films are not the only type of film CINE judges, but they are the backbone of CINE competition. Daryl Miller readily agrees that the degree of commercial exposure within film entries varies inversely with their acceptability for awards. So slickly-made sponsored films with liberal doses of commercial impact may just as well remain in the States without CINE inspection.

Because festival judges must view vast numbers of sponsored films, producers and sponsors sometimes suspect they ease their burdens a bit by viewing just the opening minutes of each film. Is that true? we asked Miller. "Not to my knowledge," he replies. "Judges recognize that many producers unleash their big guns the first few minutes of their films, the way an architect wins applause with his front-door design treatment. So to turn off the projector after the opening fireworks is foolishness. I can remember several films that were excellent, even superb not only at the beginning but all through the show, only to drop dead at the end." He imagines producers turning out first-rate creative work of ten-minute duration, then remembering their contract calls for a quarter-hour show, and padding at the end with superfluous, shallow material.

Of course, there are festivals and festivals. While CINE appears above reproach, others are spottily managed, depending on the honor of volunteers to come through with authentic judgment. I know of one producer who entered several of his better films in one of the most prestigious American film festivals, at $50 per entry. He soon received a form letter relating to one of them announcing with regret that his film had failed to pass the judge's critical eye, and try again next time, Mac. He then casually glanced at the returned print and studied it a moment.

Something was wrong. He kept looking at the print, puzzled. Suddenly he saw it. The producer's crisp new round label on the hub of the reel had never been punched through by the judge's projector. The film had not been viewed by anyone from the moment it had left the producer's offices until it was returned. The festival had clearly defrauded the producer of his particular $50 and perhaps many more $50 payments by scores of sponsored film producers.

He did not hesitate to blow the whistle. Faces quickly reddened up and down the festival pike. "These things happen," came the weak response from the Festival officials, together with a $50 refund. The judge was pictured as an absent-minded professor of high academic standing. The story hit the trade press and the producer fraternity never bought the festival's excuse.

More flagrant matters have been on industry lips for years. There are as many rumors about payoffs and friendship-born awards as one hears about the Miss-This-or-That contests. The Cannes film festival, involving theatrical films, originates stories of wild women, striking directors and political intrigue that often overshadow the merits of the sometimes brilliant films shown on the Cote d'Azur. Hunter Todd, miffed over Georgia's lack of starry-eyed investment in his festival, moved it to the Virgin Islands (sic). One member of the CINE board once confided to me that another festival would up the value of its awards one notch if the producer would assure his personal presence at the banquet.

But this is like discussing George Washington's notorious expense account instead of his priceless service to his country. One must maintain a sense of values in examining the film festival circuit and appreciate the splendid inspiration they afford the sponsored film industry. I have half a dozen underpaid directors on my staff who, I sincerely believe, value a genuine festival award above a raise. I honor those directors for such a noble and professional attitude, and pray that the festival crowd keeps its collective nose clean in order to continue to benefit filmmakers known and unknown.

A typical sponsored film festival is the International Film & TV Festival of New York. Herbert Rosen originated it in 1957, and has seen it grow in size and stature each year. It does not limit itself to sponsored films but also includes television and cinema commercials, filmstrips and slidefilms, educational and news films, filmed introductions and lead-in titles, multi-media and mixed-media productions, public service announcements and television programs. Each of the categories is individually managed, "making the annual event seven festivals in one," Rosen points out.

Its purpose is like those of the other festivals: to honor individuals and firms who contribute to the greatness of the film industry with outstanding work. The finest entry in each of the seven sections receives a Grand Award. After that, in each category, there are gold, silver and bronze medals as well as special achievement awards. That may at first blush sound like a cornucopia of trophies, but considering the fact that some 2,000 films are entered each year, one may agree that the International Film & TV Festival of New York is highly selective indeed.

The films pour in from production houses, educational institutions, sponsors and ad agencies. A panel of distinguished judges views all 2,000 films two weeks before the festival. The judges come from the same backgrounds as the sources of the films, to assure a balance of professional evaluation. Typical judges include the film department director of the Museum of Modern Art in New York, the senior art director of United Artists, production supervisor of Grey Advertising and the dean of Parsons School of Design.

Producers of sponsored films and sponsors themselves appreciate festivals like Herb Rosen's that do not look down their nose at commercialism. The U.S. Industrial Film Festival is another that does not give demerits to sponsored films where specific sponsor values are demonstrated. In a nation whose people rush to wear commercial beltbuckles, swim in beer-label pools and pay extra for the Dior name splashed all over a scarf, it is only fair to honor commercially-oriented films without shame. Rosen says it like it is. "Aesthetics will, of course, be given their due respect. But other factors will be taken into account, too, such as marketing objectives, demographics and sales achievements."

The annual awards presentation banquet of each festival comprises the climax of the annual contest. Rosen's happens at the Americana Hotel in New York. More than a thousand guests attend it because it's a social as well as professional place to be. At the opening cocktail party and reception, producers and advertising executives from many parts of the world meet and renew friendships. The dinner and entertainment start together, and then the awards presentations are interwoven. Many stage and film stars entertain and accept awards. Festival management arranges not one evening but four days of activities for visitors. They visit film labs, optical houses, computer film production houses, post-production houses, multi-media production studios, network TV facilities and ad agencies. One day is set aside for screenings of top festival entries. Those are impressive goodies for pros, and they come by subway and jet.

Herb Rosen displays unparalleled kindness in working toward having on hand all winners and excusing those who will not win. He does this by the grace of advance letters of information to the producers, agencies and sponsors. The gesture avoids the trauma of a producer inviting his sponsor to the festival affair, fully expecting an award, only to pass the evening in a crescendo of agony.

He can act blasé if he wishes, but the producer who walks to the stage to accept a shiny trophy at a film festival is savoring the essence of heaven on earth. For the moment, at least, he is a professional among professionals. He is proud to be a sponsored filmmaker. He goes home to the wife, kids and studio staff to show off his plaque and mutter, "It's nothing." The plaque ends up on the wall at the office. Maybe it's not as crowded a wall as Fred Niles', but there's always next year.

Some film contests, sad to report, will not accept sponsored films at all. This is the art film or museum circuit which holds local, regional or national festivals to commend makers of highly creative films. These festivals are tea-and-crumpet affairs attended by very few beyond the museum staff, contestants and judge. The judge is usually a film critic from a distant city willing to make the trip for carfare plus $100. Such competitions attract student films, dance films, art films and experimental films. All well and good. But sponsored films are specifically excluded as the work of the devil. *Why Man Creates* couldn't get a tin ring from a Cracker Jack box on the museum circuit because (*sotto voce*) it was sponsored by industry. The judge and director will defend their exclusion by saying that a sponsored film, no matter how expensively mounted, is dull in its commercial predictability, wall-to-wall narration and obscenely glossy cinematography. They much prefer, they proudly say, the wonderful hand-painted film frames of an 18-year-old, the ballet sequence shot through a pilsener glass or the documented, fantasy fingerpainting of a chimpanzee. *De gustibus non disputandum est.*

There are some 22 U.S. award festivals, according to Back Stage Publications' unique *Film & TV Festival Directory*. In addition, 50 more authorities of varying backgrounds issue awards to films that please them. These vary in nobility from the Oscar awards of the Academy of Motion Picture Arts and Sciences to the cash and plaques the PR man at the American Optometric Association hands out to people who gave optometry good press coverage. Then there are 10 non-professional film festivals for amateurs and independents, ranging from a Super-8 festival in Saginaw, Michigan, to the International Erotic Film Festival in, of all places, San Francisco. College and university festivals number 21. After that there are an imposing number of film competitions in other nations.

Producers could spend several thousand dollars a year entering a few films in all the competitions accepting sponsored films. Most settle on spending a few hundred dollars annually at best to see if they can hit the jackpot somewhere out there in festival land.

There are various approaches to achieving awards, just as there are certain guidelines in winning 25-words-or-less contests. Entering 10 or more films in one competition can attract enough attention to put the thought into some influential minds that at least one of them deserves to win *something*. Some festival buffs study the entry categories as closely as the tipsheets at the horseraces. If there is a very narrow category like "Animals" or "Labor Relations," some producers will shoot for those and avoid the general categories like "Documentary" and "Public Relations." They figure that they'd rather have one of their films vying for honors against seven other animal film entries than against 823 public relations films. The odds are right.

Once in a while a competition will list "Other" as a category and then the producers jump in the water. They look at this as a possibility for establishing one's own special category and winning it because no one else enters it. Of course, it is almost inevitable that several producers have that same idea at the same time, and all of them enter "Undersea" films in the same competition.

The smart money is on films that examine a new, important subject, or that look at life in an entirely fresh manner. This is as it should be. Too many producers think that festival awards go to exquisite craftsmanship and artistry. Some do, but judges are generally looking for more profound qualities. Few films really *haunt* audiences, and when a judge can say he was truly haunted by a film he just judged, you can be sure he is going to give it his finest rating. He doesn't care whether the camera was hand-held, Tyler-mounted on a chopper or atop a hydraulic dolly. He isn't enthralled by trick filters or turned into putty by opticals.

But he is profoundly impressed by a kid who creates a new animation genre with thousands of magazine clippings, adds two conflicting voice tracks and issues *Frank Film* as his *tour de force* to get a job in the film trade. That delightful film, full of style, verve and wit, won most important film awards and deserved them all.

CAREERS

Would you like to dedicate your life to floriculture? Engineering? Veterinary medicine? Is your career to be in uniform? In the sea? In space?

Whatever your vocational leaning, you are likely to find a sponsored film to warm you up. Among industry, trade associations and the U.S. Department of Labor, there are hundreds of vocational films available to the starry-eyed 'teen.

But there isn't one sponsored film that tells youth about sponsored films as a career. It's a pity, because there is much to be said and few employers are patient or candid enough to tell all to the applicants.

Tom Hope lists 4,110 sponsored films made in 1973, 3,750 in 1974 and about the same for 1975. You wouldn't call that a boom. Yet in-house production capabilities and independent production houses are proliferating like rabbits. Either each house is going to turn out fewer productions per year, or a lot of new business will have to be generated by hungry producers.

The market for new personnel is clearly limited. Competition for each opening remains fierce. It may get to the point where things were a generation ago in the advertising business. A leading New York department store had an opening for an assistant in its advertising department and ran a small ad saying that only Phi Beta Kappas need apply. Snobbery? No, just a way to filter a thousand applicants down to 200.

Job titles cover camerapersons (Am I serious? Yes, that's the word now), recordists, editors, negative cutters, gaffers, scriptwriters, directors and animators. Work varies from the highly technical, where engineering degrees are needed, to non-technical where personality qualities may be most important. Talents, not peculiar to the industry, are often part of sponsored film production: commercial art, interior design, business administration, research, musical composition. Workers may be IATSE (International Alliance of Theatrical Stage Employees) or NABET (National Association of Broadcast Employees and Technicians) union members, or non-union. They may be free-lance or full-time. Men or women. White or black.

The pay may vary from starvation to forced feeding. I know of self-employed sponsored filmmakers taking home as little as nothing to as much as $150,000 a year. The $175 a day scale for some skills of free-lance work may come in only a few days a month and the bottom line can look pretty discouraging. Many workers in the sponsored film production field "moonlight" to keep the bills paid.

In the past, skills were rather clearly divided among workers. One man would spend most of his time behind a camera and another would work principally in sound. Today the industry is looking for more all-around filmmakers, quintuple-threat people who continually switch-hit. Such a horizontal employment arrangement permits crews to be made up more flexibly, and holes to be filled easier when a man is out sick or late returning from location. A cinema *boutique* made up of three persons looking for a fourth is going to thrive better with an all-around person rather than a specialist.

To complicate even further this job market, the more highly specialized field of sponsored films presents special challenges to employer and employee. A cameraperson might be able to perform a roll-focus, zoom, pan, tilt and dolly shot all in one beautiful movement, but he might go to pieces trying to integrate a sponsor's operations into the script action. The scriptwriter who recently won a state award for short story writing can well turn to melted mozarella when it comes to blending sponsor products into the story line. Worse, he may consider himself an Artist Who Is Above All That.

There is no pat answer to the question, "Do you producers prefer employees who have completed formal college cinema training, or those who have learned through self-training or apprenticeship?" One answer, of course, is "both." My feeling is that the best young filmmakers were superb when they entered cinema school, and used the campus simply as their setting for personal excellence. The rest of the graduates come out mechanically trained to operate the hardware of the trade, but weak in the more vital values of effective storytelling on film.

Employers need to see the best work the applicant has done in filmmaking. Yet fewer than half of them have competent audition reels to present. Some worked for TV stations and their little film masterpieces were put on tape, out of reach for audition purposes. Others apply for many jobs, and have only one or two reels to bicycle among all the potential employers. Still others have worked in some film field for years without ever getting title credits.

Your heart goes out to some who simply cannot offer a sample reel. Refugees from the USSR or Czechoslovakia usually arrive in the United States with little more than a brown suitcase and a headful of memories. Some of the finest filmmakers in the world work in Prague and Moscow. When they find their way to New York, jobs really should open up to them simply on the basis of merit. But they have no reels with them. Refugee organizations and potential employers hesitate equipping them with cameras and funds to shoot their own sample material. So these marvelous film craftsmen end up loading boxes in a warehouse or hawking windup dolls on the street.

Employers with patience and a genuine wish to find fresh talent will put people temporarily on the payroll without knowing their full capabilities. After a few weeks the new employee has proved a quick study with a camera crew or has cleverly edited a film. Or he may turn out to be all talk and no talent. Either way, the employer believes he has performed a more intelligent screening of applicants by job trial than by examination of records and viewing sample reels. After all, he reminds you, a sample film could have been made by a team of several persons, of which the applicant was only one minor part. But put a person right to work and you can tell quality quickly.

Work in production of sponsored films is highly physical. Employers look for applicants who are sharply trained by the time they are 22- or 23-years old, because they have only 20 years or so of active physical service ahead of them. Carrying lighting cases, moving tripods, lifting blimped cameras, striking sets and driving the mobile unit are not the work of lightweights with back troubles.

The young applicant is also favored from a creative standpoint. The 30-year-old filmmaker who hasn't already created a dozen or more excellent sponsored films is suspected of being a perennial student or a failure. The employer wants neither. Our firm once hired a 39-year-old cameraman. He had just retired after 20 years in the Navy as a director-cameraman. Before then, in his 'teens, he had operated second camera on a Hollywood feature film crew. Now that's *experience*.

Filmmaking is among the hottest of career preferences. It's more than a passing fad. Young people were weaned on films and TV, and visual communications is like a blood factor to them. It is only natural that tens of thousands of youths state that they want to spend their lives in film. It is unfortunate for the individuals that a glut has resulted. Thousands are turned away.

As producers and operators of in-plant facilities watch the stream of applicants file by, they are tempted to sound off about the schools and organizations that send them. IATSE, the principal labor union representing workers in the filmmaking trades, castigated the American Film Institute for misleading aspiring filmmakers into thinking that the streets of Filmland are paved with gold. IATSE pointed out that the American Film Institute at once encouraged widespread training in filmmaking and failed to mention high unemployment among actors, writers, directors and technicians, and the widespread famine in the industry.

"In reality," IATSE officials were quoted as saying, "these thousands of film and TV courses are training people for non-existent jobs. Filmmaker training is a transparent program to create a vast non-union pool, which in reality simply adds to and aggravates the serious unemployment problems existing among highly qualified technicians and creative people." The union also charged that people like the AFI bring hordes of high school students to despair as they face the harsh facts of unemployment without advance warning.

Yet, producers yearn to find some brilliant new filmmaker out there and put him right to work. They might tell the state or federal employment office that they aren't hiring right now, but they will almost always find time to look at the first minutes of a new unsolicited reel that came in from a hopeful. This is not the manifestation of a bunch of softies who remembered how hard it was when they were young. It is strictly business. Producers are acutely aware of the changing fashions in filmmaking. They appreciate that the new techniques evolve from the new wave of young filmmakers. So they want to keep fresh, bright people coming in to keep their films fresh and bright.

People who apply to producers for work on sponsored films rarely get to see applications from others competing with them for jobs. They do not really ever find out why they were hired or why they were rejected. Employers, after all, know the wisdom of telling everyone he is a real pro, and the danger of spelling out an applicant's weaknesses in words.

So here are data random-selected from our Technical Personnel files, where we hold applications from more than a hundred persons at all times. We do so not to accrue fat files but to have an immediate source of help when we need it.

From the following information, the reader can form conclusions about the type of person today applying for work in sponsored film production, his age, training and capability. Names and other information that would reveal the person involved are not shown. Work descriptions cover several years and appear in date order.

Single man, 25, B.A. in filmmaking and psychology at midwestern university. Worked at TV station on floor crew, processing still film, meat delivery boy, lab aide, free-lance TV public service spot films.

Man, age unknown, B.S. cum laude southwestern university, major in broadcasting. Worked with two ad agencies as radio-TV producer, free-lance director, with TV station as writer-director-producer.

Married man, 32, M.A. in film at a New York university, B.F.A. in graphic arts and advertising. Worked as signmaker, schoolteacher, cameraman-editor at state facility, producer-director with state facility.

Man, 40, B.A. journalism and M.A. in sociology, southern university. Worked as TV news-sports editor, state department of commerce PR editor, PR man with state health association, news bureau director with state university, producer of documentaries at TV station.

Married man, 27, B.S. in radio-TV, northern university. Worked as program technician at TV stations, still photographer, A-V specialist and media assistant at school for disturbed children.

Man, age unknown, B.A. in journalism-TV-film at eastern university, M.A. in communication arts, western university. Worked as retail jewelry salesman, corporation customer service man, self-employed writer, researcher, A-V and graphics producer.

Man, age unknown, education unknown. Worked as director and producer of industrials and commercials including Detroit cars, business planes, bank.

Married man, 29, 18 months in southern business school, 4 years Air Force. Worked as Air Force cameraman, cameraman-producer-director-editor with western producer, making university films in south.

Single woman, 23, B.A. in journalism at southern university. Worked as TV news reporter-interviewer, cameraperson, editor, studio photographer.

Single man, 32, B.A. in government, eastern university, cinema courses at far western university. Worked as producer-director with Air Force, chief of Air Force film team, cameraman-director with western producer, NABET member.

Single woman, 32, attended New England and southern universities. Worked as cashier, A-V supplier at university, public affairs producer at university, TV reporter, cameraperson, editor.

Single man, 25, B.A. fine arts, far west film institute, working on M.F.A. Worked as teaching assistant at film institute, free-lance cameraman-editor, filmmaker for public TV station.

Man, 25, attended three midwestern universities, Air Force film school. Worked as film crew chief in Air Force, cameraman-editor for midwest airframe maker.

Single man, 24, attended southern film-oriented university. Worked as weekly newspaper printer-photographer, assistant cameraman in college production, portrait photographer for church directory.

Single man, 31, B.A. in languages at eastern university, attended four other campuses. Worked as teaching assistant, social worker, film lab technician, free-lance cameraman, cameraman with producer, cameraman-editor with another producer.

Man, age unknown, education unknown. Worked with southern TV stations as cameraman, cameraman with producer, free-lance cameraman.

One of the above applicants was hired; the others turned down. Among still other applications could be found a 52-year-old Academy Award winning Hollywood first cameraman, an undersea specialist, a considerable number of college film majors with no work records, TV station personnel who think film production is just a hopscotch jump from TV news production and a sad number of proficient cameramen who cannot or do not work in sound, lighting, directing or editing.

Virtually all applicants have in fact made films of their own. And virtually all have a love affair going with their own work. They seem to find new and deeper meaning in their own films each time they audition them. We employers tend to be prejudiced in the opposite; we tend, in a superior, silent way, to make note of jump cuts, shaky zooms, mike shadows and other technical errors when we should be concentrating on the total work of the applicant.

To the aspiring filmmaker, we operators of production houses have one message: show us you can make great films in a businesslike way, and you've got yourself a job. We care little about your formal training or previous work. If you have found a way to do beautiful work in our profession, you are accepted. If you made your great films when you were in federal prison, fine—so long as the film is good. If you are suffering from elephantiasis of the earlobe, come to work on a burro or wear ankle-length hair, it matters little. The work is the thing. Conversely, if you taught cinema in the most prestigious university and your films won six gold medals, and your sample films leave us depressed, we have nothing to offer you but the door.

If all this sounds somewhat brutal and impatient, try keeping a staff of professionals working well together for a generation or so, and you may come around to our state of mind.

DIRECTIONS

Zoom from closeup to protagonist and his family, walking confidently up hill, to long shot of the now-tiny figures surrounded by stunning sunset. Freeze and crawl closing title credits.

A cliché finish is not my cup of tea.

Perhaps you could proceed from classroom to laboratory. I can direct you to several excellent ones. The U.S. Library of Congress is the repository of a broad collection of sponsored films, which, thanks to fellow producers, grows stronger each year. Many universities and public libraries have assembled commendable collections worthy of examination.

Another repository of sponsored films is the National Archives and Records Service of the General Services Administration in Washington. Most of the films in the custody of the National Archives are sponsored films, according to their William T. Murphy, in that they were commissioned or produced by agencies of the U.S. government. They have about 15,000 completed productions. In addition, National Archives contain countless outtakes, camera record footage and newsreels. Altogether they have some 105,000 unique reels and, counting negatives, masters and prints, the reel total is 165,000.

The National Archives accepts transfers of films that are judged to have historical or other enduring research value. It also accepts gifts of film from private sources that relate to theatrical newsreels or to network television news. All in all, Archives presents a memorable and priceless collection. Not only does the sponsored filmmaker appreciate his best work becoming part of the National Archives, he draws on the same agency for historic footage to illustrate his films.

Thanks to the work and donation of Ott Coelln, for over 30 years editor and publisher of *Business Screen*, the sponsored film trade magazine, the American Archives of the Factual Film flourishes on the campus of Iowa State University in Ames. It is the first serious attempt by a major institution to gather together all relevant materials which document the development of factual films—non-theatrical productions—in the United States and abroad.

The Archives were established in and are administered by the library of Iowa State University of Science and Technology in cooperation with the University's Media Resources Center. Ott Coelln's donation was in the form of his own collection of films, books, journals, correspondence and other materials relating to factual films. The AAFF aims to gather, process, index and publicize all aspects of non-theatrical films for researchers. The Archives boast a growing collection of scripts, still photos, promotional materials, press clippings and oral interviews. A vigorous acquisitions program is broadening its foundations. Backing all this is the Iowa State University Library of more than one million volumes, media materials and manuscript collections.

Out of such surroundings the student of sponsored cinema can take trains in any direction. Or, if he is less deliberate, he may simply switch on his TV, watch the film program at the next Lions Club meeting, or listen to a breakfast table description by a child who has witnessed a new sponsored film in school.

The sponsored film will surely develop as one of the important educational and entertainment disciplines of the 21st century. It is comforting to have participated a little and to hope that the reader could become committed.

Appendices

(A) Standard Motion Picture Production Contract
(B) Motion Picture Specifications Outline
(C) Distribution Centers
    Association Films, Inc.
    Modern Talking Picture Service
    Modern Video Center
(D) Inforfilm—Membership Roster
(E) International Quorum of Motion Picture Producers (IQ)
    —Membership Roster

Appendix A

This Agreement is made at _____
this _____ day of _____ 19____ between _____
_____ whose address is _____
_____
hereinafter called the Client, and _____,
organized and existing under the laws of _____
_____, and hereinafter called the Producer, for the purpose of
producing a motion picture under the following specifications, terms and
conditions.

1. DESCRIPTION
The Producer shall make and the Client shall buy a sound color motion picture
with the working title of _____
on the subject of _____
which when complete will run approximately _____ minutes and is to
be photographed on _____ stock and prints are to be made
on _____ stock.

2. PAYMENT
In consideration for this motion picture the Client shall pay _____,
hereinafter called the Contract Price, according to the following terms:

        _____ percent on signing of this Agreement
        _____ percent on completion of script
        _____ percent on completion of photography
        _____ percent on Client approval at interlock showing

Invoices are payable net within 10 days of receipt. No discounts or commissions
are allowed.

3. PRODUCTION/APPROVAL SCHEDULE
The parties agree to cooperate and work in a prompt and businesslike manner to
complete this motion picture, if possible, in accordance with the following
schedule:

        Treatment or script by _____
        Client approval by _____
        Photography and recording by _____
        Interlock showing by _____
        Answer print by _____
        Client approval by _____
        Release prints by _____

4. SERVICES
The Producer shall provide all services, materials, technical personnel and
equipment necessary for the professional completion of this motion picture, as
are normally provided by a motion picture producer, and as are called for in

183

the approved script, except as to services, materials, technical personnel and equipment furnished by the Client.

5. QUALITY STANDARDS

The Producer agrees to perform under this Agreement in accordance with the trade standards and ethics of the International Quorum of Motion Picture Producers and to the quality standards of the Producer's work as previously exhibited to the Client. The Client agrees that he is satisfied with the professional competence of the Producer.

6. LIAISON REPRESENTATIVE

The Client agrees to appoint one liaison representative who shall have full power to act for the Client, including prompt and final approval of work at all stages, binding upon the Client. The liaison representative shall be available to the Producer and responsible for the Client's technical and policy decisions during photography and recording.

7. PRODUCER COOPERATION

The Producer agrees to minimize interruption or inconvenience to the Client during the Producer's work and to complete his work in a prompt and business-like manner.

8. CLIENT COOPERATION

The Client agrees to provide the Producer with such reasonable assistance as is necessary for completion of this motion picture, including but not limited to script research; arranging photography and recording locations;loan of products, technical equipment and properties; expert assistance, and making Client personnel available for appearance in this motion picture.

9. APPROVALS

The Client agrees to approve the Producer's work promptly upon submission, and where corrections are required, the Client shall be specific and constructive so that the Producer is able to make such corrections promptly and professionally.

The Producer shall obtain approval of the Client, which shall not be unreasonably withheld, at the following stages:

    A. Completion of treatment or shooting script
    B. Completion of storyboard or key drawings for animation, if any
    C. Interlock showing
    D. Delivery of answer print

10. ADDITIONAL WORK AND COSTS

A. All photography and recording necessary for completion of this motion picture are included in the Contract Price. Additional photography and recording ordered by the Client to be performed during production of this motion picture are to be charged to the Client. Such additional work would include photography and recording ordered prior to script approval and not needed in the motion picture, and extra footage for television commercials, archives, publicity, scientific study and sales.

B. The Producer shall make such reasonable changes as the Client may request without charge. If, in order to comply with additional Client changes, the Producer must depart from the previously approved work and specifications and incur additional expense as a result, the Client shall reimburse the Producer. However, the Producer shall make changes at his own expense if they are the result of his own unsatisfactory work or his material departure from specifications.

C. If the Client fails to provide facilities, personnel, properties or other requirements at the time and place agreed between the parties, thereby increasing costs to the Producer, the Client shall reimburse the Producer.

D. The Client agrees that once he has accepted one phase of work and authorized the Producer to proceed to the next, he may not revise or order revision of earlier approved work unless the Producer agrees to do so, in which case the Client will reimburse the Producer the costs of such revisions.

11. RIGHTS

A. The Producer shall obtain all rights to dramatic, literary, artistic and musical work and performance necessary for the completion of this motion picture and its uses as defined in Clause 13 herein. The Producer agrees to obtain releases wherever practical from professional talent performing and speaking in this motion picture. The Client agrees to accept responsibility for legal clearance for photography and recording of personnel and locations under its control.

B. Originals and negatives of this motion picture are to be owned by the _____. Production materials are to remain in the custody of the Producer for storage and making of prints in accordance with Producer's standards. Provision of additional prints and special versions of this motion picture shall be commissioned only from the Producer and shall be subject to separate agreement between the parties.

C. The securing of rights for this motion picture by the Producer shall not be construed to comprise rights for the Client to use such performance, work, likeness or name in any other manner.

D. Producer shall have the right to own and use prints of this motion picture for his own library, reference and demonstration.

E. The Producer shall secure at his expense copyright protection for this motion picture in Producer's name as a means of protecting both parties against outside infringement.

12. WARRANTY

The Producer warrants that his own creative work shall be original and subject to legal protection as such, and that this motion picture shall not violate or infringe on any copyright or patent right.

13. USES

A. The Client shall use this motion picture only for the following purposes: (Strike out uses not applicable)

> Theatrical
> Non-theatrical
> Television

And in the following geographical areas _____
_____. The Client shall not exhibit the
motion picture for other purposes or in other areas without first obtaining
written consent from the Producer and paying for any additional rights or
permissions necessary.

B. The parties agree that neither party may resell or syndicate this motion
picture or any part of it without prior written consent of the other party.

C. The parties agree that stock shots may be used in this motion picture and
scenes from this motion picture may be used as stock shots in other motion
pictures.

14. SCREEN CREDITS
Producer shall have the right to include in the titles of this motion picture
his own name and the names of his chief production personnel, and seals or
insignia in accordance with the Producer's obligations to labor unions or
other organizations.

15. PRINTS.
The Producer shall supply, free of any claim, lien, charge, mortgage or
encumbrance, except as mentioned in Clause 21, one answer print of this motion
picture and _____ release prints. If no release prints are provided as
part of the Contract Price, release prints will be supplied by the Producer
to the Client in accordance with the following schedule of prices and quantities:

_____
_____.
The above prices are based on a running time of _____ minutes and laboratory
prices prevailing on the date of this Agreement. Should the length and completion
date of this motion picture vary from those specified, the above release print
prices will vary accordingly.

All prints shall be mounted on standard reels head-out, packed in standard
cases, marked by title and fitted with head and tail leaders.

16. INDEMNITY AND INSURANCE
A. Producer and Client agree that both parties shall maintain normal insurance
protection against likely claims during production of this motion picture. The
Producer agrees to take reasonable precautions against damage and loss but
cannot be responsible for damage or loss to Client property involved in this
motion picture.

B. The Client indemnifies the Producer against all actions, civil or criminal,
claims or demands other than those covered by Clause 11 herein, which may arise
out of the sound or picture content of this motion picture or any exhibition of
it.

C. The Producer indemnifies the Client against all actions, claims or demands
arising from dramatic, literary, artistic or musical rights obtained by the
Producer for this motion picture.

17. TAXES
The Client agrees to pay all applicable taxes on all billings hereunder.

18. TRAVEL AND ACCOMMODATIONS
The Producer agrees to pay for all travel and accommodations for persons in
his hire for this motion picture, and the Client agrees to pay for all travel
and accommodations of Client personnel who travel in connection with the production of this motion picture.

19. SPECIAL PROVISIONS
The following special provisions are agreed to and initialed by the parties:
(Entries here may cover such matters as famous-name talent, multiple sponsorship, currency adjustment, distribution, duplicating masters, music score
details, number and identity of locations, and public print sales. If none,
write None.)

20. INDEPENDENT CONTRACTOR
The Producer warrants and agrees that in all transactions relating to this
motion picture he is an independent contractor and that all contracts and
arrangements, including those of employment, shall be made by the Producer
as principal and not as an agent for the Client.

21. TIMELY PAYMENT
A. In the event the Client fails to make timely payments, the Producer shall
have the right to suspend production until due payment is received. However
the Producer must resume immediately on receipt of such payment plus service
fee not to exceed _____ percent per annum on balance due.

B. The Producer is required to complete and release this motion picture and
related materials immediately after receipt of all due payments. The Producer
shall have a lien on all prints and other tangible property related to this
Agreement until all payments are made by the Client to the Producer.

22. DELAY AND TERMINATION
A. Delay by the Producer in production of this motion picture due to war,
fire, embargoes, strikes, laws, lockouts, government orders, industrial actions,
illness, accidents, laboratory failures, public disaster, Acts of God or other
cause beyond his control shall not give rise to any claim against the Producer.

B. In the event of unreasonable delay due to the above causes, the Client
shall be entitled to terminate this Agreement subject to payment of all costs
incurred and commitments made by the Producer to the date of termination,
inclusive of overhead, plus 10 percent of such costs. Where such total amount
is exceeded by the amounts already paid by the Client hereunder, the difference
shall be immediately reimbursed by the Producer to the Client.

C. If at any time the Client wishes to abandon production of this motion picture
for any reason whatsoever, the Client may do so by giving written notice to the
Producer and paying the Producer only the amount of profit which would have been
due had the motion picture been completed and for costs of production incurred
or committed by the Producer prior to date of termination. Immediately on
receipt of termination notice, the Producer shall acknowledge and agree to
termination, end all work, commitments and expense in the best financial interests
of the Client, and submit to the Client within 30 days of receipt of termination
notice a detailed and final claim.

23. ARBITRATION

Any dispute or difference arising hereunder shall be settled by arbitration within 60 days of receipt of written notice by one party to the other. The dispute or difference shall be referred to a single arbitrator to be agreed between the parties. Failing agreement, each party shall select an arbitrator and they together shall select the single arbitrator to settle the dispute or difference.

24. BANKRUPTCY AND LIQUIDATION

Either party to this Agreement shall be entitled to terminate this Agreement by written notice to the other party if that other party shall become bankrupt or have a receiving order made against him or shall present his petition in bankruptcy or shall make an arrangement with his creditors or shall have an execution levied on his goods or, being a corporation, shall go into liquidation (other than in connection with a plan of reconstruction or amalgamation) or have a resolution for its winding up or have a receiver appointed.

25. ENTIRE AGREEMENT

This instrument sets forth the entire agreement between the parties, all prior negotiations and understandings are merged herein, and no change or addition shall be of any effect unless in writing and signed by both parties.

In witness whereof the parties have executed this Agreement this _____ day of _____ 19_____ .

CLIENT _____

SIGNED BY _____(SEAL)

TITLE _____

PRODUCER _____

SIGNED BY _____(SEAL)

TITLE _____

WITNESSED BY _____

Appendix B

Crawley Films Limited
19 Fairmont Ave.
Ottawa, 613-728-3513

1260 University Ave.
Montreal, 514-861-9449

93 Yorkville Ave.
Toronto, 416-929-3337-8

crawleys

MOTION PICTURE SPECIFICATIONS OUTLINE

This form will help you consolidate your thinking and ensure that everyone is working precisely to your objectives. It is based on Crawley's experience in producing more than 2,000 motion pictures for marketing, information and public relations programs. All information will be held absolutely confidential. Your completion of this form in no way implies any obligation.

ORGANIZATION .... ADDRESS ....

REPRESENTATIVE .... TELEPHONE ....

TITLE .... DATE ....

1. THE PURPOSE

What is the primary purpose of the proposed film? ....

What are the secondary purposes, if any? ....

2. THE AUDIENCE

To what audience is the purpose to be conveyed?

Primary ....

Secondary ....

General public ( )   Customers/Prospects ( )   Dealers ( )   Staff ( )   Service clubs ( )   Business clubs ( )

Labor groups ( )   Farm organizations ( )   Women's groups ( )   Church groups ( )   Elementary schools ( )

High schools ( )   Universities ( )   Scientific groups ( )   Film Councils ( )

3. DISTRIBUTION

By professional distributor to television ( )   to community audiences ( )   to theatres ( )

By staff ( )   By network broadcast ( )   Other ....

In other countries? ....

By professional distributor abroad ( ) By government trade-promotion library ( ) By government travel film library ( )

By staff abroad ( )

Probable number of prints required ....

189

4. THE SCOPE

Key points of subject which would achieve the PURPOSE with the AUDIENCE.

5. TECHNICAL ELEMENTS

35mm ( )   or 16mm ( )

Color ( )   or black & white ( )

Length in minutes ....

Languages: English ( )   French ( )   Others ....

Commentary only ( )   or with synchronized sound ( )   or combination ( )

Music: existing ( )   or original score ( )

Professional actors ( )

Studio shooting ( )

Locations ....

....

....

Animation sequences?   Cartoon ( )   Diagrammatic ( )   Describe ....

....

6. CLIENT INFORMATION

Client's Representative ....

Special facilities available ....

Research material available ....

Existing footage available ....

How many years of active use should your film have? ....

Delivery date ....

Probable budget ....

Appendix C

DISTRIBUTION CENTERS

ASSOCIATION FILMS, INC.

6644 Sierra Lane
Dublin, California 94566
(415) 829-2300

7838 San Fernando Road
Sun Valley, California 91352
Los Angeles residents: 875-3242
All others phone (213) 767-7400

324 Delaware Avenue
Oakmont, Pennsylvania 15139
Pittsburgh residents: (412) 362-5011
All others phone: (412) 828-5900

8615 Directors Row
Dallas, Texas 75237
(214) 638-6791

5797 New Peachtree Road
Atlanta, Georgia 30340
(404) 458-6251

512 Burlington Avenue
La Grange, Illinois 60525
Chicagoans: Bishop 2-1898
All others phone: (312) 352-3377

410 Great Road
Littleton, Massachusetts 01460
(617) 486-3518

600 Grand Avenue
Ridgefield, New Jersey 07657
New York City residents: PE 6-9693
All others phone (201) 943-8200

915 N.W. 19th Avenue
Portland, Oregon 97209
(503) 226-7695

6420 West Lake Street
Minneapolis, Minnesota 55426
(612) 920-2095

HOME OFFICE
866 Third Avenue, New York, NY
10022

MODERN TALKING PICTURE SERVICE

Atlanta, Ga. 30308
412 W. Peachtree St. N.W.
(404) 524-1311

Boston, Mass. 02167
230 Boylston St.
Chestnut Hill
(617) 527-4184

Buffalo, N.Y. 14202
122 W. Chippewa St.
(716) 853-1805

Cedar Rapids, Ia. 52404
200 Third Ave., S.W.
(319) 363-8144

Charlotte, N.C. 28202
503 No. College St.
(704) 377-2574

Chicago, Ill. 60007
1687 Elmhurst Rd.
Elk Grove Village, Ill.
(312) 593-3250

Cincinnati, O. 45202
9 Garfield Place
(513) 421-2516

Cleveland, O. 44115
2238 Euclid Ave.
(216) 621-9469

Dallas, Tex. 75207
1411 Slocum St.
(214) 742-4106

Denver, Col. 80204
1200 Stout St.
(303) 573-7300

Detroit, Mich. 48235
15921 W. 8 Mile Road
(313) 273-2070

Harrisburg, Pa. 17105
2009 No. Third St.
(P.O. Box 3035)
(717) 238-8123

Honolulu, Hawaii 96813
Film Services of Hawaii
716 Cooke Street
(808) 536-9105

Houston, Tex. 77027
4084 Westheimer Rd.
(713) 622-3841

Indianapolis, Ind. 46204
115 East Michigan St.
(317) 635-5331

Los Angeles, Cal. 90038
1145 N. McCadden Place
(213) 469-8282

Milwaukee, Wis. 53202
1696 No. Astor St.
(414) 271-0861

Minneapolis, Minn. 55420
9129 Lyndale Ave. S.
(612) 884-5383

Philadelphia, Pa. 19107
1234 Spruce St.
(215) 545-2500

Pittsburgh, Pa. 15222
910 Penn Avenue
(412) 471-9118

St. Louis, Mo. 63043
86 Weldon Parkway
Maryland Heights, Mo.
(314) 567-4278

San Francisco, Cal. 94105
16 Spear St.
(415) 982-1712

Seattle, Wash. 98103
1205 No. 45th St.
(206) 632-8461

Summit, N.J. 07901
315 Springfield Avenue
(201) 277-6300
Serving N.J. and Southern N.Y. State

Washington, D.C. 20036
2000 "L" St. N.W.
(202) 659-9234

Don Mills, Ont. Can.
M3B 2M6 (Metro Toronto)
1875 Leslie St.
(416) 444-7347

Montreal, Quebec
485 McGill Street HY2 2H4
(514) 878-3644

Vancouver, B.C.
c/o Associated Audio-Visual Ltd.
1590 W. Fourth Ave. V5M 2Y7
(604) 736-4771

HOME OFFICE
45 Rockefeller Plaza, New York, NY
10020

MODERN VIDEO CENTER
2323 New Hyde Park Road
New Hyde Park, NY 11040

Appendix D

INFORFILM—MEMBERSHIP ROSTER

General Secretariat: J. Sibelius Avenue 16/108. 1070 Brussels, Belgium.
Tel. (02) 522.2287
AUSTRIA: Oesterreichisches Film-Service,
A - 1040 Wien, Schaumburgergasse 18,
Tel. 65.72.49
BELGIUM: Sofedi-Films, Avenue de l'Hippodrome 147,
B - 1050 Bruxelles,
Tel. 02/64.74.53 - 64.10.03 - 64.28.77
BRAZIL: Difusão de Filmes S/C Ltda.,
Av. Brig. Faria Lima, 1106, (01452)
Sao Paulo - S.P.
Tel. 210.8839
BULGARIA: Inform Film Service Bulgaria, 96 Rakovski Street, Sofia,
Tel. 88.12.91 - 88.09.51
CANADA: Modern Talking Picture Service, Inc.
1943 Leslie Street, Don Mills, Ontario,
Tel. (416) 444 - 73.59
CZECHOSLOVAKIA: Infor Film Servis, Stepanska 42, 110 00 Praha 1,
Tel. 247.109 - 243.870
DENMARK: Erhvervenes Filmcenter,
Peter Ipsens Allé 20, 2400 København NV,
Tel. (01) 19.11.44
FINLAND: Bureau for Economic Information,
Uuionkatu 14, 00130 Helsinki P.O. Box 147,
Tel. 90/174 511, Telex tttsto sf 121640
FRANCE: The combined forces of:
Céfilm, 15bis, Rue de Marignan,
F-75008 Paris, Tel. 358 35 94 - 159 40 17,
and
Cedfi, 15bis, rue Raspail, F - 92300,
Levallois-Perret, Tel. 739 50 20

GERMANY: Konferenz der Landesfilmdienste,
Rheinallee 59 D - 53 Bonn-Bad Godesberg 1,
Tel. 02221/355002

GREAT BRITAIN: Guild Sound & Vision Ltd., Woodston House,
85-129 Oundle Road, Peterborough PE2 9PZ,
Tel. (0733) 63122

ITALY Diffusione Internazionale Film Informativi,
DIFI, Viale Parioli 25, 1 - 00197 Roma,
Tel. 878.276

JAPAN: Educational Film Exchange, Inc., 6-7 Ginza - 6 Chome,
Chuo-ku, Tokyo 104,
Tel. (571) 9351-5

MIDDLE EAST: ITEM film Library,
(Lebanon, 3rd, Fl, Al-Maskan Building, Boulevard Mazraa
Jordan, Iraq, P.O. Box 8922, Beirut, Lebanon
Kuwait and *European representative:*
the Gulf States, H. K. Hughes Esq.,
Saudi-Arabia, Gatwick House, Horley, Surrey, England
Libya, Cyprus) Tel. Horley 5353

NETHERLANDS: Technisch Film Centrum (TFC)
Arnhemsestraatweg 17, Velp near Arnhem,
Tel. (085) 629188

NORWAY: Opplysningsfilm A/S,
Parkveien 62 c, Oslo 2,
Tel. (02) 55.00.28

SOUTH AFRICA: Independent Film Library (PTY) Limited,
P.O. Box 11,112, Johannesburg,
Tel. 706.1348

SPAIN: Teletecnicine Internacional,
Barcelona - 15, Avenida José Antonio 464,
Tel. 243.94.00 - 243.60.78

SWEDEN: The Swedish Council for Personnel Administration,
Sturegatan 58, S - 114 36, Stockholm,
Tel. 08/14.14.00

SWITZERLAND: Schweizer Schul- und Volkskino/Schmalfilmzentrale,
Erlachstrasse 21, CH - 3000 Bern 9,
Tel. (031) 23.08.31

UNITED STATES: Modern Talking Picture Service, Inc.,
International Building, 45 Rockefeller Plaza,
New York, N.Y. 10020,
Tel. (212) 765-3100

Appendix E

INTERNATIONAL QUORUM OF MOTION PICTURE PRODUCERS (IQ) MEMBERSHIP ROSTER

This roster has never been published before outside the organization.

Hermes Munoz
Hermes Munoz & Associados SA
Montevideo 643-Piso 3°
1019 Buenos Aires, ARGENTINA

Roy Christian
Discos Film Pdtns.
36 Seaforth Crescent
Seaforth NSW 2092 AUSTRALIA

Rudolf Kamel
West Film Pdtns.
Grosse Neugasse 8
1040 Vienna, AUSTRIA

Kobi Jaeger
Montagu Film Studios
East Bay Street
Nassau, BAHAMAS

Pierre Levie
SOFIDOC
Vieille Halle aux bles 44
1000 Brussels, BELGIUM

Pedro P. Hatheyer
Helicon
Rua Arthur Prado 82
01322 Sao Paulo, BRAZIL

Graeme Fraser
(613-728-3513)
Crawley Films
PO Box 3040
Ottawa K1Y3B5
Ontario, CANADA

Hector R. Acebes
Producciones Hector Acebes
Apartado aero 4901
Bogota, COLOMBIA

Erik Ryge
Laterna Films A/S
50 Klampenborgvej
DK 2930 Klampenborg,
DENMARK

Eduardo Palmer
Productora Filmica
  Dominicana
Apartado 1080
Santa Domingo,
DOMINICAN REPUBLIC

Aimo Jaderholm
Sektor Filmi
Tarkk' ampukank 389
Helsinki 13, FINLAND

Georges Pessis
Filmedia
48 Quai Carnot
92210 St Cloud, FRANCE

Georg Munck KG
Leonaris-Film
Meisenweg 2
Boblingen, GERMANY

S. G. Aryeetey
Ghana Film Industry Corp.
PO Box M83
Accra, GHANA

George Stamboulopoulos
Telecin Ltd
Aykabhttoy 23
Athens 135, GREECE

Pao-Shing Ting
China Film Produce
6th Floor, 236 Nathan Road
Kowloon, HONG KONG

Charles Wong
Salon Films (HK) Ltd
11 Kingston Street
Causeway Bay, HONG KONG

Magnus Johannsson
Iceland Falcon Films
PO Box 83
Reykjavik, ICELAND

A. Widodo
Safari-Cathay Films
Jalan Tenah Abang 111/19
Jakarta, INDONESIA

Pat Kavanagh
Pat Kavanagh Ltd
Granite Lodge
Cabinteely Co
Dublin, IRELAND

Cesare Taurelli
Recta Film
Via Flaminia Km 11,500
00188 Rome, ITALY

Yves Garneau
Societe Ivoirenne de Cinema
PO Box 304
Adidjan, IVORY COAST

Philip Harvey
Harvey Film Productions Ltd
PO Box 185
Kingston 9, JAMAICA

Takeji Takamura
Iwanami Film Pdtns.
2-21-2 Kanda-Misak-cho
Chiyodaku, Tokyo, JAPAN

George Nasrawl
Jordan Television
PO Box 1041
Amman, JORDAN

Michael J. Richmond
East Africa Film Services
PO Box 2818
Nairobi, KENYA

Mohamad Jannoun
Baalbeck Studios
PO Box 4665
Beirut, LEBANON

Kheng Law Ow
Urusan Cathay Films
3 Jalan Sultan Hishamuddin
Kuala Lumpur, MALAYSIA

Hans Biemler
Cine Commercial
Louisiana 81 Col Napoles
Mexico City 18, MEXICO

Mohamed Ziani
Centre Cinematographique
  Marocain
85 Rue Moulay Ismail
Rabat, MOROCCO

Jacques Eekhout
N V Cinecentrum
Postbus 508
'S Gravelandseweg 80
Hilversum, NETHERLANDS

Sanya Dosunmu
Starline Films Ltd
PMB 1212 Ikeja
Lagos, NIGERIA

Knut Jørgen Erichsen
Centralfilm A/S
Akebergveien 56
Oslo 6, NORWAY

Emil Willimetz
Audio Visual Pdtns.
Av Republica 740 San Isidro
Lima, PERU

Ernesto A. DePedro
The Multimedia Organization
PO Box 1677
Manila, PHILIPPINES

Jorge Galveias Rodrigues
Telecine Moro
Rua D Pedro V, 56/J
Lisbon, PORTUGAL

Tom Hodge
Cathay-Keris Film Pdtns.
532D East Coast Road
Singapore 15, SINGAPORE

G. H. W. Groom
Films of Africa
PO Box 70363
Bryanston 2021
SOUTH AFRICA

Santiago Moro
Moro Creativos Asociados
Valentin Beato, 3
Madrid 17, SPAIN

Hans Gelhaar
AB Europa Film
PO Box 1316
S-111 83 Stockholm, SWEDEN

Heinrich Fueter Blanc
Condor-Film
Restelbergstrasse 107
Zurich, SWITZERLAND

Kemel Baysal
Baysal Films
M Uluunlu Sokak 16
Zincirlikuyu
Istanbul, TURKEY

James Carr
World Wide Pictures Ltd
21-25 St Anne's Court
London W1V3AW,
UNITED KINGDOM

Michael Katz
TLF
91.62.48 Apto. 314
Caracas 101, VENEZUELA

D. Kolman & Z. Matko
Zagreb Films
PO Box 441
Zagreb 1, YUGOSLAVIA

J. H. Roulet
Malachite Films
PO Box 1205
Chingola, ZAMBIA

ALABAMA
Charlie Metcalfe
(205-967-1661)
Metcalfe Films
3709 Locksley Dr
Birmingham, AL 35223

Manning Spottswood
(205-478-9353)
Spottswood Studios
PO Box 7061
Mobile, AL 36607

ALASKA
Rod Thompson
(907-277-8834)
Films North
PO Box 2333
Anchorage, AK 99501

ARIZONA
Kenyon Swartwout
(602-945-8496)
Swartwout Film Pdtns.
PO Box 476
Scottsdale, AZ 85252

ARKANSAS
Monty Mann
(501-375-5561)
Monty Mann Comms.
1650 Union National Plaza
Little Rock, AR 72201

CALIFORNIA
J. Richard Butler
(916-925-6836)
Glynis Films
955 Venture Court
Sacramento, CA 95825

Philip R. Rosenberg
(714-233-6513)
Roger Tilton Films
241 West G St
San Diego, CA 92101

(LOS ANGELES AREA)
John J. Hennessy
(213-682-2352)
John J. Hennessy Motion Pictures
900 Palm Ave
South Pasadena, CA 91030

(SAN FRANCISCO AREA)
Paul B. Rich
(415-328-6516)
Films for Information
190 California Ave
Palo Alto, CA 94306

COLORADO
Jack E. Carver
(303-623-0167)
JPI
1410 Larimer Square
Denver, CO 80202

CONNECTICUT
Kevin Donovan
(203-633-9331)
Kevin Donovan Films
44 Treat Road
Glastonbury, CT 06033

DISTRICT OF COLUMBIA
Barbara Legg
(703-281-9044)
Paragon Productions
PO Box 395
Oakton, VA 22124

FLORIDA
Donald E. Barton
(904-389-4541)
Barton Film Company
PO Box 6834
Jacksonville, FL 32205

Hack Swain
(813-371-2360)
Hack Swain Pdtns.
1185 Cattlemen Rd
Sarasota, FL 33578

HAWAII
George Tahara
(808-533-2677)
Cline Pic Hawaii Corp.
1847 Pacific Heights Rd
Honolulu, HI 96813

IDAHO
Jack Williams
(208-343-1951)
IPA Photography
PO Box 315
Boise, ID 83701

ILLINOIS
Fred A. Niles
(312-738-4181)
Niles Comms. Ctr.
1058 W Washington Blvd
Chicago, IL 60607

INDIANA
Bill Sprague
(317-251-3453)
Bill Sprague Pdtns.
5833 Winthrop Ave
Indianapolis, IN 46220

IOWA
John H. Kirstein
(515-285-8863)
Kirstein Inc
661 Gepke Parkway
Des Moines, IA 50315

KANSAS
Violet Priestley
(316-682-5925)
Library Filmstrip Center
3033 Aloma
Wichita, KS 67211

KENTUCKY
Floyd Kron
(606-277-8018)
ETF Productions
PO Box 4181
Lexington, KY 40504

LOUISIANA
John Hutchinson
(504-241-3803)
Hutchinson Film Pdtns.
7211 Westhaven Rd
New Orleans, LA 70126

Henry Clements
(318-861-1477)
Clements Productions
840 Monrovia
Shreveport, LA 71106

MAINE
Everett Foster
(207-582-4607)
Foster & Associates
40 Lincoln Ave
Gardiner, ME 04345

MARYLAND
John D. A'Hern
(301-462-1550)
Monumental Films
2160 Rockrose Ave
Baltimore, MD 21211

MASSACHUSETTS
Lowell F. Wentworth
(617-354-5695)
The Film Group
2400 Massachusetts Ave
Cambridge, MA 02140

James W. Wille
(413-536-2615)
Industrial Communications
PO Box 99
South Hadley, MA 01075

MICHIGAN
Dave Seago
(313-872-4740)
Audio Visual Pdtn. Services
2832 E Grand Blvd
Detroit, MI 48211

MINNESOTA
Perry Schwartz
(612-236-8691)
The Filmakers
430 Oak Grove St
Minneapolis, MN 55403

MISSISSIPPI
Ken Parks
(601-353-5652)
KPA Films
PO Box 10654
Jackson, MS 39209

MISSOURI
Ralph Pasek
(314-225-6000)
Communico
1315 N Highway Dr
St Louis, MO 63026

MONTANA
Bob Henkel
(406-442-9500)
Sage Films
PO Box 1142
Helena, MT 59601

NEBRASKA
Don Chapman
(402-348-1600)
Chapman/Spitler/Durham
1908 California St
Omaha, NE 68102

NEVADA
Burl Kinney
(702-384-9925)
Kinney/Hancock
1048 E Franklin Ave
Las Vegas, NV 89104

Mollie Gregory
(702-329-6965)
Thunderbird Film Enters.
1420 N Virginia Ave
Reno, NV 89503

NEW JERSEY
Joe Arnold
(609-829-2262)
House of Arnold
835 Homewood Dr
Riverton, NJ 08077

NEW MEXICO
Robert Stevens
(505-242-2679)
Bandelier Films
2001 Gold Ave
Albuquerque, NM 87106

NEW YORK CITY
Bill Bryant
(212-682-2013)
FWB & Associates
6 East 45th St
New York, NY 10017

Alex Massis
Israfilm
527 Madison Avenue
New York, NY 10022
(212-752-3015)

NEW YORK
Richard C. Cressey
(315-446-1151)
Cressey Productions
102 Woodside Dr
Syracuse, NY 13224

John Gates
(716-856-3220)
Ent/Gates Films
200 Chicago Street
Buffalo, NY 14204

Bill McAleer
(516-433-2035)
Matt Farrell Pdtns.
17 Gables Dr
Hicksville, NY 11801

NORTH CAROLINA
Walter J. Klein
(704-542-1403)
Walter J. Klein Co. Ltd
6301 Carmel Road
Charlotte, NC 28211

Mike Howard
(919-489-7356)
Shadowstone Films
1402 Duke University Rd
Durham, NC 27701

OHIO
Larry Ward
(513-721-1462)
Brand Photographers
1203 Central Parkway
Cincinnati, OH 45210

Edward Feil
(216-771-0655)
Edward Feil Productions
1514 Prospect Ave
Cleveland, OH 44103

Ed Lang
(513-433-3133)
Ed Lang Inc
73 Westpark Rd
Dayton, OH 45459

OREGON
Robert M. Lindahl
(503-224-3456)
Northwestern Inc
011 S W. Hooker St
Portland, OR 97201

PENNSYLVANIA
Walter G. O'Connor
(717-534-1000)
Walter G. O'Connor Co
Hershey, PA 17033

George Romero
(412-261-5589)
The Latent Image
247 Pitt Blvd
Pittsburgh, PA 15222

(PHILADELPHIA AREA)
John Beck
(215-674-1080)
Creative Film Pdtns.
26 Meadowbrook Lane
Chalfont, PA 18914

RHODE ISLAND
Mark Edmunds
(401-943-2333)
Mark Edmunds Inc
2 Needham St
Johnston, RI 02919

SOUTH DAKOTA
Charles W. Nauman
(605-673-4071)
Nauman Films
PO Box 232
Custer, SD 57730

TENNESSEE
Jacob Eleasari
(615-385-0061)
Eleasari Productions
2106 19th Avenue, S.
Nashville, TN 37212

Elston S. Leonard
(901-774-4383)
Fotovox
PO Box 4386
Memphis, TN 38104

W. Fleming Reeder
(615-693-0871)
Reeder Motion Pictures
P. O. Box 10191
Knoxville, TN 37919

TEXAS
J. Philip Knight-Sheen
(512-824-3548)
Piccadilly Films Intl
PO Box 16255
San Antonio, TX 78246

Zack Belcher
(817-753-6852)
Educational Services Inc
PO Box 3020
Waco, TX 76707

Bill Stokes
(214-363-0161)
Bill Stokes Associates
5642 Dyer St
Dallas, TX 75206

UTAH
Fred Edwards
(801-322-2505)
TeleScene Inc
179 Social Hall Ave
Salt Lake City, UT 84111

Robert Davison
(801-772-3390)
Expedition Films
Shadow Canyon
Springdale, UT 84767

VERMONT
Robert Campbell
(802-869-2547)
Campbell Films
Saxtons River, VT 05154

VIRGINIA
George Haycox
(804-855-1911)
Haycox Photoramic
1531 Early St
Norfolk, VA 23502

WASHINGTON
R. W. Cameron
(206-623-4103)
Cameron Film Pdtns.
222 Minor Ave North
Seattle, WA 98109

WISCONSIN
Ervin L. Penkalski
(414-374-7900)
Omega Productions
3788 N. Humbolt Blvd.
Milwaukee, WI 53212

WYOMING
Bob Dorn
(307-235-6108)
Bob Dorn Photography
PO Box 1191
Casper, WY 82601

HONORARY LIFE MEMBERS
Lillian Farrell
(203-264-8706)
PO Box 201
Southbury, CT 06488

Ott Coelln
(417-264-7151)
PO Box 184
Thayer, MO 65791

HEADQUARTERS OFFICE
(703-281-9044)
PO Box 395
Oakton, VA 22124

Index